Posterity

Doubleday

NEW YORK LONDON TORONTO

SYDNEY AUCKLAND

Posterity

LETTERS OF
GREAT AMERICANS TO
THEIR CHILDREN

Dorie McCullough Lawson

PUBLISHED BY DOUBLEDAY
a division of Random House, Inc.

DOUBLEDAY and the portrayal of an anchor with a dolphin are
registered trademarks of Random House, Inc.

Library of Congress Cataloging-in-Publication Data

Posterity : letters of great Americans to their children /
Dorie McCullough Lawson.—1st ed.
p. cm.
Includes bibliographical references.
1. United States—History—Sources. 2. United States—Civilization—Sources. 3. United
States—Biography. 4. American letters. I. Lawson, Dorie McCullough.

E173.P77 2004
973—dc22
2003055494

ISBN 0-385-50330-X

May 2004

5   7   9   10   8   6   4

For my parents,
David and Rosalee McCullough

CONTENTS

Love

Good Work

Struggle

Contents

Strength of Character

The Pleasures of Life

Brace-Up

A Place in Time

Loss

Aging

Rules to Live By

FOREWORD

This is an uncommonly wise and important book full of much wonderful writing and invaluable observations on life. It is also unprecedented,
the first rich anthology of letters from eminent Americans to their children, selected from many thousands of letters written down the years in
times of peace and war, flush times and times of extreme hardship and
stress.

The authors of the letters include a number of the giants of American
literature—novelists, poets, playwrights—as well as soldiers, explorers,
artists, and inventors. Eight of the authors were presidents of the United
States. Three were first ladies. Two were the mothers of presidents, and
two, the fathers. At least one, Thomas Edison, was an acknowledged
"wizard."

There are besides a pioneering physician, a world-famous industrialist,
a brilliant lyricist, an actor, a photographer, a clergyman of the eighteenth
century, the most influential physicist of the twentieth century, a legendary
president of Harvard—altogether sixty-eight acclaimed Americans, each
of whom did something exceptional in a multitude of fields over a span
of more than three hundred years. But here they sign themselves "Ever
yours, Father and Friend," "Your affectionate Mother," "Papa," "Dad,"
"Daddy," "Your Old Pal," or "Mama Bess." For that was who they were,

heart and soul, when composing these letters, and so, inevitably, understandably, they expressed themselves in ways they did not in other correspondence, often saying things that they never would to anyone else.

To get the most from the letters, one needs, of course, to know something of the setting and circumstance in which they were written—the sometimes surprising context—which makes the clear, perceptive biographical material provided here of the utmost interest and value.

Had the letters been written by people of no particular renown, one would still, I think, be struck by their great range and variety. But because the affectionate father happens to be Benjamin Franklin or General Patton, or the affectionate mother Abigail Adams or Barbara Bush, the force and importance of the letters are enormously compounded. And so it was, too, very often, for the recipients. Imagine being told by General John J. Pershing that it was past time for you to shape up!

Naturally, as parents, they were of many moods and wrote from a range of motives. They exhort and they sympathize. They caution, upbraid, tease, joke, teach, preach. They take pride and they take offense. And, of course, they offer no end of advice. Some of the letters are supremely entertaining. A few, written in anger, are hard to bear. Yet over and over, in ways obvious and subtle, even at times unkind, they are missives of love.

Often the authors want only to save their children from making the mistakes they have. When photographer Ansel Adams writes, "I have spent a good part of my life trying to understand the obligations of a parent," he could be speaking for the authors of many of the letters, not to say all of us who in raising our children have had to learn as we go.

The oldest letter in the collection was written by the seventeenth-century poet Anne Bradstreet, who with her husband, Simon Bradstreet, was among the early settlers of the Massachusetts Bay Colony, arriving from England in 1630. Other letters date from our own time.

Some of the letters go on for pages, while one of the most moving in the collection, by Robert E. Lee, is only two paragraphs. And nearly all come from a time when writing letters was considered part of life. It was something you did as a matter of course. It was expected of you. "Write no matter how tired you are, no matter how inconvenient it is," Theodore Roosevelt tells his son Quentin in a letter dated 1917.

For his part Theodore Roosevelt was one of the most prolific correspondents ever, pouring out more than 150,000 letters in one lifetime, and those to his children are among the most charming he ever wrote. Even in his busiest days as president, he would take time to write to his sons and daughters and always with infectious enjoyment, as his letters included here well demonstrate.

That so few of us write to our children any longer, that we so rarely write personal letters of any sort, is a shame. I think often of how little we will leave about ourselves and our time in our own words. Maybe some of the e-mail will survive, but I doubt it. How will future generations ever come to know us? Historians and biographers a hundred or three hundred years hence will have almost nothing of a personal kind to work with. Our story, consequently, will be a lot less interesting, less human, perhaps even impossible to write.

Beyond that we're denying ourselves the pleasures and benefits of putting our thoughts and feelings down in words of our own. Nothing so focuses the mind as writing. We've all known the experience of a new idea or insights coming suddenly, almost miraculously to mind, as we write, and as probably they never would were we not writing. Working your thoughts out on paper, it used to be called.

In this spirit, many of the authors here are writing as much for themselves as for the recipients of their letters. Jack London's rant about his first wife, the mother of the daughter to whom he is writing, is a case in point.

By contrast there are the selections in the chapter called "The Pleasures of Life" written mainly for fun, and what a different side they show of the eminent figures who penned them. I'll never think of the renowned landscape architect Frederick Law Olmsted the same way again, having read his exuberantly playful speculation to a four-year-old on the reproductive capacities of cats. Nor do I know of a more ingenious example of how to tell a child no.

The unabashedly corny jokes shared by Alexander Graham Bell with his grown daughter are pure gold to me, as I suspect they will be to other readers. And my fondness for Groucho Marx is greater than ever, now that I have read what he had to say in the voice of his dog.

The quantity of sound advice offered is considerable. That life is short and uncertain is a repeating theme. The importance of one's work is stressed again and again. "Work you know is your work, which belongs to you. That's the best thing about it," writes Eugene O'Neill. "Because any fool knows that to work hard at something you want to accomplish is the only way to be happy."

In an effort to convey to his gifted son Andrew what his work means to him, the great illustrator N. C. Wyeth quotes a line from Michelangelo: "It is only well with me when I have a chisel in my hand." "But work, real work for what we call duty or the truth, that is more fun than tennis," writes Lincoln Steffens.

It is gratifying, also, to find that some of the comeuppance delivered had good effect, as in the case of young Warren Pershing.

Many of the letters make one want to know more of the lives and achievements of those who wrote them, or in the case of the professional writers, to read more of their work. Anyone who could convey with such understanding to a nine-year-old the meaning of Valley Forge as does William Henry Seward was plainly a good deal more than just the man who bought Alaska.

I've not thought of John O'Hara's novels since college, but his letters to his daughter Wylie make me eager to read him again. And the same goes for Sherwood Anderson. The guidelines he gives on art and life, for the son studying painting in Paris, ought to be pinned up as reminders for all who paint or write or teach. "Try to be humble. Smartness kills everything," Anderson says. "The point of being an artist is that you may live."

But then nearly all the writers here are trying in one way or other to impart what life has taught them, and it's the sum total of such observations, and the sincerity of expression, that give these pages their inordinate value.

"If you feel the blues coming on you, get a book and a glass of wine," advises the august, learned Charles W. Eliot, the president of Harvard. "Know history," George Patton tells his son. "Great necessities call out great virtues," Abigail Adams reminds young John Quincy Adams.

The trials and suffering of life, the horrors of disease and war, the fierce inner struggles many suffer, are all to be found in these letters. It is hard to imagine, for example, anyone ever forgetting Woody Guthrie's letter as he was being destroyed by Huntington's chorea.

Every reader will have his or her own favorites. To my mind what W. E. B. Du Bois writes to his daughter Yolande is both a surpassing lesson in human understanding and a beautiful expression of a father's devotion. The letter should be required reading everywhere. I love Sidney Lanier's letter about his newborn son. Oscar Hammerstein's beautiful, autobiographical letter to his son Bill may be my favorite of all.

Dorie McCullough Lawson is my daughter, I'm proud to say, and I have thought often of a comment she made as she first embarked on the research for the book. "Think how much I'm going to learn," she said. I know how much I have learned from the collection and from her very skillful editorial commentary.

This is a book to pick up and read at almost any page, a book to keep close at hand, to return to for nourishment and guidance, yes, but also for reassurance and pure pleasure.

—David McCullough
West Tisbury, Massachusetts

Posterity

Preface

In the fall of 2000, I began compiling an anthology of letters from great Americans to their children—a collection of the personal letters from those we, as a nation, admire most, those whose lives have mattered in the long run. Included are letters from artists, writers, politicians, scientists, actors, businesspeople, activists, and explorers. From the outset I wondered: What did these Americans tell their children? And how did they tell them? What lessons did they feel were important for their children to learn? What might the letters reveal about the writer and the time in which he or she lived? And, perhaps most importantly, what can we as parents, children, and Americans learn from their words?

These letters of our fellow Americans are treasures. They are genuine, of the moment, free of self-consciousness, and, with the exception of an important letter from Henry Louis Gates to his two young daughters, none included here was written explicitly for publication. Nearly all are a pleasure to read, but there are some that are tough to take—heartbreaking, shocking, hypocritical, mean. Yet, it is through some of these most unkind and difficult letters that we are provided with an immediate and unique access to times past and significant personalities. Overall the letters are full of heart, temper, wisdom, sensitivity, disappointment, humor, heartbreak, joy, and again and again the thoughtful, beautiful use of the English language.

Take, for example, lines from the nineteenth-century poet Sidney Lanier to his twelve-year-old son, "I admire the sight of a man fighting his own small failings, as a good knight who never ceases to watch, and war against, the least blemish or evil: You may therefore fancy how my heart warms with loving pride in you and for you." Or, from photographer Ansel Adams during the Korean War to his son in the U.S. Air Force, "I am wondering, in the afternoon of my own life, just what your day will be."

With the intention of creating something more like a gallery of fine and important pieces, rather than a comprehensive catalog, I chose letters for the book using essentially two guidelines. First, the letters had to be written by a person who made substantial and worthwhile contributions to our country. Second, they had to reveal something of value. For a variety of reasons, many undisputed American greats are not included: Abraham Lincoln, because his letters to his children were mostly brief communications of a logistical nature; Martin Luther King, because there are no letters to his children; Rachel Carson, because she destroyed all of her letters to her adopted son. Then there are many, many greats who are not here for the obvious reason that they had no children at all—Henry David Thoreau, Mahalia Jackson, Dr. Seuss, Louisa May Alcott, Winslow Homer, Martha Graham, Margaret Bourke-White, Louis Armstrong, Willa Cather, Billie Holiday, Orville and Wilbur Wright, Janis Joplin, Oliver Wendell Holmes, Walt Whitman, Mary Cassatt, and the list goes on and on.

There are very few letters from modern or living Americans. Numerous requests were sent out, and over and over came the response—there are no letters. From the brilliant economist Milton Friedman came an answer that clearly describes our contemporary predicament, "I am sorry to say I have [no letters] that I would be able to contribute. We have always been close to our children, have been able to communicate with them more directly by personal conversation, telephone calls, and the like so that we have no systematic collection of letters. Sorry." Sorry indeed are we all, and future generations may be sorrier still.

This raises the question of e-mail, as people have often asked if I would include electronic messages in the book. I made the decision that I would not. E-mail is efficient, inexpensive, and instantaneous, but it is not the same as sitting down and composing a letter. Letter writing is generally a thoughtful art and typing e-mail often is not.

Letters in the book are arranged thematically, with chapters such as "The Developing Mind," "Love," "Loss," "Aging," and "Rules to Live By"—categories that evolved from the letters themselves. Within each section, the letters are in chronological order. Printed in their entirety, the letters appear as they were composed. Asterisks or ellipses shown here also appear in the actual letters. I have not corrected misspellings, grammatical errors, missing words, idiosyncrasies, or repetitions, nor have I cut any lines or passages. A single exception is the letter from Anne Bradstreet where some now unusual seventeenth-century spellings were updated for ease of reading. Occasionally, it may seem that the writer goes on too long or too often repeats a point, but these letters are as they were written, as they were read, and as they were intended. Sometimes kernels of true wisdom are embedded within the pedestrian, but that is how it was—it's authentic, and often it is just that quality that makes the letters so wonderful. For example, it is important for the reader to know that when Theodore Roosevelt, while president of the United States, wrote his son a stern dissertation on the proper role of athletics in one's life and the importance of character above all, that he concluded the letter with a jovial update on the doings of the younger siblings and news about several of the family animals. It says so much about what kind of father he was, what kind of man.

There are several previously published letters included that were, or may have been, cut or "cleaned-up" by another editor at another time. Every effort was made to find the originals for inclusion here, but in some instances it proved impossible. For clarity, I have included, in brackets, information that is now available, but did not appear on the original, such as the date, or approximate date, or where the parent was when he or she was writing. Nothing else but the bracketed information has been added.

Letters illuminate emotion, humanity, and fortitude in a way that is always fresh and enduring. They are the color, heart, and personality of history. Families, good or bad, are a vital force in most every life and they certainly have been so in the life and ideals of our country. Parents everywhere and throughout the ages know firsthand the visceral sentiment expressed by Sherwood Anderson in a letter to his son, John, "My heart is set on you." As I worked with the following letters from American parents from many walks of life, spanning centuries, again and again I came back to the realization that family ties and compelling stories surround us—in history, in the lives of those around us, and in our own lives.

—*Dorie McCullough Lawson*
Rockport, Maine

Wilmington in the State of
Delaware October 9th 184[?]
Monday.

My dear Boy, I am very much obliged
to you for your letter which gives me
much interesting information. I will try
to procure in New York a filterer
which will purify the water of the
new pump.

I have been at many places
in Pennsylvania when I wished that
you were strong enough to be with me.
When you grow strong enough I shall want
you to travel with me. I saw on the
Banks of the Schuylkill, Valley Forge the
place where General Washington had
his camp during one of the most severe

First page of William Henry Seward's letter
to William Henry Seward, Jr.

Continuity

WILLIAM HENRY SEWARD TO
WILLIAM HENRY SEWARD, JR.

"How good and virtuous and just ought we to be and how thankful to God that we have blessings secured by the virtue and sufferings of our ancestors."

One of the most important political figures of the mid-nineteenth century, William Henry Seward was governor of New York, then senator, then secretary of state under Abraham Lincoln. As a leading voice in the condemnation of slavery, it was he who delivered the courageous line on the floor of the Senate evoking a "higher law." Later, in 1867, it was Seward, the ever-devoted proponent of American expansion and progress, who secured the purchase of Alaska for the United States. With thick, disheveled hair and a prominent nose, Seward, according to Henry Adams, looked like a "wise macaw." Charming and relaxed, he was a welcome guest and a favorite among the Washington hostesses.

In the fall of 1848, he was running for the first time for a seat in the United States Senate. He campaigned in his home state, New York, and traveled about the East Coast speaking on behalf of the Republican Party. Here, with his characteristic broad sense of time, William Seward, the grandson of a Revolutionary War colonel, writes to his son Willie, a nine-year-old boy at home with persistent eye troubles.

7

[October 7, 1848]
Wilmington in the State of Delaware, Monday

My dear Boy

I am very much obliged to you for your letter which gives me much interesting information. I will try to procure in New York a filter which will purify the water of the new pump.

I have been at many places in Pennsylvania where I wished that you were strong enough to be with me. When you grow strong enough I shall want you to travel with me. I saw on the banks of the Schuylkill, Valley Forge the place where General Washington had his camp during one of the most severe winters which occurred during the American Revolution. His camp extended four miles long with two entrenchments in front and high mountains on the one side and a deep creek on the other. From the mountain in rear he could see with his spy glass the British army in Philadelphia seventy miles off. He was almost destitute of ammunition to protect himself. The Congress was not able to supply him with money, the army was in deplorable want of bread and meat clothes and shoes. They suffered exceedingly. The poor horses and dogs died of hunger and diarrhea and death extended to the men, a dozen were buried in a day and in one place, scarcely beneath the frost in the surface of the ground. The farmer now often turns up the bones of the lost men when plowing his fields. Mrs. Washington was a good woman, she spent the winter in the camp and she served and consoled the sick and dying. It was by such sacrifice that Liberty was obtained for the American people. How good and virtuous and just ought we to be and how thankful to God that we have blessings secured by the virtue and sufferings of our ancestors. I hope you will get Peter Parley's history of the Revolution and ask Ma to read to you the account of the Revolution and then I hope you will re-solve to be a good man like General Washington that all people may love and bless you.

I saw canal boats on railroad cars in Pennsylvania loaded with freight, and what is very strange is that as the boats are too long for the curves of the Rail Roads, they build the boats into three pieces, and when they get on the mountains they put them together with hooks and let them down into the Canal and float them to Lake Erie. Yet they do not take in a drop of water. Can you guess how this is done?

Your affectionate father
William H. Seward.

Elizabeth Cady Stanton to
Margaret L. Stanton

*". . . I feel that . . . I am making the path smoother for
you and Hattie and all the other dear girls."*

Elizabeth Cady Stanton, a plump and jolly mother of seven, was a revolutionary. Dressed in yards of black silk and lace, with her white hair curled neatly beneath her bonnet, she charmed and excited audiences across the country. She often began with talk of children and motherhood and then deftly moved on to property rights, divorce reform, and the right to vote. "You may never be wives, mothers or housekeepers," she explained, "but you will be women."

Nineteenth-century American women could not vote, could not sign a contract or serve on a jury. Married women were not permitted to own or inherit property, or to earn or invest money, and in the case of a divorce, the custody of the children automatically went to the father. For fifty-four years, from 1848 until her death in 1902, Elizabeth Cady Stanton fought vehemently for overall social justice for women. In organizing meetings and writing speeches, she was tireless; for eight months of each year during the 1870s, she toured the country lecturing. Spreading the word and earning a living, Stanton delivered one speech a day and two on Sundays in town after town. Here, describing a typical day on the road, she writes from Austin, Minnesota, to her twenty-year-old daughter, a student at Vassar.

To Margaret L. Stanton
Au[st]in, Minnesota, December 1, 1872

Dear Madge:

Imagine me to-day sitting in a small comfortable room in the railroad hotel about a half mile from this little Minnesota town, where I do not know one soul. But as everybody is polite and attentive, I suppose they all know me. I spoke last evening at Waterloo, and in order to reach here, my next place, I was obliged to leave at midnight. So after my lecture, I had an oyster supper, packed up my finery, and, all ready to start, took a short nap on the sofa. I was called at two. But as the horses were sick and I was the only guest going from the hotel westward, I was toted, I and my baggage, in a little cart drawn by a mule through a fearful snow storm, the wind cutting like particles of glass. Having arrived safely at the depot, my escort, a good natured, over-grown boy, deposited me and mine beside a red-hot stove. Learning then and there that the train was two hours behind, I rolled my cloak up for a pillow, laid down on the bench and went to sleep, listening to a discussion in an adjoining room on the merits of my lecture. One man vowed in a broad Irish brogue that he would leave the country if the women voted. Gracious, I thought to myself as I dozed into slumber, what would become of our experiment if one "white male" should desert the flag! In due time I was waked by some gentle Patrick,— perhaps my very critic—tickets bought, valise checked and I transferred to a sleeping-car, where, in a twinkling, I at once "flopped" asleep again, without even taking my bonnet off. At eight, I was roused by an African for this place, where, it being Sunday, the train lies over. So I ordered a fire, washed my face, ate breakfast, undressed regularly, went to bed and slept soundly until one, when I arose, took a sponge bath, had dinner, read all the papers I could procure and now sit down to answer your letter, which was the only one I received at Waterloo. I read it alone at midnight, and, though I am always advising you to write short letters, I did wish this time you had written more at length. You ask if it is not lonely travelling as I do. It is indeed, and I should have enjoyed above all things having Hattie with me. But you see, dearest, that would double my expenses, and as I am so desirous of making money for the household, I must practice economy in some direction. And above all considerations of loneliness and fatigue, I feel that I am doing an immense amount of good in rousing women to thought and inspiring them with new hope and self-respect, that I am making the path smoother for you and Hattie and all the other dear girls. You would laugh to see how everywhere the girls flock round me for a kiss, a curl, an autograph. They all like so much my lecture, "The Coming Girl." I am so glad, dearest, to know that you are happy. Now, improve every hour and every opportunity, and fit yourself for a good teacher or professor, so that you can have money of your own and not be obliged to depend on any man for every breath you draw. The helpless dependence of women generally makes them the narrow, discontented beings so many are. With much love for yourself, kind regards for your chums and pleasant dreams for all in Vassar,

Good night,
Mother.

ALBERT EINSTEIN TO
HANS ALBERT EINSTEIN

*"What I have achieved through such a lot of strenuous
work shall not only be there for strangers but
especially for my own boys."*

When Albert Einstein first arrived at Princeton University in 1933, he was asked what equipment he needed for his office. "A desk or table, a chair, paper and pencils. Oh yes, and a large wastebasket . . ." he replied. In essence, all the Nobel Prize–winning scientist really needed was his brain. His mind operated at the highest reaches of human capability and his theories of relativity thoroughly revolutionized our understanding of light, matter, and energy.

He was an endearing character who loved his violin and said that he thought and daydreamed in music. He was inherently shy, utterly disinterested in the "trivialities of living," and emotionally he was often indifferent, even with his own family.

In November 1915, Einstein was living in wartime Berlin with his cousin Elsa, the woman who eventually became his second wife. His estranged wife, Mileva, lived in neutral Zurich along with his two sons, Hans Albert and Eduard, "Tete." Following eight years of effort, Einstein spent a final five weeks in the fall of 1915 completing "one of the most beautiful works of [his] life," the theory of general relativity. The theory—supreme thought expressed in just two pages—was the work that launched him into worldwide celebrity and secured his place among the greatest thinkers of all time. Here the thirty-six-year-old Einstein, flush with his recent accomplishment, writes to his eleven-year-old son, Hans Albert.

[Berlin,] 4 November [1915]

My dear Albert,

Yesterday I received your dear letter and was very happy with it. I was already afraid you wouldn't write to me at all any more. You told me when I was in Zurich, that it is awkward for you when I come to Zurich. Therefore I think it is better if we get together in a different place, where nobody will interfere with our comfort. I will in any case urge that each year we spend a whole month together, so that you see that you have a father who is fond of you and who loves you. You can also learn many good and beautiful things from me, something another cannot as easily offer you. What I have achieved through such a lot of strenuous work shall not only be there for strangers but especially for my own boys. These days I have completed one of the most beautiful works of my life, when you are bigger, I will tell you about it.

I am very pleased that you find joy with the piano. This and carpentry are in my opinion for your age the best pursuits, better even than school. Because those are things which fit a young person such as you very well. Mainly play the things on the piano which please you, even if the teacher does not assign those. That is the way to learn the most, that when you are doing something with such enjoyment that you don't notice that the time passes. I am sometimes so wrapped up in my work that I forget about the noon meal. Also play ringtoss with Tete. That teaches you agility. Also go to my friend Zangger sometimes. He is a dear man.

Be with Tete kissed by your

Papa.

Regards to Mama.

John D. Rockefeller, Jr., to John III, Nelson, Laurence, Winthrop, and David Rockefeller

". . . it is not too early for you to begin preparing and training your children to bear their share in these responsibilities . . ."

With commitment, originality, and principle, John D. Rockfeller, Jr.—the son of Standard Oil tycoon John D. Rockefeller—made philanthropy his life's work. He distributed more than half a billion dollars for the public good over the course of his career. With utmost respect and admiration for his father's accomplishments, he perceived himself as the steward—not the owner—of the vast Rockefeller fortune. For future generations of the family, wherever money and social conscience were involved, he never missed an opportunity to instruct. "To whom much is given, much is expected" was his motto.

Here, in a typically straightforward and controlled manner, he writes to his five sons, John, Nelson, Laurence, Winthrop, and David, who ranged in age from thirty-seven to twenty-eight years old.

Rockefeller Center
New York
Room 5600
30 Rockefeller Plaza
December 21, 1943

Dear Boys:

From the time Grandfather Rockefeller, a lad of about sixteen, got his first position, his "Ledger A" records the fact that he was making current contributions to worthy causes and needy people although the amounts were sometimes not more than three or five cents. This practice he continued all his life, increasing the amounts thus devoted to the betterment of his fellow men as his own resources increased. One of the earliest recollections of my childhood is Grandfather's reading to us at the table letters of appeal which he had received from individuals or on behalf of causes and discussing with us their merits and what answers should be made. He began to teach us to give and to save regularly when our allowances or the money we earned by doing various family chores amounted to not more than ten cents a week. With this inheritance and early training it was natural that we children should have commenced to give away money for the benefit of other people and causes in our early youth and that our gifts should have increased as Grandfather's did with increasing resources.

After I had worked with Grandfather and his other associates for a few years in developing and organizing his philanthropic gifts on an ever-broadening scale, and it had become apparent to him that I was seeking with what means I then had to be helpful to my fellow men as he had always been, Grandfather gave me, from time to time, increasingly large sums. These gifts he made, as he said in making them, because he felt confident he could count upon my continuing to do for my fellow men as he had done, thus adding to the extent and diversity of the gifts for public purposes which he had been making.

These monies received from Grandfather, I have always regarded as a trust. As he sought to develop in his children the desire and ability to conserve their funds and to use them for the benefit of mankind, so, from an early age, I have sought to do the same with you children and have added, from time to time, to your resources as I have noted the wisdom as well as the generosity with which you have used a substantial portion of them for the betterment of your fellow men.

Some years have passed since I set up trust funds for you. The full in-

13

come as well as the principal of these funds became available for each of you as you reached 30, and will be available for David when he is 30. I have observed with profound satisfaction that by and large you have not let these larger resources affect the simplicity of your living, although your growing families have of necessity increased your living expenses, but that on the other hand you have drawn upon them in ever larger amounts for the benefit of the worthy causes to which you have individually related yourselves. In other words, you have shown the same sense of stewardship and the same sense of responsibility that Grandfather, by his example, inspired in me. It is, therefore, with confidence and satisfaction that I am planning to share with you still further, from time to time, this trusteeship reposed in me by Grandfather. The wise course you are all pursuing in the use of your resources and your deep and earnest desire to make your lives and your means count as fully as possible for the betterment of humanity would, I know, give Grandfather as great satisfaction as it gives me.

In the meantime, it is not too early for you to begin preparing and training your children to bear their share in these responsibilities. In the hope that it will be helpful to that end, I am setting up a trust for each of your children with the securities listed in the accompanying memorandum. I have chosen this time to set up these trusts because it is the spirit of Him Whose birth the world is about to celebrate, that inspires all worthy living and generous giving.

Affectionately,
Father.

ANSEL ADAMS TO MICHAEL ADAMS

*"I am wondering, in the afternoon of my own life,
just what your day will be."*

Photographer and environmentalist, Ansel Adams had a vision of America that was precise and certain. He was an artist and masterful technician who combined, in his words, "machine, mind and spirit" to create powerful, unforgettable images of the American landscape. His photographs are so widely known and appreciated that, in a sense, his vision has become our national view of America's natural beauty.

Thoroughly committed to his work, Adams often put in eighteen-hour days for weeks on end. He was a gregarious fellow, brimming with energy and enthusiasm. An exuberant correspondent (his letters are filled with exclamation points), it's estimated that over the course of his life he wrote in the neighborhood of one hundred thousand letters and cards.

Michael, Adams's son, was raised in Yosemite National Park in a house teeming with artists and creative people. As a boy, he often traveled with his father, and in 1941 he was there when Ansel Adams made what was to become his most well-known photograph, Moonrise, Hernandez, New Mexico. *Here at the end of 1953, during the Korean War, Ansel Adams writes to twenty-year-old Michael, who had just joined the Air Force.*

Yosemite National Park
Christmas 1953

Dear Mike—

I began this letter in San Francisco but am just finishing it up today in Yosemite. I never wrote a letter of this kind before, because I never had a son joining the Air Force before! The idea of Christmas is very strange to me at this time, but we have to keep up the illusion. I want to give you everything—but I can't think of a single thing you really need! That telephoto lens sounds good to me!

You are now a man, joining up with a very important part of our national defense. What is more important, you are taking your place in the pattern of our time (which exists whether we like it or not). I never joined up with anything; I have missed the peaks of such experience, and I envy you considerably. Now you are quite far from the little boy in *Michael and Anne in Yosemite Valley*—and yet I wonder how far you can get—or really want to get—from that particular kind of reality. I doubt if you can ever realize the advantages of being raised in Yosemite—only outsiders could grasp the potentials. But such a life would have value only if it instilled in you some awareness of intangible qualities beyond the ordinary. I think it has done this for you, and that you will fully appreciate them in the future.

I have spent a good part of my life trying to understand the obligations of a parent! The conventional idea of a parent is very obnoxious to me. We gave you considerable freedom of being—it was a pet theory of ours. I think it worked out quite well; I see nothing about you that I am not proud of!

If you are man enough to join the Air Force, you are man enough to comprehend the problems surrounding us. I have never talked much about

15

"morality" because I trusted your innate sense of values to carry you through and I distrust words written or spoken about wordless things. I have had quite a lot to do with the external world—and quite a lot with the internal world, too. I am wondering, in the afternoon of my own life, just what your day will be. It will take much effort, devotion and compassion—something beyond the thin skin of morality—to bring you to a full realization of what it is to be a man in the face of the world as it now is and in the face of a perplexing future. You cannot be misled by the obvious "easy" way—there isn't any!

When you go to Fresno on the 28th you take on a whole new world of experience—and you carry a lot of the experience of your mother and father with you—which is there to help you if you need it. You are entering a bright new world of your own. The skies are the new land—I envy you, and if I were younger I would like to be up there, too.

We cannot grasp the full meaning of your new life to you, but we would like to share just a little of it with you. Please make a special effort to write us often—to your mother especially. I don't think this is too much to ask.

Good luck—all our love!!!
Ansel

HENRY LOUIS GATES, JR., TO MAGGIE AND LIZA GATES

"I hope that it brings you even a small measure of understanding, at long last, of why we see the world with such different eyes . . ."

With a rare combination of intellect and entrepreneurial spirit, Henry Louis Gates, the W. E. B. Du Bois Professor at Harvard, has worked tirelessly and successfully to elevate African-American studies to the scholarly level of an independent academic discipline. He is a writer, a teacher, a literary critic, an outspoken educational reformer, and through his scholarship we now have the earliest known literary works by African-American women—two novels written in the 1850s—Hannah Crafts's The Bondswoman's Narrative *and Harriet Wilson's* Our Nig.

We study literature, culture, and history so that we may better understand. In 1994 Gates published a book about his growing-up years in the 1950s and 1960s in West Virginia. The book began as a series of letters to his two young daugh-ters—letters written so they might better understand from where and from whom they had come. The following letter to Maggie and Liza Gates is also the intro-duction to Gates's memoir, Colored People.

Dear Maggie and Liza:

I have written to you because a world into which I was born, a world that nurtured and sustained me, has mysteriously disappeared. My darkest fear is that Piedmont, West Virginia, will cease to exist, if some executives on Park Avenue decide that it is more profitable to build a completely new paper mill elsewhere than to overhaul one a century old. Then they would close it, just as they did in Cumberland with Celanese, and Pittsburgh Plate Glass, and the Kelly-Springfield Tire Company. The town will die, but our people will not move. They will not *be* moved. Because for them, Pied-mont—snuggled between the Allegheny Mountains and the Potomac River Valley—is life itself.

I have written to you because of the day when we were driving home and you asked your mother and me just exactly what the civil rights move-ment had been all about and I pointed to a motel on Route 2 and said that at one time I could not have stayed there. Your mother could have stayed there, but your mother couldn't have stayed there with me. And you kids looked at us like we were telling you the biggest lie you had ever heard. So I thought about writing to you.

I have written for another reason, as well. I remember that once we were walking in Washington, D.C., heading for the National Zoo, and you asked me if I had known the man to whom I had just spoken. I said no. And, Liza, you volunteered that you found it embarrassing that I would speak to a complete stranger on the street. It called to mind a trip I'd made to Pitts-burgh with my father. On the way from his friend Mr. Ozzie Washington's sister's house, I heard Daddy speak to a colored man, then saw him tip his hat to the man's wife. (Daddy liked nice hats: Caterpillar hats for work, Dobbs hats for Sunday.) It's just something that you do, he said, when I asked him if he had known those people and why had he spoken to them.

Last summer, I sat at a sidewalk café in Italy, and three or four "black" Italians walked casually by, as well as a dozen or more blacker Africans. Each spoke to me, rather, each nodded his head slightly or acknowledged me by a glance, ever so subtly. When I was growing up, we always did this with each other, passing boats in a sea of white folk.

Yet there were certain Negroes who would avoid acknowledging you in this way in an integrated setting, especially if the two of you were the ones doing the integrating. Don't go over there with those white people if all you're going to do is Jim Crow yourselves—Daddy must have said that to me a thousand times. And by that I think he meant we shouldn't cling to each other out of habit or fear, or use protective coloration to evade the risks of living like any other human being, or use clannishness as a cop-out for exploring ourselves and possibly making new selves, forged in the crucible of integration. Your black ass, he'd laugh, is integrated already.

But there are other reasons that people distrust the reflex—the nod, the glance, the murmured greeting.

One reason is a resentment at being lumped together with thirty million African Americans whom you don't know and most of whom you will never know. Completely by the accident of racism, we have been bound together with people with whom we may or may not have something in common, just because we are "black." Thirty million Americans are black, and thirty million is a lot of people. One day you wonder: What do the misdeeds of a Mike Tyson have to do with me? So why do I feel implicated? And how can I not feel racial recrimination when I can feel racial pride?

Then, too, there were Negroes who were embarrassed about *being* Negroes, who didn't want to be bothered with race and with other black people. One of the more painful things about being colored was being colored in public around other colored people, who were embarrassed to be colored and embarrassed that we *both* were colored and in public together. As if to say: "Negro, will you *pul-lease* disappear so that I can get my own white people?" As if to say: "I'm not a Negro like other Negroes." As if to say: "I am a human being—let me be!"

For much of my adolescence and adulthood, I thought of these people as having betrayed the race. I used to walk up to them and call them *Brother* or *Sister*, loud and with a sardonic edge, when they looked like they were trying to "escape." When I went off to college, I would make the "conversion" of errant classmates a serious project, a political commitment.

I used to reserve my special scorn for those Negroes who were always being embarrassed by someone else in the race. Someone too dark, someone too "loud," someone too "wrong." Someone who dared to wear red in public. Loud and wrong: we used to say that about each other. Nigger is loud and wrong. "Loud" carried a triple meaning: speaking too loudly, dressing too loudly, and just *being* too loudly.

I do know that, when I was a boy, many Negroes would have been the first to censure other Negroes once they were admitted into all-white neighborhoods or schools or clubs. "An embarrassment to the race"—

phrases of that sort were bandied about. Accordingly, many of us in our generation engaged in strange antics to flout those strictures. Like eating watermelon in public, eating it loudly and merrily, and spitting the seeds into the middle of the street, red juice running down the sides of our cheeks, collecting under our chins. Or taking the greatest pride in the Royal Kink. Uncle Harry used to say he didn't *like* watermelon, which I knew was a lie because I saw him wolf down slices when I was a little kid, before he went off to seminary at Boston University. But he came around, just like he came around to painting God and Jesus black, and all the seraphim and the cherubim, too. And I, from another direction, have gradually come around, also, and stopped trying to tell other Negroes how to be black.

Do you remember when your mother and I woke you up early on a Sunday morning, just to watch Nelson Mandela walk out of prison, and how it took a couple of hours for him to emerge, and how you both wanted to go back to bed and, then, to watch cartoons? And how we began to worry that something bad had happened to him on the way out, because the delay was so long? And when he finally walked out of that prison, how we were so excited and teary-eyed at Mandela's nobility, his princeliness, his straight back and unbowed head? I think I felt that there walked the Negro, as Pop might have said; there walked the whole of the African people, as regal as any king. And that feeling I had, that gooseflesh sense of identity that I felt at seeing Nelson Mandela, listening to Mahalia Jackson sing, watching Muhammad Ali fight, or hearing Martin Luther King speak, is part of what I mean by being colored. I realize the sentiment may not be logical, but I want to have my cake and eat it, too. Which is why I still nod or speak to black people on the streets and why it felt so good to be acknowledged by the Afro-Italians who passed my table at the café in Milan.

I want to be able to take special pride in a Jessye Norman aria, a Muhammad Ali shuffle, a Michael Jordan slam dunk, a Spike Lee movie, a Thurgood Marshall opinion, a Toni Morrison novel, a James Brown's Camel Walk. Above all, I enjoy the unselfconscious moments of a shared cultural intimacy, whatever form they take, when no one else is watching, when no white people are around. Like Joe Louis's fights, which my father still talks about as part of the fixed repertoire of stories that texture our lives. You've seen his eyes shining as he describes how Louis hit Max Schmeling so many times and so hard, and how some reporter asked him, after the fight: "Joe, what would you have done if that last punch hadn't knocked Schmeling out?" And how ole Joe responded, without missing a beat: "I'da run around behind him to see what was holdin' him up!"

Even so, I rebel at the notion that I can't be part of other groups, that I can't construct identities through elective affinity, that race must be the most important thing about me. Is that what I want on my gravestone: Here lies an African American? So I'm divided. I want to be black, to know black, to luxuriate in whatever I might be calling blackness at any particular time—but to do so in order to come out the other side, to experience a humanity that is neither colorless nor reducible to color. Bach *and* James Brown. Sushi *and* fried catfish. Part of me admires those people who can say with a straight face that they have transcended any attachment to a particular community or group . . . but I always want to run around behind them to see what holds them up.

I am not Everynegro. I am not native to the great black metropolises: New York, Chicago, or Los Angeles, say. Nor can I claim to be a "citizen of the world." I am from and of a time and a place—Piedmont, West Virginia—and that's a world apart, a world of difference. So this is not a story of a race but a story of a village, a family, and its friends. And of a sort of segregated peace. What hurt me most about the glorious black awakening of the late sixties and early seventies is that we lost our sense of humor. Many of us thought that enlightened politics excluded it.

In your lifetimes, I suspect, you will go from being African Americans, to "people of color," to being, once again, "colored people." (The linguistic trend toward condensation is strong.) I don't mind any of the names myself. But I have to confess that I like "colored" best, maybe because when I hear the word, I hear it in my mother's voice and in the sepia tones of my childhood. As artlessly and honestly as I can, I have tried to evoke a colored world of the fifties, a Negro world of the early sixties, and the advent of a black world of the later sixties, from the point of view of the boy I was. When you are old enough to read what follows, I hope that it brings you even a small measure of understanding, at long last, of why we see the world with such different eyes . . . and why that is for me a source both of gladness and of regret. And I hope you'll understand why I continue to speak to colored people I pass on the streets.

Love,
Daddy

Piedmont, West Virginia
July 8, 1993

Elsie, Mabel (wife), Daisy, and
Alexander Graham Bell

Lincoln Steffens and son Pete

The Developing Mind

John Adams to
Abigail "Nabby" Adams Smith

*"In your solitary hours, my dear daughter, you will
have a delightful opportunity of attending to the
education of your children . . ."*

John Adams knew firsthand what education could do for a person. The son of
a farmer and a mother who was likely illiterate, he was granted a scholarship at age
fifteen to Harvard College and the world opened before him. With his own children he was constantly advising them on what to read, what to learn, and what
was important to know, and when he became a grandfather his interest in the education of his grandchildren was strong indeed. He was, too, a man of his times and
he believed, most respectfully, that it was the mother's duty and "delightful opportunity" to educate her young children.

Here, Adams writes to his thirty-two-year-old daughter, Abigail—known as
"Nabby"—about her role in the developing minds of her three sons. Newly elected
president of the United States, he would be inaugurated on March 4, 1797, less
than two weeks hence. The election to replace George Washington was bitterly fac-
tional. As well, no precedent had yet been set for how a new president would select his cabinet. It all weighed heavily upon him.

Philadelphia, Feb. 21st, 1797

Dear Child:

I believe I have not acknowledged your favour of the 20th January, which I received in its season.

I hope your apprehensions that "the party who have embarrassed the President, and exerted themselves to divide the election, will endeavour to render my situation as uncomfortable as possible," will be found to be without sufficient foundation; I have seen, on the contrary, a disposition to acquiesce, and hope it will increase. I am not at all alarmed; I know my countrymen very well.

If the way to do good to my country, were to render myself popular, I could easily do it. But extravagant popularity is not the road to public advantage.

By the 4th of March I shall know what to do. I cannot build my house till the foundation is laid; at present I know not what house I shall have, nor what means to furnish it. These things will be determined in ten days. At present I believe it will be best for your mother to remain where she is until October. I shall go to her as soon as I can.

Your brother John continues to give the highest satisfaction to government by his great industry, his deep discernment, his independent spirit, and his splendid talents. I hear such commendations of him as no other man abroad obtains.

In your solitary hours, my dear daughter, you will have a delightful opportunity of attending to the education of your children, to give them a taste and attachment to study, and to books. A taste for science and literature, added to a turn for business, never can fail of success in life. Without learning, nothing very great can ever be accomplished in the way of business. But not only a thirst for knowledge should be excited, and a taste for letters be cultivated, but prudence, patience, justice, temperance, resolution, modesty, and self-cultivation, should be recommended to them as early as possible. The command of their passions, the restraints of their appetites, reverence for superiors, especially parents, a veneration for religion, morals, and good conduct.

You will find it more for your happiness to spend your time with them in this manner, than to be engaged in fashionable amusements, and social entertainments, even with the best company.

But I must restrain myself, and subscribe the name of your affectionate father,

John Adams

Alexander Graham Bell to Elsie and Marian (Daisy) Bell

"I cut off the tail and sent it to Elsie by mail today so that you might see it."

By inventing the telephone in 1876 at the age of twenty-nine, Alexander Graham Bell changed the world. Imaginative and extremely industrious, throughout all of his seventy-five years, he was continually inventing and creating. Sound, communication, aviation, architecture, genetics, geography, geology, geometry, current affairs, linguistics, and, most importantly, the education of the deaf—he was interested in it all. He invented a metal detector and the first respirator, he was a founder and president of the National Geographic Society, he warned about environmental pollutants and coined the phrase "greenhouse effect," and he was integral in bringing the teachings and methods of Maria Montessori to the United States.

Bell was convinced that children learn through their play and by doing. He believed that education was "a leading forth from within rather than a putting in from without" and that "exercise of the mind is just what children need. It develops their reasoning powers and arouses their interest."

Here, at forty, Alexander Graham Bell writes to his two daughters, nine and seven years old.

Edgartown, Martha's Vineyard
Sunday, November 13th, 1887

My dear Elsie and Daisy

I wish you could be here with me in Martha's Vineyard, for I am sure you would enjoy playing on the sandy beach, and watching the great big waves dashing on the shore. I am sure you would enjoy looking for the beautiful shells and pebbles that are thrown on the beach after every storm.

I was walking on the beach this afternoon with Mr. [Hity?] when I saw a funny black object on the shore. It looked like a book with a long tail!!

What do you think it was? It was the dead body of a fish—and it was the funniest fish I ever saw! It was flat like a book. Its eyes were on the top of its head, and its mouth was in its stomach! But where do you think its teeth were? I opened its mouth—but there were no teeth there. Guess where they were. Did you ever hear of a fish with teeth on its tail?!!!! I never did, but this fish had teeth all over its tail, and all over its back. It was covered with teeth so that you could not touch it without being bitten.

It could bite you by wagging its tail. I cut off the tail and sent it to Elsie by mail today so that you might see it. I hope it will reach you safely.

The mouth of this wonderful fish was very beautiful. Its lips were not soft like yours but quite hard and covered all over with beautiful little ivory pearls. I cut off the lips so that you might see them. I sent them to Daisy by mail.

The people here call the fish the "Stingaree" though its proper name is "The stinging ray." The fish I saw was only a baby. Captain Osborne says he has seen one with a tail four feet long covered with teeth an inch long. He says that the teeth have poison on them when the fish is alive, so that it is dangerous to touch them. He knew a man who tried to catch one in the water, but the fish stuck its long tail into his leg and hurt him so much that he was glad to let it go. The leg swelled up and he was unable to walk for months. You need not be afraid of the tail I have sent you, because the fish has been dead for a long time, the teeth are dry and there is now no poison on them. Now my dear little girls I must say good-bye. I hope you are both good and gentle. I hope you are trying to learn as much as you can from Miss Hudson and I hope you try to make Mamma very happy and proud of you both. I expect Grandpapa and Grandmamma Bell to-morrow. Won't you write a nice letter to Grandmamma? I am sure she would be glad to hear from you—and so would I. Good bye for the present.

Your loving father
Alexander Graham Bell

JACK LONDON TO JOAN LONDON

"Do you, desiring to be a success, think your success depends on the advice of a failure?"

Jack London was the most successful writer of his generation. Over his lifetime he produced an astounding quantity of work: two hundred short stories, four hundred pieces of nonfiction (essays, articles, war correspondence reports, and book reviews), and twenty novels. Yet, by 1913, at the age of thirty-seven, London was dying, his body failing. He was still writing, but by his own admission, only churning out pieces for the money. Years of excessive drinking and extravagant living had left him with kidneys diseased beyond hope.

Bitterly divorced from his two daughters' mother, Bess, London was a mostly distant father. High living kept him from his children, as did Bess's refusal to allow the girls ever to see their father in the presence of his second wife, Charmian.

Here London writes his twelve-year-old daughter, Joan. It is interesting to note that Joan's mother, Bess, was a teacher.

Glen Ellen,
Aug 17 1913

Dearest Joan:—

I have just dispatched a telegram to you, telling you that letter follows.

(1) Regarding bulkhead—I havent the money now. In another year I'll have the money. In the meantime we'll have to endure the damage of the winter rains. Tell mother, by digging drainage ditches, this damage can be minimized at the cost of several dollars for a day-laborer. Ask Uncle Ernest to indicate where the drainage ditches should be dug, how deep, how wide, etc.

Now (2). Please remember that an English teacher is a teacher of English, for not very many dollars a month salary for two reasons: (a) She has failed to get married & have a man buy her clothes & food for her; (b) she can't write stuff that brings money from the editors and publishers. In short, no matter how good an *"English"* teacher she may be, she has proved that she can't write salable English. Again, in short, she is a failure. Do you, desiring to be a success, think your success depends on the advice of a failure?

Now, Joan, when your Daddy tells you he is a top-writer in the world, do not think he is bragging. He is telling you in order to show that he has succeeded where teachers of English have failed. He is telling you this in order to prove that he *knows* where literary success lies, and where the failure—English teachers do not know.

I must talk this over with you at length. I can't write it. I can't leave the ranch now. Ask mama, from me, if you can run up on the train to the ranch when here and have a few hours talk with me about your education.

If mama says "no," & I hope for your sake that she will not, then, anyway, select your French & German & cut out Latin & Greek (as we previously planned), & wait until I can come down & talk with you.

Of course, remember, & tell mother so, that you are my first-born; that your life is largely at stake here; that I know; that teachers of English do not know; and that the greatest thing in the world right now for *you* would be to have this talk with me. It is not a case of mother; of me; but of *you & your whole life welfare.*

You can come on a morning train and leave on an afternoon train; better would it be to stay one night over, because I work all morning.

Of course, have mama read this letter and talk the whole matter over with her.

Remember that your daddy is a very busy daddy these day.

Daddy.

P.S.—Always write your letters in *ink*, on *one side* only. Always address your letter in *ink*. Always know the postal laws.

First class postage is reckoned in *units of two cents*. 3cts is no good on a letter. 2–4–6–8—is the way to stamp letters. 3 cts. means that you lose 1 ct., and that the recipient must pay the difference between 2 cts. and 4 cts., or 2 cts.

Daddy

Lincoln Steffens to Pete Steffens

*"Nobody understands things as they are and the proof
of this is that nobody,—not the greatest scientist,
not the tenderest poet, not the most sensitive painter;
only for a moment, the kindest lover can see
that all is beautiful."*

Journalist, radical, and reformer, Lincoln Steffens was among the first of America's muckrakers. In a series of articles for McClure's *magazine, later published together in 1904 in his well-known book* The Shame of the Cities, *Steffens exposed to the nation the widespread corruption of local governments. His work changed the way Americans viewed the establishment and introduced a new kind of journalism to the country: investigative reporting.*

A father only late in life, to Steffens's great surprise, he was delighted and fascinated by fatherhood and created a gentle, affectionate atmosphere for little Pete. "The father's place is in the home," he wrote, "and there I am and there I mean to stay—on guard—to protect my child from education."

Here, while in Germany working on his autobiography, sixty-year-old Steffens writes a letter of guidance for the future to his two-year-old son, Pete.

Carlsbad, June 23, 1926

Dear Pete:

This place will suit you I think. Down three flights of stairs is a restaurant through which you will go to either an open cafe in front or on a side toward the town to a large graveled playground. There is not much for a little fellow like you to do on this playground. It is the grown-up idea for a place for kids. A bare yard where there is nothing to break and nothing to get hurt on. Safety first is the law for children, but you will have your ball and we will find you a half-developed *Deutsches Madel* [German girl] to play with, so that you can learn to think in another language. Sometimes we can go in back of the house to a playground for grown-ups. That has a net and balls 'n' everything to amuse the big children who can't play with nothing like a baby. They have a game called tennis which they work at hard rather than do anything useful. It's thought to be degrading to work; and it is. It is a sure sign that your father was an honest man and never got any graft, if you have to work for your living. I hope to arrange it so that you will not be ashamed of me; I leave you my graft and I'll show you how to get more if you need it. If you work, you will work as a scientist or an artist, for fun, not for money. Money *cannot* be made by labor. But work, real work, for what we call duty or the truth, that is more fun than tennis. Sometimes we will sit, you and I, and look at the human beings that crawl around here, and when we have had our fill of that sight we will walk away a few hundred feet and look at the trees, the beautiful, tall straight trees that have no bellies and no bad tastes. They are dignified and well-dressed. I'd like to have you appreciate trees, appreciate the difference between them and men, and then, some day, believe that, under decent conditions it will be possible for human beings to also have souls. They haven't now; only bellies, pockets and the poor beginnings of a mind.

Your mother and your Cousin Jane will explain this to you, if I am gone. They will tell it to you honestly and humorously, Pete; they will not propagand with you; with all others maybe; but not with Pete. You are to have the straight of it my boy; and the straightest of the straight is that we don't know anything; not any of us; not Jane, not Peter, not I. Nobody understands things as they are and the proof of this is that nobody,—not the greatest scientist, not the tenderest poet, not the most sensitive painter; only for a moment, the kindest lover can see that all is beautiful. I can't, I only believe that.

It may be wrong; there may be ugliness, like the sick bellies these miserable *Kurgaste* [spa guests] come here to cure, but I have a funny old faith that, if a little fellow like you is shown everything and allowed to look at everything and not lied to by anybody or anything, he, even Pete, might do better even than Joyce did what *Ulysses* was meant to do; he might see and show that there is exquisite beauty everywhere except in an educated mind.

And an educated mind is nothing but the God-given mind of a child after his parents' and his grandparents' generation have got through molding it. We can't help teaching you; you will ask that of us; but we are prone to teach you what we know, and I am going, now and again, to warn you:

Remember we really don't know anything. Keep your baby eyes (which are the eyes of genius) on what we don't know. That is your playground, bare and graveled, safe and unbreakable.

Love your mother, but don't you believe and revere her; and as for your father, laugh at him as he laughs at himself till the tears start.

L. Steff.

EUGENE O'NEILL TO SHANE O'NEILL

*"Because any fool knows that to work hard at
something you want to accomplish
is the only way to be happy."*

*In July 1939, playwright Eugene O'Neill had just completed notes and out-
lines for two of his masterworks,* The Iceman Cometh *and* Long Day's Journey Into Night. *At fifty years of age he had already won the Nobel Prize and
three Pulitzer Prizes (a fourth Pulitzer was awarded to him after his death).*

*O'Neill was the father of three children—Eugene, Jr., with his first wife, and
Shane and Oona with his second wife. A shy, often depressed and extremely driven
man, he was not particularly affectionate nor involved with any of his children. His
second child, Shane, was a sweet but troubled boy who idolized his father. For
O'Neill, Shane's lack of commitment and his dependence on others were persistent
sources of frustration. Here O'Neill, who was living in California with his third
wife, Carlotta, writes to nineteen-year-old Shane, who over the preceding several
years had been asked to leave one school after another.*

July 18, 1939

Dear Shane,

I wrote Oona a couple of days ago to tell you to expect an answer to
your letter soon and here it is.

My feeling, that Harry spoke to you about—and by the way, I didn't
tell him to say anything to you—was based on the fact that you had let me
hear so little from you at Lawrenceville. But forget it. I appreciate a lot the
frankness of this last letter of yours and I hope you will always write to me
in just that spirit. What you say of your feeling a new understanding had
sprung up between us on your last visit was exactly what I felt. Which
made it doubly hard to comprehend why later on you went ahead with a
complete change in your plans without consulting me and were all booked
for Lawrenceville by the time I heard from you.

My advice on the subject of raising horses would not be much use to
you. I don't know anyone in that game, what conditions or prospects are,
or anything else about it. All I know is that if you want to get anywhere
with it, or with anything else, you have got to adopt an entirely different
attitude from the one you have had toward getting an education. In plain

words, you've got to make up your mind to study whatever you undertake, and concentrate your mind on it, and really work at it. This isn't wisdom. Any damned fool in the world knows it's true, whether it's a question of raising horses or writing plays. You simply have to face the prospect of starting at the bottom and spending years learning how to do it. The trouble with you, I think, is you are still too dependent on others. You expect too much from outside you and demand too little of yourself. You hope everything will be made smooth and easy for you by someone else. Well, it's coming to the point where you are old enough, and have been around enough, to see that this will get you exactly nowhere. You will be what you make yourself and you have got to do that job absolutely alone and on your own, whether you're in school or holding down a job.

After all, parents' advice is no damned good. You know that as well as I. The best I can do is to try to encourage you to work hard at something you really want to do and have the ability to do. Because any fool knows that to work hard at something you want to accomplish is the only way to be happy. But beyond that it is entirely up to you. You've got to do for yourself all the seeking and finding concerned with what you want to do. Anyone but yourself is useless to you there.

I'm glad you got the job on the party-fishing boat. It's a start in the right direction of independence. The more you get to know of independence the better you will like it, and the more you will get to know yourself and the right aim for your life.

What I am trying to get firmly planted in your mind is this: In the really important decisions of life, others cannot help you. No matter how much they would like to. You must rely on yourself. That is the fate of each one of us. It can't be changed. It just is like that. And you are old enough to understand this now.

And that's all of that. It isn't much help in a practical advice way, but in another way it might be. At least, I hope so.

I'm glad to know of your doing so much reading and that you're becoming interested in Shakespeare. If you really like and understand his work, you will have something no one can ever take from you.

We are looking forward to Oona's visit. I appreciate your writing about her as you did. It is so long since I've seen her. Too long. Ordinarily I would have been coming East every year or two to put on new plays and would have seen her then. But a Cycle of nine plays is another matter. It brings up complications that keep me tied down to the job, especially as I have not yet caught up on my schedule from the delay my long illness of two years ago caused.

Don't talk of dry spell! We know all about that! We hardly had any rain last winter and now we live in dread our springs will get so low before summer ends that a lot of the stuff we have planted around the house can't be watered and will have to die. It's rotten. Natives tell us there was less rain this year than at any time for forty years.

Carlotta joins me in love to you. Let me know as soon as you have any definite plans for the immediate future. And keep your chin up! You will be all right as soon as you get yourself organized along one set line.

As ever,
Father.

N. C. WYETH TO NAT AND CAROLINE WYETH

"To keep alive and to intensify his sense of wonderment and his curiosity about the simplest things—these will become and remain the most potent factors in his life, no matter what he is destined to do."

N. C. Wyeth's enthusiasm for the world around him was apparent in nearly all he did. The celebrated illustrator, whose classic paintings illuminated the pages of such books as Treasure Island *and* Kidnapped, *loved adventure, nature, and action. He was known to stand for hours on the rocky coast of Maine just watching the crashing waves, sensing the power of the ocean. Wyeth delighted in his family and encouraged his five gifted children to stretch their imaginations and creativity to their fullest. Three of his children—Henriette, Caroline, and Andrew—became artists. His daughter Ann became a composer and painter, and son Nat, an engineer and inventor.*

Here N. C. Wyeth writes to his eldest son, Nat, and Nat's wife, Caroline, about their nearly two-year-old son, Newell.

Chadds Ford, Pennsylvania
October 19, 1943

Dear Nat and Caroline,

The memories of last week with you all are not dimmed as each event stands lens-clear. The beautiful and powerful little figure of Newell dominates it all however. His personality, for one so very young, is truly astonishing to me; the clarity of it remains in my memory, as does his blonde face and figure, cameolike—in sharp preciseness and ultimate delicacy. I like to think mostly of the glow of his hair and face in the cavernous gloom of that cathedrallike woods of "the grotto." I shall never forget him there.

Obviously he is blessed with a quick and attentive spirit. Nourish these traits by every means you can think of. This will comprise his greatest and profoundest education, no matter what imposing institutions he may encounter later on. To keep alive and to intensify his sense of wonderment and his curiosity about the simplest things—these will become and remain the most potent factors in his life, no matter what he is destined to do.

Two years after the above letter was written, N. C. Wyeth and his grandson, Newell, were killed together when a train struck the car N. C. was driving.

WILLIAM O. DOUGLAS TO
MILDRED DOUGLAS WELLS

"The only dangerous people in the world are those who are rebels without a cause . . ."

William O. Douglas was appointed to the Supreme Court of the United States by Franklin Roosevelt in 1939. A spirited champion of liberty, Douglas believed the government should interfere in people's lives as little as possible. He was a protector of civil liberties, worked for religious and racial tolerence, and fought for equality of opportunity. As a westerner and an outdoorsman, Douglas was a modern-day environmentalist who traveled, camped, hiked, and was an ardent advocate of conservation. Energetic and controversial, he was known through his thirty-six years on the Supreme Court as a liberal dissident. He married four times, twice to women very much younger than he, and he was quite distant from his two children. Douglas once said, "I doubt I rated high as a father . . ."

Here he writes to his thirty-two-year-old daughter, herself a "rebel" in earlier days, about her son, Tyrone.

December 16, 1961

Dear Millie:

I am glad that Ty is turning out to be a rebel. Any boy who is any good has that spark in him when he is about Ty's age. The problem is to see that it does not die out, and that he retains the capacity to tell his old lady or his old man where to get off.

The only dangerous people in the world are those who are rebels without a cause, and the problem is as the years go by to find a good cause to which Ty can tie his rebellion. On that you and he can get together and come up with something pretty special and I am sure it will all work out to the best of the order.

Merry Christmas to you all.

Love,
[William O. Douglas]

Do not read this
till you are quiet in
your own room

Newport

July 9. 1890

My dear Helen:

Mamma has told me
that you had asked her how you could
make yourself care for persons whom
you do not naturally love. The question
shows a recognition, on your part, of a
feature of your disposition which we
have noticed for some time, and
concerning which you need some advice.

In the first place, my dear child,
you must not allow yourself to be

First page of Alfred Thayer Mahan's letter
to his daughter Helen

Love

THOMAS JEFFERSON TO
MARTHA "PATSY" JEFFERSON RANDOLPH

*"The happiness of your life depends now on the
continuing to please a single person. To this all other
objects must be secondary . . ."*

*In early 1790, Thomas Jefferson was in New York beginning his term as the
first secretary of state of the United States under President George Washington. His
eldest daughter, eighteen-year-old Martha Jefferson Randolph (known as Patsy),
remained in Virginia with her new husband, Thomas Randolph, and her only living sibling, Maria (known as Polly). To his daughters, Jefferson was totally dedicated—particularly so since the death of their mother eight years earlier. He
approved of Martha's marriage, thought his son-in-law a "young gentleman of genious, science and honorable mind" and in this missive encourages his daughter to
make her husband her priority.*

*Although Martha and Thomas Randolph went on to have eleven children, all
of whom were named by their "Grandpapa" Jefferson, their marriage was a disappointment. Thomas Randolph eventually became a congressman for the state of
Virginia and later its governor, but he was considered by some to be a failure—
dependent, perilously in debt, an ineffective manager of property. In the end,
Martha Jefferson Randolph remained unquestionably devoted to one man above all:
her father.*

New York April 4, 1790

My Dear Daughter

I saw in Philadelphia your friends Mrs. Trist and Miss Rittenhouse. Both complained of your not writing. In Baltimore I inquired after Mrs. Buchanan and Miss Holliday. The latter is lately turned methodist, the former was married the evening I was there to a Mr. Turnbull of Petersburg in Virginia. Of course you will see her there. I find it difficult to procure a tolerable house here. It seems it is a practice to let all the houses the 1st of February, and to enter into them the 1st of May. Of course I was too late to engage one, at least in the Broadway, where all my business lies. I have taken an indifferent one nearly opposite Mrs. Ellsworth's which may give me time to look about me and provide a better before the arrival of my furniture. I am anxious to hear from you, of your health, your occupations, where you are etc. Do not neglect your music. It will be a companion which will sweeten many hours of life to you. I assure you mine here is triste enough. Having had yourself and dear Poll to live with me so long, to exercise my affections and chear me in the intervals of business, I feel heavily these separations from you. It is a circumstance of consolation to know that you are happier; and to see a prospect of it's continuance in the prudence and even temper both of Mr. Randolph and yourself. Your new condition will call for abundance of little sacrifices but they will be greatly overpaid by the measure of affection they will secure to you. The happiness of your life depends now on the continuing to please a single person. To this all other objects must be secondary; even your love to me, were it possible that that could ever be an obstacle. But this it can never be. Neither of you can ever have a more faithful friend than my self, nor one on whom you can count for more sacrifices. My own is become a secondary object to the happiness of you both. Cherish then for me, my dear child, the affection of your husband, and continue to love me as you have done, and to render my life a blessing by the prospect it may hold up to me of seeing you happy. Kiss Maria for me if she is with you, and present me cordially to Mr. Randolph: assuring yourself of the constant and unchangeable love of your's affectionately,

TH: JEFFERSON

SAM HOUSTON TO SAM HOUSTON, JR.

*"Your Ma loves you more, than she does any one else,
so you should love her, more than any one."*

*Congressman and governor of Tennessee, adopted son of a Cherokee chief,
frontiersman, commander of the Texas revolutionary army responsible for freeing
Texas from Mexican dictatorship, twice president of the Republic of Texas, and
later senator and governor of the new state, Sam Houston is an American legend.
He stood six feet, two inches tall, wore unusual and sometimes dramatic clothes,
spoke the Cherokee language fluently, loved classical literature, and, in the days
before his marriage, had the reputation of being a hard drinker often in pursuit of
women. At forty-seven years old Houston married the young and beautiful Margaret Lea, whose religious piety and belief in temperance had great influence in reforming her husband's way of life. Married for twenty-three years, the couple had
eight children, the first of whom, Sam Jr., was born when Houston was fifty
years old.*

*In 1846, when Sam Houston wrote the following letter, he was just beginning
his first of nearly fourteen years as senator from the brand-new state of Texas. The
issue of the day was the Oregon Country: should it be a slave territory or free. The
freshman senator from Texas broke with his southern colleagues and voted for Oregon to be free. Here he writes to his son, three-year-old Sam, at home with Margaret in Huntsville, Texas.*

15th June, 1846.

My dear Son,

Your Father loves you, and hopes you are a good boy. He is very anxious to see you, and your dear Mother, as well as your dear Uncles, and
aunts, and cousins. These your Pa hopes to see at home. You have not forgot, your dear Grand Ma, Uncle Vernal, and Aunt Ann. These you ought
to love as much, as those who are with you, every day. You ought as a
good and dear Son, to love your dear Ma, more than all others, and next
to her, you should love your dear Grand Ma, and then your Pa!

Your Ma loves you more, than she does any one else, so you should
love her, more than any one. You should love and obey your Father & hear
all that he says to you. Your Ma, took care of you, when you were a little
helpless *babe*. She did not sleep, when she thought you were not well, but

43

watched you in the night. Now my son, you can never do enough for your dear Ma. Your Grand Ma, too took care of you, and loved and still, loves you, as much, as if you were her own son!

So you see my son, why you should love, your Ma, & Grand Ma, more, than all others! You should love me, too, and when I do good, you should do like me. You ought to love all your *relations*, and all good people, and then your good father in Heaven, will love you, and when you die, He will take you to Heaven, where you will always be happy.

My son, I send you some poetry, and if Ma, thinks well of it, she, and cousins, will learn you to repeat it to Pa, if he lives to meet his dear boy.

You must give Pa's love to ma; and a kiss to Aunt & Cousins. Thy devoted Father,

Sam Houston

SALMON P. CHASE TO
KATE CHASE SPRAGUE

*"How wrong it is for those who love
not to express their love."*

A leader in the fight to end slavery, Salmon P. Chase was secretary of the United States Treasury at the time of the Civil War and chief justice of the Supreme Court during Reconstruction. He was thought to be overly ambitious; yet clearly apparent, too, were his determination and moral courage.

By the time he joined Lincoln's cabinet, Chase had suffered the nearly unimaginable loss of three wives and four daughters. To his surviving children, Kate and Nettie, he was utterly devoted. Kate Chase emerged from a lonely childhood riddled with death to become a spirited young woman. She became a companion and hostess for her father and her unbridled ambition seemed to equal his. Her marriage to one of the wealthiest men in the nation, the former governor, then senator from Rhode Island, William Sprague, was a celebrated social event in Washington during the dark days of the Civil War. Yet the Spragues' marriage was not a happy one and Chief Justice Chase, who resided in the same house with the volatile couple, tried to be the peacemaker.

Here, during the impeachment trial of Andrew Johnson, in which both he and Senator Sprague were involved, Salmon P. Chase writes to his daughter, Kate.

Washington, May 10, 1868.

My dear dear Katie,

I am ashamed that your affectionate letter has remained so long unanswered; but you know how prone I am to procrastination, and what excuses—(not sufficient however I admit)—I have lately had for it.

But my duties connected with the Impeachment are nearly over, and I *will* write you a few words today:

The Governor tells me that you will probably leave Narragansett very soon. He is anxious about you, and talks of going south with you as soon as the trial is ended. If he does go I will and go at once; so if you incline that way and wish Nettie to go with you please write her immediately and come home.

I was dreadfully frightened about your cold, and very uneasy about your going north when you did. The Governor says you have found the Narragansett air too bracing and his uneasiness increases mine. You *must* take care of yourself.

How I wish you would take a different view of your social duties, & cease exposing yourself, by attending those wretched night parties. You could do so, I think, & lose nothing in any respect.

Most of all I long to see you an earnest Christian woman—not only religious but happy in religion. I realize painfully how far short I come of my own ideal; but I am not on that account the less desirous that you should excel where I fail. One thing I am sure of that true faith in Christ is the only thing on earth really worth having; and the only thing that we can carry from earth.

How I do love you my darling! My whole heart seems to go toward you while I write and tears come into my eyes. How wrong it is for those who love not to express their love. I remember how often you have felt hurt by my apparent indifference to what interested you: and I feel sorry that I ever occasioned any such feelings to you. I see now in your husband something of that which I blame on myself. But I know how strong my love really was, and I know how strong his is. And I am very glad that, while you have sometimes forgotten that the happiness of a wife is most certainly secured by loving submission & loving tact, you, generally, conquer by sweetness. I never saw him so much affected as by the difference that occurred between you just before you went away. He was almost unmanned—moved to tears. I have not thought it best to refer to it; but try to make my society pleasant for him & hope I succeed. You must *love away all his reserve*—and help yourself to do so by reflecting how generous, self sacrificing & indulgent a husband he has been to you. How few husbands would consent to such absences, & be at once so liberal & thoughtful. If he were only a true Christian he would be nearly perfect.

The final question on the impeachment is ordered for Tuesday—day after tomorrow, and it is probable that it will then be taken. My own judgment & feeling favors acquittal; but I have no vote & do not know how the Senators will vote. It seems to be that there is very little balance of probability either way. It is not impossible that something may occur to postpone the question a day or two. It will require parts of two days probably to complete the vote when begun. The question is to be taken on each article and it may be that some articles will be divided. The form of the question to be put by me on each article to each Senator is "Mr Senator——— How say you? Is Andrew Johnson President of the United States guilty or not guilty of a high misdemeanor as charged in this article?": and each Senator must rise in his place & answer "guilty" or "not guilty." It will take about half a minute for each Senator & there are fifty four Senators—say 25 minutes to each article & there are 11 articles, making with the time required for reading about 6 hours. Shan't I be tired?

Goodbye my darling—kisses & dear love for Willie—don't let him forget grandpa.

Your affectionate father
S P CHASE

After Kate engaged in a well-publicized affair with Senator Roscoe Conkling, her marriage to William Sprague ended. Her life went into a tailspin, and by the time of her death at fifty-eight years old, she had become a social recluse living in destitution.

ALFRED THAYER MAHAN TO
HELEN EVANS MAHAN

*"Like yourself, I am naturally indifferent to others;
and for many years I thought it almost
something to be proud of."*

Adm. Alfred T. Mahan, naval officer and historian, was the world's greatest authority on sea power. His book The Influence of Seapower Upon History, *published in 1890, revolutionized the way military and political leaders worldwide considered the importance of their navies. In it, Mahan convincingly demonstrated for the world that "command of the sea" determined the power of a nation.*

Slender and erect with blue eyes, a bald head, and a carefully trimmed Vandyke beard, Alfred T. Mahan lectured his three children on everything from medical practices to which authors were acceptable to read. (William Shakespeare and Walter Scott were approved; Mark Twain was not.) Mahan's manner was shy and reserved, cold even, and he himself never successfully established close friendships. Yet he readily advised his daughters on the subject. Here he writes to his eldest child, seventeen-year-old Helen.

Newport
July 9, 1890

Do not read this
till you are quiet in
your own room.

My dear Helen:

Mamma has told me that you had asked her how you could make yourself care for persons whom you do not naturally love. The question shows a recognition, on your part, of a feature of your disposition which we have noticed for some time, and concerning which you need some advice.

In the first place, my dear child, you must not allow yourself to be worried about this trait of your character, which renders you indifferent to most persons, as though it were a *fault*, or a sin, for which you are originally responsible. It was born in you, without your will. But while it is not a fault, it is a very serious *defect*, against which you are bound as a Christian to strive, as earnestly as you would against any other natural defect, or weakness.

You will notice that indifference to other people, the failure to be moved by their happiness or sorrow, though not as bad as hatred, or ill-will, to them, is nevertheless as much opposed to that charity, or love, which our Lord and His apostles dwell upon as the great distinctive grace of the Christian character. It is well to note this. Like yourself, I am naturally indifferent to others; and for many years I thought it almost something to be proud of. I did not meddle with other people's business, which is undoubtedly a good thing; unfortunately, in me it was due to the fact that I did not care anything about their business, whether it went well or ill. It is only very lately that I have realized that it is not enough to refrain from, and keep under, bad or unkind feelings toward others; charity demands that we have toward them feelings of kindly interest; of sympathy; even of affection, in accordance with the relationship which they bear to us, as relatives, as friends, or as neighbors.

You have in your Aunt Rosie a very good example of what this charity should be—in her affection for her mother. You know how devoted it is. I have heard her say that it is no merit in her to do all she does for her mother *because she loves her so*; and in that she is quite right, it is no *merit* in her any more than your indifference is a *fault* in you; it is a natural trait. But do you not see what a lovely trait it is, and how far better we all would be if we by nature loved others as Rosie loves her mother; not so much, of course, in every case, but having for every one a degree of interest and love proportioned to their relationship to us. That we have not, is because our nature is fallen.

Now as to the means of gaining this better nature, it is necessary to distinguish between your part and God's part. Your part is to give care and thought as to your loving duty to others, and then to try earnestly and carry it out. First of all in your home; next among your other relatives, then extending to others about you. For instance, at Bar Harbor, there is Grannie and Marraine. The former can go about but little, and though she has many friends who either from natural affection, or Christian kindness, go to see her, yet every little visit is an incident and a pleasure in her day. I know that she has shown such a very marked partiality for Lyle, that it is not to be wondered at she has lost the affection of her other grandchildren; but the evidence of her love for you is not the measure of your duty of kindness to her. Go to see her frequently, and not grudgingly or of necessity; remembering that God loves a cheerful giver. This is less hard than you may think; a moment of prayer and effort of the will will scatter all sense of inconvenience and reluctance.

But doing this, and such like things, though necessary, will not of themselves give you the spirit of love which you desire. They are external acts, though good acts; and are of the nature of those "works," of which St. Paul says they cannot save us. They are done against our nature, which seeks its own welfare or pleasure rather than that of another person; whereas that which we are to desire is that change of heart, or change of nature, through which we will naturally and without effort do right and kind things. By our present nature we seek self; by our new nature we shall seek the good of others. Here you may see the value of that instance which I have used, of Rosie's love to her mother. Rosie doubtless dislikes some people, and is indifferent to many; but in one particular she affords a very beautiful example of what our redeemed and new nature will be. She does her kindnesses to her mother, not because she ought to, but because she loves her by nature; her acts of kindness therefore are not "works," but "fruits"; they spring naturally from what she is, and therefore, though not meritorious, they are evidence of a character that in this particular is lovely.

Such a change of nature, from indifference to love like this, is beyond a man's power. Works we can do, but change our nature we cannot. This is God's part. He requires of us our will and wish, which if we have we will doubtless do works of love; but do what we will, He only can change the heart.

Therefore, to become what you wish, to have kindly interest in and sympathy with others, you must: 1st do works of kindness, and 2d pray continually to God to change your nature in this respect and give you a loving heart. It will take time, but never despair of it. I believe you do try not to have unkind feelings toward others, but dont stop content with that; aim at having kind interest in them.

Both your mother and I think of you, my dear child, among your present surroundings. Your friends seem to be very kind and fond of you; but we cannot be without some apprehension, believing that they are in their aims and principles entirely worldly—living that is for this world, and not for the next. It is not for me to judge them in this respect, but only to caution you to be careful, and not allow yourself to attach undue importance to, and care too much for, the comforts and pleasures of this world. We are all too apt to do this, but particularly when surrounded by them, as you now are. The "deceits of the world," as the Litany calls them, are very pleasant, particularly in youth; but the deceit is there, for they are found on experience to be unsatisfying in the end. Yet the strange thing is that even those who have by experience found this hollowness, and even talk of their emptiness, still cling to them by force of habit. I trust you may escape their taking such hold upon you. Remember that life is not only uncertain, but that it is *short*. You may or may not have a life of average length; but even if you live long—at the longest, life is short; and long before its end pleasure ceases to please. And at the end, but one thing gives pleasure; and that is a nature which, having been renewed by God, brings forth those fruits which are pleasant here, love, joy, peace, and which endure beyond the grave.

Lovingly
A. T. M.

WASHINGTON A. ROEBLING TO JOHN ROEBLING

"It sounds queer to talk about my wedding; the wedding of an old man who ought to be thinking about his grave rather than the vanities of life."

Between the years 1870 and 1883, the Brooklyn Bridge took shape, spanning the East River and finally linking Manhattan to Brooklyn. During the last eleven of those fourteen years, the chief engineer, Washington A. Roebling, was never able to visit the construction site. He was suffering from "the bends," or "caissons disease," and a general collapse of the nervous system brought on from too rapid an ascent from the base of the Brooklyn Bridge towers under the East River. His body was riddled with pain so savage and excruciating, he found it difficult to write and speak. As well, his eyesight was failing. In building the bridge, Roebling was fulfilling his late father's vision and if he, too, were to falter, it was likely there would be no one to continue the work. In his pain and incapacitated state, communication with the world outside of Roebling's Brooklyn home was accomplished by his wife, Emily Warren Roebling. It was Mrs. Roebling who took his dictation and handled his correspondence, she who kept him abreast of the news and progress on the bridge, she who met in the living room with bridge officials and contractors, and she who delivered messages to the site where the massive bridge was being erected. It was a marriage like no other, he the invalid mastermind of the greatest engineering project of the day, and she the arms, legs, eyes, and voice connecting him with the world.

But for all Washington Roebling's physical ailments, it was the sturdy Emily Roebling who was the first to die. After thirty-eight years of marriage, Washington Roebling was left alone. Alone for the next five years he was miserable and, as always, in pain. Then, at nearly seventy-one years old, to the surprise of most who knew him and to the delight of his only child, John, Washington Roebling announced that he was to marry again.

More About the Proposed Marriage
and the Bride-Elect

W.A.R. to John.
191 West State Street,
Trenton, N.J., March
21/08

It sounds queer to talk about my wedding; the wedding of an old man who ought to be thinking about his grave rather than of the vanities of life.

But these relationships are those of the heart, not governed by reason or judgement (fortunately so perhaps)—A second marriage late in life cannot be judged by the standard of the first because its motives are usually quite different, and if it should not prove happy, death soon remedies all troubles.

I expect to be married about 15th to 20th of April—The wedding will take place at Dalton near Pittsfield, Mass. (provided my health don't break down)—The bride elect is Mrs. Cornelia Farrow, a widow of about 40, with one son of 16 or 17—Her winter home is in Charleston, S. C. where her mother lives—In summer she abides with her friends & protectors, the Cranes at Pittsfield—(The Cranes make all the bank notes of the U. S. Sen. Crane is one of them, so is Fred Crane.)

Mrs. Farrow's grandfather was a Connecticut Yankee who came South after the war and entered business.

She is thin, slender, brown-haired, of my height, with much personality and extremely amiable, speaking with a strong Southern accent. You will like her like a sister presently—

As regards our mutual relations you know that I am just and no wrong will come to you or yours—How these things come about is always a mystery, and I feel somewhat guilty in inflicting myself upon Cornelia.

At any rate I invite you most cordially to come up and attend the simple ceremony—I am not strong and feel like breaking down without some support—I have no one to help me and must do everything myself—

There are a number of your mother's photographs about, at your service. Her mobile face would never photograph well—the painted miniature on my table is mine, and stays there—

[Washington A. Roebling]

THEODORE ROOSEVELT TO QUENTIN ROOSEVELT

"Write no matter how tired you are, no matter how inconvenient it is . . ."

At a patriotic rally at the beginning of World War I, Theodore Roosevelt was faced with a heckler who demanded to know what he, the former president of the United States, was doing for the war effort. "What am I doing for my country in this war? I have sent my four boys for each of whose lives I care a thousand times more than I care for my own, if you can understand that . . ." The heckler and the entire audience were silenced.

In fact, the four Roosevelt boys, with the encouragement and help of their father, began serving in World War I as quickly as they could. The older three, Ted, Kermit, and Archie, were already married when they went overseas and the youngest, Quentin, became engaged to Miss Flora Whitney just before he sailed for France. Here Theodore Roosevelt advises twenty-year-old Quentin about corresponding with his fiancée.

Oyster Bay, December 24, 1917

Dearest Quentin,

Mother, the adamantine, has stopped writing to you because you have not written to her—or to any of us—for a long time. That will make no permanent difference to you; but I write about something that may make a permanent difference. Flora spoke to Ethel yesterday of the fact that you only wrote rarely to her. She made no complaint whatever. But she knows that some of her friends receive three or four letters a week from their lovers or husbands (Archie writes Gracie rather more often than this—exceedingly interesting letters).

Now of course you may not keep Flora anyhow. But if you wish to lose her, continue to be an infrequent correspondent. If however you wish to keep her write her letters—interesting letters, and love letters—at least three times a week. Write no matter how tired you are, no matter how inconvenient it is; write if you're smashed up in a hospital; write when you are doing your most dangerous stunts; write when your work is most irksome and disheartening; write all the time! Write enough letters to allow for half being lost.

> Affectionately A hardened and wary old father
> [Theodore Roosevelt]

"Why do'n't you write to Flora, and her father and mother, asking if she wo'n't come abroad and marry you?"

Oyster Bay, March 17, 1918

Dearest Quentin,

In a Rochester paper appeared a note from one Whaley, a superintendent of a post office "somewhere in France," who writes "Young Quentin Roosevelt is as modest as a school girl, but as game as they make 'em in aviation. Keep tabs on this game young chap."

Early in the week we were greatly depressed to learn that gallant young Tommy Hitchcock had been captured by the Germans; it is said that he was not hurt. Then came the excitement about Archie. The first news—whether true or not we do not know—was that he had been given the croix de guerre by a French General "under dramatic circumstances"; then the War Dept notified us that he was slightly wounded; then Ted cabled that he had been hit in the leg, and his arm broken, by shrapnel, but that he was in no danger, and that Eleanor would take care of him. Our pride and our anxiety are equal—as indeed they are about all of you.

Why do'n't you write to Flora, and to her father and mother, asking if she wo'n't come abroad and marry you? As for your getting killed, or ordinarily crippled afterwards, why she would a thousand times rather have married you than not have married you under those conditions; and as for the extraordinary kinds of crippling, they are rare, and anyway we have to take certain chances in life. You and she have now passed your period of probation; you have been tried; you are absolutely sure of yourselves; and I would most heartily approve of your getting married at the earliest possible moment.

Mr. Beebe is out here, he has just come from France; on the French front he was allowed to do some flying and bombing—not fighting the German war-planes.

Your loving father,
Theodore Roosevelt

On July 14, 1918, Quentin Roosevelt was shot in the head and killed by the Germans at Chemery, France. He was not yet twenty-one years old.

RICHARD E. BYRD TO RICHARD E. BYRD, JR.

"My last words to you my boy are to beg you to concentrate on your life to two things . . ."

On April 28, 1926, Commander Richard E. Byrd sat down in his cabin to write his six-year-old son. His ship, the S.S. Chantier, amidst ice fields and snow squalls, was steaming for Spitzbergen, Norway. In "a rough following sea" they had endured hard work and seasickness for days. The commander was about to attempt the first flight ever over the North Pole. He knew of the dangers of flying over ice, and in high winds, and through polar fog. He knew the greatest dangers were in the unknown, and he knew, too, that he might not survive. Here, in an unsteady hand, across six pages, Commander Byrd writes to his son.

En route Spitzbergen
April 28, 1926

My Precious Boy—

This letter is to be read twice by you on your eighth birthday then again on your fourteenth birthday, your sixteenth and once more every four years after that.

I want to tell you about your mother I am writing at sea in my cabin. The sea is very rough and icy winds are blowing from the ice fields of the polar sea. We arrive at Kings Bay tomorrow and from there I am to take a hazardous airplane flight over the Polar sea which is a cold and frozen ocean.

If by hard luck I do not get back this is my farewell to you my dear boy—which I know you will take very seriously and all your life I hope you will try to follow what I ask you to do.

When you reach manhood I will be only a vague memory to you—like a dream it will be. But now I am a very real factor in your life. Your sweet mother can tell you how I adore you. But even she does not realize the depth of my affection for you. You are everything a son should be—devoted, unselfish, thoughtful, generous and honorable with an unusual sense of justice. You have I am very thankful to say many of your mothers traits.

Your mother has been perfect to you absolutely devoted, unselfish and untiring where you are concerned. She has sacrificed herself for you ever since you were born and what I like most about you is that you appreciate her and love her above everything. You call her "sweet mommie" and every day when you return from playing outside you bring her something. When you walk with her you walk outside—nearest the street—to protect her from automobiles. You help her across the street and warn her not to stumble over stones, etc. Those little things my boy show that you are made of the right stuff. It is infinitely gratifying to me that you have sense enough and character enough to appreciate your mother. You have made her very happy. She may not need your help now but if I do not come back home she will need your help—you will have to take my place as much as you can.

I have loved your mother since we were little children and I have never known her to do an unkind or unjust thing. She is the sweetest, purest human being I have ever known or have ever heard of. She is an angel—too good I am afraid for this world. My boy I worship her. She is the kind who never hesitates to sacrifice herself for those she loves and then think nothing of it nor look for credit.

Youth is cruel and thoughtless and has little consideration for age, but I believe you will be an exception to this rule. I believe that you will always try to help your mother over the rough places just as you would like to do even now as a child. She is very, very proud of you and so don't let shadow or stain ever darken your name. Anything dishonorable that you would do would break her heart.

Whatever comes up you will find her the best sport you have ever known. I have never met a man whose sense of fair play and sportsmanship equaled hers. She is a thoroughbred—every inch of her.

My last words to you my boy are to beg you to concentrate on your life to two things—first to understand, cherish and protect you mother—and secondly to emulate her in all matters. model yourself as much as you can after her for she is the finest person in the world.

Don't forget the small attentions. Don't stop bringing her things when you go away and come back to her. If you marry for Gods sake dont select a woman who will not like your mother or who might come in between you and her. Women are jealous of each other—specially a wife of a mother. Do not marry too hastily.

Your mother has an extraordinarily logical mind so you cannot go wrong if you will always take her advise. I have done so as a rule and she has never made a mistake.

Dickie old boy do what your mother wants you to do. She is the only one in the world who will advise you with only your own good in view. But don't let her be too unselfish with you as she has with me.

And so my boy I will end where I began—follow your mothers advise and try to make yourself as much as possible like her with her great sense of honor. She is the very soul of honor.

Remember always that whatever she does is right. She can do no wrong. You and I want her happiness more than anything else in the world. Therefore *whatever* she may do to make her happy you must back up whole heartedly.

Always put honor and your mother first. Goodbye my darling boy.

Your devoted father
Richard E. Byrd Jr.

On May 9, 1926, Commander Byrd and Chief Machinist's Mate Floyd Bennett flew for sixteen hours, 1,360 miles, from King's Bay, Spitzbergen, over the North Pole and back. He returned home to a hero's welcome and a ticker-tape parade in New York City. Byrd later went on to lead five expeditions to Antarctica and to make the first flight over the South Pole.

Sherwood Anderson to John Anderson

*"In the end perhaps a man can only remain
devoted to the intangible."*

Sherwood Anderson, author of the classic Winesburg, Ohio, *was one of the
most influential writers of the twentieth century. In that his fiction was driven by
the lives and psychology of ordinary people, rather than by plot, Anderson broke
new ground for future generations of American novelists.*

*He was happiest when he was in solitude writing, and found marriage, time and
again, a disappointment. While married to his first wife, the mother of his three
children, he became desperate to "escape out of marriage and into life," and to begin writing. "Most women simply frighten me," he wrote to a friend. "I feel hunger
within them. It is as though they wished to feed upon me."*

*Here Sherwood Anderson, between his third and fourth marriages, writes to his
twenty-year-old son, an art student at the University of Wisconsin.*

[1929]

Dear John—

the very capacity you have for feeling will inevitable make it burst into
a flame occasionally about some woman. My own experience will, I am
afraid, be of little help. In the end art is the essential thing, I think.

It is so difficult. The road is so long. Sometimes it is a tremendous ease-
ment to center it on some other person.

Women want that, of course. I do not believe that, at bottom, they
have the least interest in art. What their lover gives to work, they cannot
get.

In the end you may prove a great disappointment to women, as I have
and as most artists have.

Suddenly you go off. What was all-absorbing is no longer so. It is more
terrible for the woman than going to another woman.

You go into something indefinite, into a place where they cannot follow.

I dare say you will have to go through these cycles. Who has escaped
them. Read the history of all men who had devotion. In the end perhaps a
man can only remain devoted to the intangible. Nature serves the purpose
and woman is sometimes an exquisite manifestation of nature. I would not
want you to miss that, but can understand it's confusion.

I dare say sometimes you will be disgusted at yourself as I have been when you find yourself turning even this fine feeling into work.

You did not give me an address at Madison.

S. A.

EUGENE O'NEILL TO EUGENE O'NEILL, JR.

"Keep your love affairs free from all relatives and their homes if you want to avoid complications with your love or with your relatives or both."

Of familial entanglements with affairs of the heart, Eugene O'Neill was quite familiar. As a young man of twenty-two he secretly married Kathleen Jenkins when she disovered she was pregnant. Both Kathleen's and Eugene's own parents were upset when they learned of the pregnancy and marriage, and their behavior and influence combined to keep the young couple apart even after the birth of Eugene O'Neill, Jr. Having never lived with Kathleen and having seen his son only once or twice, Eugene was officially divorced from Kathleen when the boy was two years old. It would be nearly a decade before he saw his son again in 1921.

In the years following their reunion, O'Neill and Eugene, Jr., corresponded frequently and a genuine kind of camaraderie developed between them.

In 1930, a newlywed for the third time, O'Neill was living a secluded existence in France and was at work on his play Mourning Becomes Electra. *He was somewhat distracted by what turned out to be an unjustified plagiarism suit, and he was concerned about keeping up financially with his new wife's way of life. Here he responds to nineteen-year-old Eugene, Jr., who had asked to bring a girlfriend to visit his father and stepmother in France.*

Feb. 20th 1930

Dear Eugene:

I have been waiting to answer your last letter to Carlotta that was meant for both of us until I had finished the first draft of the huge job. Well, I finished it today. Thank God! It has been a terrific job and I have never worked so hard on anything before. But I am pleased with the results. Of course, there is the devil of a lot yet to do before the final result is reached—as much again and then some. When I will have the final version ready, quien sabe? Certainly not in time for any production next season. I am now going to Italy for a rest. I need it. I am all "washed up" and on edge and need a change of scene to get my mind off the obsession of this job that I have been living with night and day for the past four months.

Now as to your coming over: I am sorry to say that it doesn't look as if it would be possible this year. In the first place, the way things are stacking up, I simply cannot afford to stake you to the trip. There will be no play next year, *Interlude* will be finished, and I doubt if I will have more than enough income in the season of '30–'31 to pay alimony. And my expenses this past year, what with the divorce—a costly affair—and other stuff have been abnormally large. The pity is they promise to be even larger this coming twelve months. The damned plagiarism suit is due to cost me a pile of money. And so forth. You know that I will always give you a break and that I am not talking through my hat about this but have reason. But even laying aside the matter of expense, there are other matters. For one thing, there is a prospect that I may have to go to New York this summer about the suit. Then there is the eminent probability that Carlotta's mother and daughter will come for a visit—or if they don't that she will have to go to California to see them, in which case I will come to New York with her. You will understand that this family business has to be arranged in a sort of schedule with certain periods assigned to each party. You were over last year and it is her turn to shoot now. This doesn't imply that Carlotta wouldn't welcome you with shouts of joy no matter who was here—but the point is that we can't have too much of a crowd here at once. Carlotta couldn't stand the strain of the elaborate housekeeping entailed and if I was trying to work, which I will be, it would bawl me all up. So you see. That's the answer. So I think you will agree that it is only fair that you should stay where you are this summer. If there is anything special you figure out you want to do in the States in the summer, let me know and I will help you to the best of my ability. Another thing I feel strongly is this: You owe your mother a hell of a lot more than you do me in the way of giving you the background to become what you are, and I think you ought to take a good look inside yourself and figure out whether you don't owe her a bit more of your time, and whether you shouldn't see a lot of her during her vacation. You are an only child, you know, and that makes it a bit tough for her. I don't mean to do any lecturing but the above is worth a thought.

As for the other matter you brought up—that of bringing Betty here—even if you had come over I wouldn't have advised that. What I am writing now is strictly between you and me, sabe? It is the fruit of whatever worldly sagacity various kicks in the pants, my own pants and others, have given me. Keep your love affairs free from all relatives and their homes if you want to avoid complications with your love or with your relatives or both. Why run the risk with your love of forcing it into human interrelationships where you never can foretell what the answer may be? For example, how do you know Betty would like me or Carlotta, or that we would like her? You may say that you know but that [is] only because you *feel* affection for all concerned. And if one dislike crept into this combination, then all the slumbering prejudices would awake and the complications would start—and spread! Ideally this sounds rather crass but practically all it amounts to is that everyone is human and more or less petty in small things no matter how nobly they may respond to soul-trying crises. My dope is emphatically that love should be kept on a pedestal and not made to run unnecessary risks, for it is very fragile and has a hard struggle to endure even with all the breaks one can give it. Family contact I rate as risk A One. Please understand me right. I respect your love for Betty and she sounds like a brick to me and I would sure like to meet her if I come to New York. Also understand that Carlotta has nothing to do with what I am writing and doesn't even know I am writing this. It is honestly for the sake of your preserving the glamour of your love that I am writing. It is for Betty's sake most of all. You shouldn't want her to be put in such a position, that's my notion. It might work out all right, but then again it mightn't and my whole idea is the practical one that when you are happy as it is why run any risks? If you were married it would be different—only because it would have to be different. But even in the case of marriage you have only to go back to your Mother and me. If families had been kept out of it we might have had a chance. I must confess, with the guy I was then, the chance was slim and she was probably well rid of me—but you never can tell how much family interference and prejudices had to do with it.

Well, that's off my chest. What I have written is far from clearly stated but I rely on you to get the gist of it and give me credit for good intentions even if you think I am all wrong in this particular case. One of the principal reasons for my caution, as I hope you will guess, is that your and my relationship is too fine for us to place it in a position where, through neither your fault or mine, it might be hurt or messed with. Put that one in your pipe and smoke it!

Well, there's no news except work. I have been writing every day for four months half the day and thinking about it the other half so there wasn't much chance for anything to happen.

Good luck and all love to you! Write me and let me know how everything is coming at Yale. I expect to be back here on the job in three weeks, or at most four. I hope this vacation will buck me up. I'm fagged out.

As ever,
Father

N. C. WYETH TO ANN WYETH McCOY AND JOHN McCOY

"To sustain the integrities which you are both generously endowed with, to keep alive that sense of charity toward one another, to be sensitive with a purpose, and with vast energy and deep-laid ambitions, you two will go far—and by this I mean you will go far into the realms of human happiness."

That marriage might take one away from art and work was always a concern for N. C. Wyeth. The great American illustrator worried about his painting when he himself married and he was equally apprehensive about the effects of matrimony on his creative and productive children.

By the time of her wedding at twenty years old, Ann Wyeth was already an accomplished composer whose piece A Christmas Fantasy *had been performed by Leopold Stokowski of the Philadelphia Orchestra. Her new husband, John McCoy, was a painter and a student of N. C. Wyeth.*

Nine days after they were married in his studio in Chadds Ford, Pennsylvania, N. C. Wyeth wrote to Ann and John McCoy.

Studio
Chadds Ford, Pennsylvania
November 4, 1935. Monday

Dear Ann and John,

Your splendid letters came in this morning!

The time, since you left, has been strangely vacant and strangely full to repletion. We all go around with a hollow feeling and yet our thoughts, and actions too, fairly teem! We seem to be vaguely seeking to pick up the loose strands and in some way to seek a new combination that we may tie them together again to start anew. At the same time our lives are actually very full and each one is accomplishing something.

The canvas I thought sure was a failure has turned into one of my good ones. Andy has done his strongest landscape as well as several superb life drawings. Carolyn has come out of the dark woods with a powerful still-life and her bust. Henriette painted a corking portrait of John Wyeth and on the side captured first prize in the Wilmington show with her "Miss Flaherty" (and Andy sold his "Seiners" to Mrs. Meeds). And Ma has been turbulently busy in the home and making many dashing visits to your homestead beyond the brook.

Back of it all are the resurgent echoes of the wedding, memories of which will never fade. It is all a massive dream to me, real and unreal as all dreams are.

As John truthfully said, the procession of events on that evening of the 26th left a deep mark on most of the friends who were here. There was a poignancy about it all which I believe transcended the vast majority of similar occasions. The surroundings were indeed happy and felicitous, but the important ingredient was the great sympathy and the great faith in you two—in you, as individuals, and together as builders of a new generation. To sustain the integrities which you are both generously endowed with, to keep alive that sense of charity toward one another, to be sensitive with a purpose, and with vast energy and deep-laid ambitions, you two will go far—and by this I mean you will go far into the realms of human happiness. All else, by comparison, is nothing.

I am sorry, of course, that the fog has persisted. Perhaps Nature herself has conspired to give you privacy on your honeymoon!

But if I know you two, even persistent fog will not be lost and it will always take on a certain hallowed beauty and character which never existed before.

Our weather here has been dark, wet, lowering and commonly called *lousy*. But no! It has been like a great gray curtain dropped after a magnificent "third act." It has given us a remoteness—a chance to get our emotional breath. It has been gorgeous!

[N. C. Wyeth]

Clare Boothe Luce to Ann Brokaw

"If you don't love him that's your business—if you do it becomes partly mine, darling."

Sharp-tongued and hard-driven, Clare Boothe Luce succeeded in the professional world of men in a way no woman ever had. Blonde and athletic, she was striking in appearance and when in the company of men, she made sure her good looks, ambition, and bold mind were not overlooked. She was the managing editor of Vanity Fair, *an original and popular playwright, congresswoman, the first woman ever to deliver the keynote address at a national political convention (Republican National Convention, 1944), and she was the American Ambassador to Rome. Her husband was Henry Luce, the creator of TimeLife, Inc., and one of the most influential publishers of all time.*

She had one child, a daughter, Ann, with her first husband, a wealthy playboy named George Brokaw. The girl was attractive and smart and so admired her mother that she once wrote in her diary. "Was that glorious woman really my mother?"

Here Clare Boothe Luce writes a conversational letter of advice to eighteen-year-old Ann, a sophomore at Stanford University. Two days before receiving her mother's endorsement, Ann had told her boyfriend, Walton Wickett, that she didn't want to see him again. The following letter from her mother "threw [her] into a tailspin . . ."

November 24, 1942.

Ann darling:

Thank you so much for your lovely flowers, my sweet, for the beautiful red picture frame, for the McArthur bowl, and above all for your telegram on our anniversary.

We had the loveliest party in one of the big suites upstairs in the Waldorf. I am enclosing a list of the guests. Everybody made wonderful speeches about how nice Dad and I were, cracked a lot of jokes and toasted us in champagne. And then afterwards we all went to Noel Coward's movie, "In which we serve" which was very fine indeed. And then we came home and yammered some more and went to bed. We missed you as we always do!

Now I would like to tell you for your own information, and not for his, about your young friend Walter. As you know, I told you when you first began to speak of him that in spite of all the hard things you said of him, he somehow or other "came through" as a very nice guy indeed. He sounded pretty nice to me although I thought at the time, and still do, that he is a little on the old side for you. However, you made the thing sound so unexpectedly serious when I spoke to you on Sunday that I reacted rather spontaneously as a loving Mama might be expected to do and made certain inquiries through the heads of Panam on the subject of your young man. I am glad to report that the Panam tycoons and bigwigs gave him a remarkably fine bill of endorsement. They said he was not only a young man of complete sobriety and dependability but that he had plenty of brains and marked ability. They said also that he had a great future in the airways—which as you know is one of the businesses with the greatest future of all in the postwar world. They said, in short, that he was a swell guy, that his family was as nice as it could be—all of which is very reassuring to me. My instincts at the time when you told me about him were that he was a very nice beau for you to have, and it seems to me very nice that you should have one. If you don't love him that's your business—if you do it becomes partly mine, darling. If the young man is really serious about you and you think there is a chance you might get serious about him, I wish that you would urge him to come East shortly and let Dad and me look him over and see if we really think as highly of him as his business associates seem to. I think you had better bring a couple of snapshots of him when you come home, because I would like to see what kind of a creature I am discussing with you. Well, that's all there is to that. I am, as I say, very much more comfortable in my mind about it than when I talked to you on the telephone because he sounds so nice and so clever.

I am looking forward so eagerly to seeing you on the 20th. We will be here in the Waldorf until a day or so after Christmas and then instead of going down to Mepkin, we will go down to Washington and you will have a chance to look that over and see what you think of it.

Don't worry about your studies. When you want to do them well you will do them superbly but for the moment the main thing is to get what little happiness there is out of life in this wartorn world because "these are the good old days" now.

With bestest love to you,
[Clare Boothe Luce]

*". . . any time you want to make an ogre out of mama,
in order to get rid of some wretched youth,
I am only too happy!!"*

Less than two weeks later, with the relationship between Ann and her "young man" deteriorating even further, Luce writes again.

December 4, 1942.

Ann darling—

Your young man sent me a sad little note, the purport of which was that I was not only threatening to wreck his chances of persuading you on the subject of matrimony, but I was spoiling your college career by urging you to come to Washington. Now, I have written him a little note which I am enclosing. I don't know what you have told him. It is conceivable to your old ma that you are using me as an excuse to spare his feelings, and any time you want to make an ogre out of mama, in order to get rid of some wretched youth, I am only too happy!!

So, o o o o, I leave it entirely up to you whether or not you want to send him this letter after you have read it. He will probably think I am even more of an old meany for not answering him at all, so you had better let me know if you don't want to send this one, and tell me what you would like me to say to help you out in the best way possible.

Always (you wretched little flirt),
Your adoring,

P.S. If you want this letter sent, drop it in the box yourself.

Ann sent Clare Boothe Luce's letter to Walton Wickett. (It has since disappeared.) Wickett felt it was a "kind and eminently sensible letter," and he and Ann eventually went their separate ways.

JOHN STEINBECK TO THOM STEINBECK

"Glory in it . . ."

"I like to write. I like it better than anything." From the time he was a teenager in California, John Steinbeck wrote, and wrote all the time. He produced a wide breadth of material, ranging from Of Mice and Men, *to* The Sea of Cortez, *to* Travels with Charley—*some twenty-six volumes of fiction and nonfiction in all. For* The Grapes of Wrath, *he won the Pulitzer Prize, and in 1962, for his entire body of work he was awarded the Nobel Prize. At the time of his death in 1968, Steinbeck was the most popular novelist in the world. A shy man, awkward, and built large, he wanted people to care about his words but often resented their interest in him. He was married three times and the father of two sons.*

He once wrote, "We are lonesome animals. We spend all our lives trying to be less lonesome." In the following letter to his eldest son, fourteen-year-old Thom, who was away in Connecticut at boarding school, Steinbeck identifies two kinds of love, both of which he himself had experienced firsthand: the "crippling kind" with Gwyn Conger, the boys' mother, whom he had grown to despise; and the "outpouring of everything good in you," which he felt he had found with his third wife, Elaine.

[New York]
November 10, 1958

Dear Thom:

We had your letter this morning. I will answer it from my point of view and of course Elaine will from hers.

First—if you are in love—that's a good thing—that's about the best thing that can happen to anyone. Don't let anyone make it small or light to you.

Second—There are several kinds of love. One is a selfish, mean, grasping, egotistical thing which uses love for self-importance. This is the ugly and crippling kind. The other is an outpouring of everything good in you—of kindness, and consideration and respect—not only the social respect of manners but the greater respect which is recognition of another person as unique and valuable. The first kind can make you sick and small and weak but the second can release in you strength, and courage and goodness and even wisdom you didn't know you had.

You say this is not puppy love. If you feel so deeply—of course it isn't puppy love.

But I don't think you were asking me what you feel. You know better than anyone. What you wanted me to help you with is what to do about it—and that I can tell you.

Glory in it for one thing and be very glad and grateful for it.

The object of love is the best and most beautiful. Try to live up to it.

If you love someone—there is no possible harm in saying so—only you must remember that some people are very shy and sometimes the saying must take that shyness into consideration.

Girls have a way of knowing or feeling what you feel, but they usually like to hear it also.

It sometimes happens that what you feel is not returned for one reason or another—but that does not make your feeling less valuable and good.

Lastly, I know your feeling because I have it and I'm glad you have it.

We will be glad to meet Susan. She will be very welcome. But Elaine will make all such arrangements because that is her province and she will be very glad to. She knows about love too and maybe she can give you more help than I can.

And don't worry about losing. If it is right, it happens—The main thing is not to hurry. Nothing good gets away.

Love,
Fa

Eugene O'Neill and Eugene O'Neill, Jr.

Laura Ingalls Wilder

John D. Rockefeller and John D. Rockefeller, Jr.

Good Work

John Adams to John Quincy Adams

*"Go and see with how little Wisdom
this World is governed."*

"All my hopes are in him, both for myself and my country," Vice President John Adams wrote of his eldest son in 1794. Of admirable character and extraordinary intellect, John Quincy Adams was a Boston lawyer and one of the most prolific political writers of the day. At just twenty-seven years old, he was widely read and traveled; he had been educated in Paris, Amsterdam, Leyden, and Harvard; he was fluent in seven languages; and he had served with the American minister to Russia. That John Quincy Adams was prepared for his first political appointment—Minister to Holland—his father was certain.

Here John Adams, the vice president of the United States under President George Washington, writes a confidential letter to his son.

Philadelphia May 26. 1794

My dear Son

The Secretary of State called upon me this morning to inform me by order of the President, that it is determined to nominate you to go to Holland as Resident Minister. The President desired to know if I thought you would accept. I answered that I had no Authority from you. But it was my Opinion that you would and that it would be my Advice to you, that you should.

The Salary is 4500 Dollars a Year and as much for an Outfit.

Your knowledge of Dutch and French; Your Education in that Country; your Acquaintance with my old Friends there will give you Advantages, beyond many others. It will require all your Freedom and all your other Virtues as well as all your Talents.

It will be expected that you come here to see the President and Secretary of State, before you embark. I shall write you as soon as the Nomination is made and advised by Senate. Be Secret. Dont open your Mouth to any human Being on the Subject except your Mother. Go and see with how little Wisdom this World is governed.

Adieu,
John Adams

JOHN JAMES AUDUBON TO VICTOR AUDUBON

". . . every exertion in our power should be kept up, with truth, firmness, dignity and consistency from begainning to end."

John James Audubon was the illegitimate son of a French slave-dealing sea captain. By the time he was thirty-four, he had been jailed for unpaid debts. In 1819, after he admitted bankruptcy and was released from jail, he redirected his efforts away from business and began painting portraits and teaching. During the following year, 1820, he concluded that his ambition was to publish a series of paintings of all of the birds of North America. From that point forward, with passion and single-mindedness, he pursued his dream. "My Birds, My Beloved Birds of America fill all my time and nearly all my thoughts," he wrote.

Searching for specimens, he spent weeks and months in the woods, at times sleeping on the snow wrapped in a buffalo robe and eating everything from red-winged blackbirds to roasted wasps. When his two sons were young, Audubon's work kept him from them and his wife for years at a time and when the boys grew older he brought them in on the project. John, the younger son, often traveled with his father and served as his assistant. The elder, Victor, helped with editing and with the business of publishing. Audubon felt that Victor had "become [his] Right Arm and hand." In writing to his sons, he referred not to "my work," but to "our work."

Here America's most celebrated naturalist-artist writes to Victor, twenty-six years old, who was in England supervising the engraving, tinting, and printing of his father's plates and soliciting subscriptions for the work.

Charleston S.C. Jan'y 14th, 1834

My Dear Beloved Victor.—

God willing we will be with you about the 4th of July next!—

I have been much tormented for some weeks passed on account of the requisitions which you have made that I should return to England as early in the Spring as possible—no *reasons* have you given and sorry indeed will I be, if on our arrival in England I find, as I have done on a former occasion, that I should have been recalled to Europe for the mere gratification of a few Friends & acquaintances; the whole of whom I dare say may long to see me, but none of whom, *can know* the Intentions, the Cares, and the Anxieties which Your Father feels toward *Your* welfare, that of your Brother and equally that of your most kind Mother—The Die is however cast.—I have given up my urgent wishes to revisit the Floridas, and a certain portion of the Western & Northwestern portion of our own beloved Country—and unless you write in answer to my last letters to you on this subject, *with open thoughts of your own* that *I* may remain in America, depend upon what I say at the begaining of this—God willing I and us will be (God willing) with you on the 4th of July next.—

Fearing that you are troubled for the want of money, I will exert myself to the very utmost to send you forthwith 2. or 3. or 4 hundred pounds to alleviate the difficulties (if any there are) in your calls for cash.—I have already written to Docr Parkman to exert himself in trying to have some advances made on a/c of the 2*d* Volume at Boston & have requested to forward you if successful whatever he may get immediately. I shall in a few days go to Savannah to try with W*am* Gaston to do the same there.—I wish you had made it *a point* to have sent me the 20 Volumes for which I have so often written to you.—through these I could have sent you per-haps one thousand pounds—but now this is all over and I must do the best I can without any of them but 2 Copies—

I can do no more in England than you have done—depend upon it the Southern part of that Country will be of no effect when I go there.—America I am sure is the Country that will support us after all.—

This day the Nos 34 & 35 for this City and for Columbia College have arrived in Port—*but I have not seen them yet*.—All the Nos by the President were *Wet* & good for nothing—These have been sold at auction in New York and have I been vexed enough on that account.

I ask of you most earnestly not to ship any thing more in this *slack man-ner*—If Havell will not see that our Work is properly packed, *see to it your-self*.—

I shall reach England I hope with as many Drawings of Water Birds as will compleat the 3*d* Volume of our Work—but to tell you the truth it will prove a most wonderful thing if the 4*th* Volume does contain 100 plates. You are afraid of New Species coming in—I am greatly afraid of the want of them—but enough of this—when we meet all will be understood in a few weeks, and in *a few months* I must return to Our Country to compleat my researches, and procure *here* (America) subscribers to enable us all to become one day independent of the World & *particularly of England!*

Long ere this reaches you I hope you will have received the Duplicate pa-per sent you for Louden's Magazine, and that also Mr Louden will have in-serted it in his Journal—that, that paper may produce *some* effect on the mind of many, I have no doubt, but that it will be an equivalent to the representa-tions of my character being false is quite another affair. —*here Rattlesnakes* are known to climb trees—to feed on Squirrels—&c—*here* Vultures are known to have *no sense* of *Smell* &c but all that *we* know of these matters will require a Century of Time to establish these *facts in the Eyes of the British Public*.—

Our Work will become *important* even long ere it is compleated; for this reason it is imperiously necessary that every exertion in our power should be kept up, *with truth, firmness, dignity and consistency* from begainning to end—that the World and Naturalists especially will become satisfied that when finished, Our Work will be the standard of American Ornothology, I have no doubt, but as this will in all probability only appear after my Death, you & your Brother are the ones that will reap the benefits of the Worthiness of my *practical Studies*, therefor I strongly advise you to believe in Your Father's thoughts, that through this Publication *You & John may ex-pect* to become rich, respected and highly thought of—

Twenty Years since, my writing in the present style would have been ridiculous in me—but now, I am *sure* of what I say, and proud that when that I express my feelings freely to my Sons, I am equally sure that I tell them the truth & nothing but the truth; connected with my most ardent wish that they should become most happy, through my exertions connected with theirs—I will finish this as soon as possible after I have seen and delivered the Nos 34 & 35 for this place and the first Volume for Mr. Rees which is also arrived here—Good night

My Dear Victor—

16*th*—This morning I brought Nos 34 & 35 for the subscribers here, & the Columbia College—I have opened them, and I tell you with pleasure that I think them *very fine*. all I regret is the *errors* in nomenclature, which however may be corrected so that you may have them correct for those persons who have not yet been supplied.—as follows.—plate [—] instead of Grey Tyrant have Titirit Fly Catcher—Muscicapa *Matinatus*—Plate [—] *Muscicapa Cooperii*—also have the *black headed Titmouse* as follows (*for it is a new Species*) The Lesser black headed Titmouse—*Parus Caroliniensis*. My letter press will do the rest. —I will write to Havell.—

On the 18*th* Instant I ship to New York 5 Numbers of Water Birds to be forwarded to London by London Packet (I hope that the 1*st* of Feb.y.—When you receive them, write by duplicate from London & way of Liverpool that you have them, to relieve my anxiety about them. Inclosed is a list of them and of 3 more numbers composed of Drawings which you have in England, *and which* should you not receive the present 5 Numbers; have published rather than to stop the Work from going on regularly—but I hope the 5 Numbers will reach you safely.—

One of the 2 Volumes you sent is also received here and I have sent John to deliver it to *Mr Rees'* agent who I expect will pay John.—*In a few days* I will send you a Draft or Bill for some money.—

Show all the Drawings at once to Havell when you receive them—it will prove to him that *the Water Birds* have not more work upon them than the Land ones.—As many Birds have been *Pasted*, take great care of those Drawings and shew them to *a very few* of your Friends.—

The 3 Small Drawings of Land Birds being *New Species I wish you to give them for the 3 extra small plates.* —be sure that these go instead of hitherto known Birds which I have sent you and which you have, but which will come in the 4*th* Volume, a Volume which will be composed of both Land & Water Birds.—take good heart attend strictly to the Publication &c & all will go on well.—

Friend Bachman has finished another paper on Buzards, notes for this Country—and I shall have 200 Copies of it struck in a few days, for all our Subscribers here and others whom it may concern—

Good night God bless you.—

Make arrangements with Mrs Russel for us.—

Ever yours Father & Friend
John J. Audubon.

CHARLES W. ELIOT TO
CHARLES ELIOT, JR.

*"If you feel the blues coming upon you,
get a book and a glass of wine . . ."*

Following the Civil War the United States went through a period of astounding progress in industry, science, and engineering. Yet there was no greater advancement made than in the world of ideas. From 1869 to 1909, leading the way of advancement and reform in American education was Harvard president Charles W. Eliot. Modern American universities, as we know them today, were largely structured and shaped by the changes Eliot instituted during his forty-year tenure.

He believed individual interests, rather than requirements enforced by the university, should be the driving force guiding curriculum. He wanted students to be treated as adults. He felt that those Harvard students who were from modest means were "the very best part" of the university and he took great interest in their welfare. When word of a death in a student's family reached the university, it was the president himself who delivered the news to the young man. On more than one occasion he gave his house over to a student who was gravely ill.

With his eldest son, Charles, he had an unusually close friendship. Recognizing their differences, Eliot described himself as "sanguine, confident, content with present action," whereas he thought his son to be "reticent, self-distrustful" and "speculative." In 1886, having just finished an apprenticeship with Frederick Law Olmsted, twenty-six-year-old Charles was in Europe studying landscape architecture. He wrote to his father referring to himself as "incompetent in dealing with men." Here Charles Eliot responds.

April 20, [18]86

Dear Charles,

Don't imagine yourself deficient in power of dealing with men. Such dealings as you have thus far had with boys and men you have conducted very suitably. There is no mystery about successful business intercourse with patrons and employés. Nobody can think, and at the same time pay attention to another person, as you seem to expect to do. On the contrary, exclusive attention to the person who is speaking to you is a very important point in business manners. Nothing is so flattering as that. Some audible or visible signs of close attention are of course desirable. Then there is very seldom any objection to the statement, "I should like to think that over." . . . I wish you were tough and strong like me. But you have nevertheless an available measure of strength, and within that measure an unusual capacity of enjoyment. In this respect you closely resemble your mother. She enjoyed more in her short life than most people in a long one; and particularly she delighted in natural scenery. You get a great deal more pleasure out of your present journeyings than I ever could have. I should not have your feelings of fatigue and weakness, but neither should I have your perception of the beautiful and your enjoyment of it. When you come to professional work, you will have to be moderate in it. Where other men work eight hours a day, you must be content with five. Take all things easily. Never tire yourself out. If you feel the blues coming upon you, get a book and a glass of wine, or go to bed and rest yourself. The morbid mental condition is of physical origin. Take comfort in the thought that you can have a life of moderate labor,—the best sort of life. You will have a little money of your own, and need not be in haste to earn a large income. I am strong and can work twelve hours a day. Consequently I do; and if it were not for Mt. Desert, I should hardly have more time for reflection and real living than an operative in a cotton mill. For a reasonable mortal, life cannot truly be said to have "terrors," any more than death. The love of beauty is a very good and durable correspondence between your soul and the world; but the love of purity, gentleness, and honor is a better one.

[Charles Eliot]

FREDERICK LAW OLMSTED TO FREDERICK LAW OLMSTED, JR.

"I have all my life been considering distant effects and always sacrificing immediate success and applause to that of the future."

Americans owe Frederick Law Olmsted an enormous debt of gratitude. Through his genius of design, his capacity to manage enormous projects, his ability to get things done, and his remarkable foresight, landscapes of his design and execution serve as oases of serenity stretching from coast to coast: from New York City's Central Park, to Oakland's Mountain View Cemetery, to Chicago's village of Riverside, to the grounds of the United States Capitol. He was a pioneer in his field who elevated landscape architecture to a respected profession and redirected the focus of the work from decoration to creating spaces for the enjoyment, health, and well-being of people, especially for those residing in the new and growing American cities.

The son of a well-respected Connecticut merchant, Olmsted, as a young man, jumped again and again from one line of work to another. He had been a merchant seaman, a farmer, a travel writer, an editor, the chief executive officer of the U.S. Sanitary Commission during the Civil War, the manager of a California gold mine, and a publisher. In hindsight, Olmsted considered the time before he settled into landscape architecture to be a "sad waste" and thought his own father to have been "overly-indulgent to my inclinations." He would not make the same mistake with his son, Rick. In fact, he even went so far as to change the boy's name at seven years old from Henry Olmsted to Frederick Law Olmsted, Jr., because he knew it would serve him well in his future career as a landscape architect.

"Looking forward several generations" was what Olmsted always did in his design work and it seems, too, he took the same long view for his children. Here sixty-eight-year-old Frederick Law Olmsted writes to twenty-year-old Frederick, Jr., who was about to begin his freshman year at Harvard.

5th September 1890

Dear Rick:

I found your letter of the 12th [J]ul[y] when I came back here from the West. I should have replied to it sooner but I knew that you had left Lake George and had no clue to your address. John and I have both been away since in different directions on business and we only came together this morning. If I am well eno' I start again tomorrow morning for North Carolina and from there may have to go on to Chicago, so I may not be able to see you before you are matriculated. Hence, I write, though I can not say nearly what I would like to say. I enclose the paper containing Professor Shaler's remarks to which I referred (accidentally omitted, I suppose, from my former note).

Your letter pleases me very much as showing that you have sought sound advice and have used personal judgment and have been cautious and considerate. I am not disposed to differ with your conclusions. My only question is whether you are not undertaking too much in the regular college lines to allow you to give the time that you should to others. I want you to systematically give a good deal of time, thought and management to other sorts of education than the college provides. I cannot fully say what and why but can perhaps show some of the stems of my wishes in these respects. My life is pretty nearly run out. At the best I shall be disabled from all business long before you are to enter upon it. I wish that it were otherwise so far that your professional education could proceed with my actual work as John's has and Eliot's, Codman's and Coolidge's. As that cannot be reckoned upon, it is consolation that you must have acquired a good deal of knowledge of my principals and methods unconsciously, and it is to be hoped that you will henceforth be much more than you have been in an attitude of interest and intelligence to take in more. I want you to keep up a certain regular methodical reading and thinking on the subject, I will say at least five hours a week. I reckon that in four years you would thus have read everything not ephemeral in English, French and German and would be the best read man as to this Art in the world. I want you at the same time to keep such knowledge of what is going on in our office that you will gradually be led to an understanding of practice in relation to theory and of theory in relation to practice. What I want now is that you adopt this wish of mine and let it enter into your plans and expectations and habit, in the same way that the cut and dried requirements of the college course will enter into them.

One reason of this wish has this foundation. I have, with an amount of forethought, providence, sacrifice and hardship of which you can hardly have an idea, been making a public reputation and celebrity of a certain kind, which at last has a large money value. We have, as a consequence, more business than we can manage. The business increases faster than we can enlarge our organization and adjust our methods to meet it. And it is plain that this depends as yet almost entirely on me. Clients insist on having my personal examination and personally conferring with me. I do not mean that the process of shifting the business more and more to Jno. and Harry is not going on successfully. After a work has started I am surprised to find how they come gradually to be accepted, and indeed I am loosing the run of a good deal of business and occasionally small commissions from the start carried on independently of me. Yet all of our large and profitable commissions come to us from those who know no one but me and who are prepared at the outset to take advice from no one else. Hence whenever I drop out the business will fall off greatly, the more so that there are so many young men lately starting in it. Of the income from the present business more than half comes to me and with my share of it we are able to live as we do and are now putting a thousand dollars or more to windward every year. But a large share of my earnings laid up otherwise in various indirect ways, making the business, have been lost in fitting out Owen and the beef business, and so when my name no longer attracts clients, your mother, Marion and you will be in comparatively very straitened circumstances. You and Jno. will have to support them and John is entitled to marry and have others to support. That's sufficient indication of the business side of the matter. You ought to have it in mind, however, that we are getting much higher prices and larger works and works that relatively to what they yield us cost less, than any others of our profession are getting. I do not suppose any one, or any three working together, earn a quarter as much as we do in L[andscape] A[rchitecture]. I say this with reference to what you have to expect as to your own future earning capacity. The measure of this capacity will depend on the capital you can acquire in no inconsiderable degrees in five hours reading a week during the next four years and the insight you obtain of the manner in which business is conducted in our office.

Another foundation of my wish is the modest pride and satisfaction I have in what, against great difficulties, I have accomplished in—if not elevating the art and profession of L. A., at least in contending for a much higher standard than could, but for what I have done, been maintained. I feel that I have been rather grandly successful in this respect, and yet only successful in holding the fort as it were. It is as if the war had just begun and my part had been to keep the enemy in check until reinforcements could arrive. These young men, John and Harry, Eliot and Coolidge, with Sargeant and Stiles and Mrs. Van Renssalaer are the advance of the reinforcements. I want you to be prepared to be a leader of the van. How much abler should I have been had I had your education, to this time of your education. How much more had I had that education that you may have ten years hence. I would speak of myself and what I have done, as I have to no one but you, and to you, only under these circumstances. I have all my life been considering distant effects and always sacrificing immediate success and applause to that of the future. In laying out the Central Park we determined to think of no results to be realized in less than forty years. Now in nearly all of our work I am thinking of the credit that will indirectly come to you. How will it as a mature work of the Olmsted school affect Rick? I ask, and then, with reference to your education, How is Rick to be best prepared to take advantage of what in reputation I have been earning? Reputation coming as a result of what I shall have done, but not coming in my time. How best prepared to carry on the war against vulgarity and continued further and successfully against ignorance and prejudice and meanness. How best to make L. A. respected as an Art and a liberal profession.

Of course the main thing is solid strength in the art itself, to gain which the course of college studies with the atmosphere into which the pursuit of these studies will bring you, and the reading and the rapport that you may secure with the office will be the best means. This with as much familiarity as you can gain in holidays and vacations with good natural scenery and the study of landscape paintings.

But with reference to success as a landscape architect, to obtaining business and gaining a name, you must just as systematically study to acquire social power. You must be storing up through your college acquaintances social opportunities. Be not lazy or shy to avail yourself of opportunities, first to earn friendly acquaintances, second to train yourself in social art. It is as necessary to success as anything else that you should be able to make yourself pleasing and entertaining in any society but more especially to be at home and ready to contribute the general entertainment of the most cultivated society. You need to be well-informed, thoughtful and familiar with the literature of all topics of conversation likely to come up in such a society. For this reason you must set apart hours for keeping up with the world by reading certain books as they come out, certain periodicals and certain newspapers, and by looking at works of art as they become prominent, considering criticisms upon them, attending public entertainments,—all this and more, I mean, besides cultivating social standing assiduously in the ordinary way of parties, balls and "calls." Do not think that you have only to follow your inclination in this respect. Use discrimination. Seek the best society. Seek to enjoy it. Seek to make yourself desirable in it. Make yourself well-informed on matters of conversation of the best and most fortunate sort of people. This is an essential element of your education. Follow it systematically. Arrange other studies and occupations with reference to it. You have disappointed me in not training yourself more to acquire better manners in respect to the small change of social grace. It is entirely a matter of will. You have it in your power to greatly increase your value in this respect, your power to be useful and through usefulness respectable to others and yourself, which is the chief defense against misery in life. You have your defects and weaknesses but on the whole you are in capital condition at the starting point of the University period of your life-work.

Your affectionate father

JOHN D. ROCKEFELLER TO JOHN D. ROCKEFELLER, JR.

"Go carefully. Be conservative. Be sure you are right—and then don't be afraid . . ."

The controversial industrialist John D. Rockefeller, creator of the giant Standard Oil Company, was America's first billionaire and perhaps the greatest philanthropist this country has ever known. To his only son, John D. Rockefeller, Jr., he entrusted his fortune and his dream to "promote the well-being of mankind throughout the world." Here the eighty-seven-year-old father writes to his nearly forty-eight-year-old son at a time when managing the family's charitable giving was becoming an increasingly complicated and enormously demanding responsibility. Over the course of their lifetimes John D. Rockefeller and John D. Rockefeller, Jr., gave well over a billion dollars for philanthropy.

Ormond Beach
Florida
January 26, 1922

Dear Son:

As to the sums which I have handed you from time to time, it is to be remembered that I have already set aside large amounts in our different trusts, for benevolent purposes, in addition to my regular giving personally, and with the careful and protracted study which I give to each object of any considerable moment, it is evident that I shall not fulfill to the complete extent, my heart's desire to make everything that I can give to the world available, for many years to come.

As you are in touch with the world from a somewhat different angle from mine, and there have been ample means left by a kind Providence, I have hoped that with your constant and careful studies, and wide and broad knowledge of the needs of the world, you would have the fullest enjoyment in personally determining and carrying out plans of your own for helping the world, and I rejoice to afford you this opportunity, in the confident assurance that great good will result therefrom.

I am indeed blessed beyond measure in having a son whom I can trust to do this most particular and most important work. Go carefully. Be conservative. Be sure you are right—and then don't be afraid to give out, as your heart prompts you, and as the Lord inspires you.

With tenderest affection,

Father

SHERWOOD ANDERSON TO JOHN ANDERSON

"Next to occupation is the building up of good taste. That is difficult, slow work. Few achieve it. It means all the difference in the world in the end."

What Sherwood Anderson needed to sustain him was to be writing, and to be writing well. Throughout his career, as he tried to reveal the lives and psyches of ordinary Americans, he did writing of all kinds—novels, short stories, lectures, articles, autobiography, plays, and poems. By the mid-1920s, although he continued to forge ahead, he was struggling unsuccessfully to make a mark that would surpass his earlier work.

Here, at forty-nine years old, he writes to his second child, seventeen-year-old John, a young man contemplating his future.

[Spring, 1926]

Dear [John]:

It's a problem all right. The best thing, I dare say, is first to learn something well so you can always make a living. Bob seems to be catching on at the newspaper business and has had another raise. He is getting a good training by working in a smaller city. As for the scientific fields, any of them require a long schooling and intense application. If you are made for it nothing could be better. In the long run you will have to come to your own conclusion.

The arts, which probably offer a man more satisfaction, are uncertain. It is difficult to make a living.

If I had my own life to lead over I presume I would still be a writer but I am sure I would give my first attention to learning how to do things directly with my hands. Nothing gives quite the satisfaction that doing things brings.

Above all avoid taking the advice of men who have no brains and do not know what they are talking about. Most small businessmen say simply—"Look at me." They fancy that if they have accumulated a little money and have got a position in a small circle they are competent to give advice to anyone.

Next to occupation is the building up of good taste. That is difficult, slow work. Few achieve it. It means all the difference in the world in the end.

I am constantly amazed at how little painters know about painting, writers about writing, merchants about business, manufacturers about manufacturing. Most men just drift.

There is a kind of shrewdness many men have that enables them to get money. It is the shrewdness of the fox after the chicken. A low order of mentality often goes with it.

Above all I would like you to see many kinds of men at first hand. That would help you more than anything. Just how it is to be accomplished I do not know. Perhaps a way may be found.

Anyway, I'll see you this summer. We begin to pack for the country this week.

With love,
Dad.

"The thing of course, is to make yourself alive."

At the end of 1926, Anderson and his third wife took his two younger children, John and Marion, to Europe. Eighteen-year-old John remained in Paris to study painting. Understanding the parallels between writing and painting and having painted himself, Sherwood Anderson sent his son the following advice.

[April 1927]

Something I should have said in my letter yesterday.

In relation to painting.

Don't be carried off your feet by anything because it is modern—the latest thing.

Go to the Louvre often and spend a good deal of time before the Rembrandts, the Delacroixs.

Learn to draw. Try to make your hand so unconsciously adept that it will put down what you feel without your having to think of your hands.

Then you can think of the thing before you.

Draw things that have some meaning to you. An apple, what does it mean?

The object drawn doesn't matter so much. It's what you feel about it, what it means to you.

A masterpiece could be made of a dish of turnips.

Draw, draw, hundreds of drawings.

Try to remain humble. Smartness kills everything.

The object of art is not to make salable pictures. It is to save yourself.

Any cleanness I have in my own life is due to my feeling for words.

The fools who write articles about me think that one morning I suddenly decided to write and began to produce masterpieces.

There is no special trick about writing or painting either. I wrote constantly for 15 years before I produced anything with any solidity to it.

For days, weeks, and months now I can't do it.

You saw me in Paris this winter. I was in a dead, blank time. You have to live through such times all your life.

The thing of course, is to make yourself alive. Most people remain all of their lives in a stupor.

The point of being an artist is that you may live.

Such things as you suggested in your letter the other day. I said—"don't do what you would be ashamed to tell me about."

I was wrong.

You can't depend on me. Don't do what you would be ashamed of before a sheet of white paper or a canvas.

The materials have to take the place of God.

About color. Be careful. Go to nature all you can. Instead of paint-shops—other men's palettes, look at the sides of buildings in every light. Learn to observe little things—a red apple lying on a grey cloth.

Trees—trees against hill—everything. I know little enough. It seems to me that if I wanted to learn about color, I would try always to make a separation. There is a plowed field here before me, below it a meadow, half-decayed cornstalk in the meadow making yellow lines, stumps, sometimes like looking into an ink bottle, sometimes almost blue.

The same in nature is a composition.

You look at it, thinking—"What made up that color." I have walked over a piece of ground, after seeing it from a distance, trying to see what made the color I saw.

Light makes so much difference.

You won't arrive. It is an endless search.

I write as though you were a man. Well, you must know my heart is set on you.

It isn't your success I want. There is a possibility of your having a decent attitude toward people and work. That alone may make a man of you.

S. A.

Tell Church that David Prall finally got the Cezanne prints.

Also tell the man at the shop where you go for the Picasso book—or if you have been there, drop him a note—the shop, I mean.

EUGENE O'NEILL TO SHANE O'NEILL AND TO EUGENE O'NEILL, JR.

"You write as if these were normal times, in which a young man of twenty-one could decide exactly what job he should choose as offering him the pleasantest prospect for a normal peacetime career."

During April of 1941, when Eugene O'Neill was completing revisions on The Iceman Cometh, *he wrote to each of his sons, twenty-one-year-old Shane and thirty-one-year-old Eugene, Jr., about their respective careers and futures. The letters, written only ten days apart, are at opposite ends of a spectrum from one another—but then too it seems were O'Neill's sons. Shane, who had thought superficially about careers in fishing, horse-training, and art had been expelled from a number of schools and was using drugs. Eugene, Jr., on the other hand, earned a Ph.D. in Classics from Yale, knew six languages, and taught at his alma mater where recently he had been promoted from instructor to assistant professor. Signs of trouble, however, were becoming apparent. Drinking heavily, Eugene, Jr., was often disillusioned with his work and, at thirty-one years old, he was already on his third marriage.*

Eugene, Jr., and Shane both ultimately took their own lives.

April 18th 1941

Dear Shane,

Your letter is comprehensable to me only if I assume that you have decided to forget every word I said to you when you were here a year ago. And it is pretty evident by what you haven't done in the past year that you did not think any of my advice worth taking. Well, that is your priviledge and I am not questioning your right to decide for yourself, but on the other hand you have no license to ask my help as long as you continue to live as you are living.

There is no use in my repeating all I said to you last year. You certainly remember the points I emphasized, because I know damned well you realized then that what I said was true. It is even truer now, considering the disasterous way the world crisis has developed since then. That's one thing I can't understand about your letter. You seem to have no realization of what is going on in the world. You write as if these were normal times, in which a young man of twenty-one could decide exactly what job he should choose as offering him the pleasantest prospect for a normal peace-time career. Don't you know the country will almost certainly be in the war soon? Don't you know that those who became twenty-one since the draft law passed will soon be included in the draft? Don't you know that if this country gets into the war, it will probably go on for years, and that no one can possibly predict what conditions will be like even a year from now? The one sure thing is that for years to come the big opportunities for young men will be in one of the branches of the United States Service or in the industries directly connected with the Defense Program.

Until you show you have some conception that all this affects you—as it affects me and every person in this country—and that you are making some decision which faces realistically the crisis we are all in, I simply don't know what to say to you. But I am absolutely certain that planning to start a career in the movies at this time is no answer to anything. In fact, at any time, I would not regard it as an answer for you. The farther you stay away from any job that has to do with the theater, the better off you will be. And I certainly will not give you a letter to Kenneth Macgowan. It wouldn't do you the slightest good, anyway. I happen to know something about Kenneth's job. It is extremely specialized and he has nothing to do with hiring anyone.

What happened to the job you were to get in Texas? Or was that just a phony tale?

I don't like to pan you but it is a big disappointment that after all the talk a year ago you have done so little to make yourself independent.

My health has been extremely poor during the past winter. It was the lowest I've felt since I was laid up in '37. The fact that the weather has been lousy, with record rains, had something to do with it. And, natually, like everyone else with any sense or imagination, I'm worried as hell about the future—which doesn't help any.

Carlotta joins me in love to you and please give our love to Oona. I owe her a letter and will write before long.

As ever,
Father

"Work you know is your work, which belongs to you!"

April the 28th 1941

Dear Eugene,

I am delighted to learn about the promotion. My sincerest congratulations! It is a deep pleasure and pride and satisfaction to know you are progressing steadily and that your fine work is appreciated. Work you know is your work, which belongs to you! That's the best thing about it. It seems to me I so rarely meet anyone who *knows* that the work he does *is* his work, a part of him, and not an extraneous support for his living. Even with people who are extremely successful, I feel this. Their work is an exterior job, not an inner necessity. They may possess a pleasant affection for it but no love and pain. I feel you love yours—in its deeper aspects, I mean, the devotion to knowledge and culture.

I hope you will be able to come out here this summer. There are a lot of things I'd like to say—and hear. I'm a louse not to have written you in so long. I meant particularly to tell you ages ago how deeply moved I was by the letter you wrote way back around my last birthday. "Deeply moved," is right, not merely words! It was a grand letter to get from a son. I kept waiting for a mood in which I could answer as it should be answered, but the mood continued consistently indigo all winter. Poor health plus world crisis pessimism—but mostly poor health—the lowest prolonged period since my crack-up in '37. The weather was no help. For three months or more it rained four out of every five days, or more, and the flu epidemic closed the schools, etc.

This health business wouldn't bother me so much if it did not affect work. I've been able to get little done since last December except a lot of notes and outlines. However, the stride seems to be coming back now, with sun and warmth. And my work is one of the few things I don't feel depressed over. In the past two years I've written two plays I'm really enthusiastic about: *The Iceman Cometh* and *Long Day's Journey into Night*. They will rank among the finest things I've ever done, I know. But they— particularly the second—are emphatically not plays I want produced or published at this crisis-preoccupied time. They could not be understood. Not their real meaning or truth. *The Iceman Cometh* might be a big success, if done well, but it would be for its least significant merits and its finest values would be lost, or dismissed because the present psychology would not want to face them. Moreover, conditions in the New York theater are a mess, from all I hear, and due to grow increasingly worse. My health isn't up to bucking the strain of that kind of battle, even if there were no other reasons for remaining unproduced. So I'm staying partly aloof, and ignoring all Theater Guild persuasions.

In addition to the two plays, the Cycle, although on the shelf, is still very much alive. I constantly make notes of fresh angles I get on individual plays, or on the nine as a whole, and these will be a big help when I return to it. I've also written detached outlines for four new plays outside the Cycle (one, a comedy) which look damned good to me. So you see, crisis or no crisis, I don't feel blocked at all in my work, no matter what my intuitions are about its lack of timeliness! Bum health is my only real block—the periods when there just isn't the vitality for the grind of intensive day after day labor. When you live through the play you write, you have to have a lot of reserve life on tap.

I enclose a check for your birthday. Again, much paternal pride and congratulations! And love to you and Sally.

As ever,
Father

F. SCOTT FITZGERALD TO
FRANCES SCOTT "SCOTTIE" FITZGERALD

*"Nobody ever became a writer
just by wanting to be one."*

At forty years old, drunk and defeated over the financial failure of Tender Is the Night, *F. Scott Fitzgerald felt his life as a novelist was over. He retreated to North Carolina, lived in various hotels near the sanatorium where Zelda, his wife, was institutionalized for schizophrenia, and wrote a series of essays for* Esquire *about his failure and "emotional bankruptcy." Echoing the title of his* Esquire *essays, the years 1936 and 1937 became known as "The Crack-Up."*

In September 1936, with a broken shoulder from a diving accident, Fitzgerald was emotionally devastated further by an article in the New York Post. *The front-page headline read: "The Other Side of Paradise Scott Fitzgerald, 40, Engulfed in Despair, Broken in Health He Spends His Birthday Regretting That He Has Lost Faith in His Star."*

Here he writes to his nearly fifteen-year-old daughter, who had just begun at the Ethel Walker School in Connecticut.

Grove Park Inn
Asheville, N.C.
October 20, 1936

Dearest Scottina:

I had already decided to go up Thanksgiving which I will do, God willing, and so on your own suggestion I have killed the idea of going up on your birthday. You seem to understand the fact that I cannot afford at the moment to make two trips within the same month; so I know you won't be unduly disappointed.

To finish up news of me, the arm is really definitely out of danger and I am going to be able to use it again, which I doubted for three or four weeks. Went out to football game with the Flynns last Saturday, the same sort of game exactly that we went to last fall at very much the same time. Lefty was his usual handsome self and Nora was charming as always. They asked about you repeatedly, and not because they thought they ought to but because they have a real affection for you, and I mean both of them. They were so happy to know that you are getting along so well at your school.

Confirming my Christmas plans, they are, briefly: that we shall have a party for you in Baltimore at the Belvedere or the Stafford, if we can afford it! Then the actual Christmas day will be spent either here with your mother (it won't be like that awful Christmas in Switzerland), or else you and your mother and the trained nurse will go to Montgomery and spend Christmas with your grandmother; perhaps with a little time afterwards in Baltimore before you go back to school.

Don't be a bit discouraged about your story not being tops. At the same time, I am not going to encourage you about it, because, after all, if you want to get into the big time, you have to have your own fences to jump and learn from experience. Nobody ever became a writer just by wanting to be one. If you have anything to say, anything you feel nobody has ever said before, you have got to feel it so desperately that you will find some way to say it that nobody has ever found before, so that the thing you have to say and the way of saying it blend as one matter—as indissolubly as if they were conceived together.

Let me preach again for one moment: I mean that what you have felt and thought will by itself invent a new style so that when people talk about style they are always a little astonished at the newness of it, because they think that is only *style* that they are talking about, when what they are talking about is the attempt to express a new idea with such force that it will have the originality of the thought. It is an awfully lonesome business, and as you know, I never wanted you to go into it, but if you are going into it at all I want you to go into it knowing the sort of things that took me years to learn.

Why are you whining about such matters as study hall, etc. when you deliberately picked this school as the place you wanted to go above all places? Of course it is hard. Nothing any good isn't hard, and you know you have never been brought up soft, or are you quitting on me suddenly? Darling, you know I love you, and I expect you to live up absolutely to what I laid out for you in the beginning.

Scott

LAURA INGALLS WILDER TO ROSE WILDER LANE

"To think that I could have forgotten all this which comes back to me now. That's why the sooner I write my stuff the better."

In 1932, Missouri farm wife Laura Ingalls Wilder had her first book published. She was sixty-five years old. Her Ma, Pa, and sister Mary were all gone, younger sisters Carrie and Grace lived far away and she was afraid the story of her family and the world of her childhood would be lost forever. She wrote, too, hoping her work "might sell a good deal more than farm stuff" as she and her husband, Almanzo "Manly" Wilder, weren't quite making it at Rocky Ridge Farm with their chickens and fruit alone.

Her books, eight in all, did sell—and they keep selling, some thirty million copies in twenty-six languages—and through her work Wilder gives us, perhaps better than any other, a sense of what it was like to have been an American pioneer girl. She crossed the prairie by covered wagon. She lived in Indian Territory, a dugout hut, a frontier hotel, and a log cabin. She knew what it was like to make her own clothes, to build a house, to survive a long winter in near-starving condi-

tions and to celebrate with almost nothing. And she knew what it meant to move on to new land and new horizons.

It is hard to know whether Wilder's books would have come to pass without the help of her only surviving child, Rose Wilder Lane. It was she who first encouraged her mother, back on the farm in Missouri, to write, and it was she who diligently served as her mother's agent, editor, and teacher. The correspondence between mother and daughter reveals just how involved Rose was with the books—with story line, rhythm, point of view, and character development—and how much she supported her mother in her work. Here, on the eve of the publication of On the Banks of Plum Creek, *with the work on* By the Shores of Silver Lake *under way, nearly seventy-year-old Laura Ingalls Wilder writes to fifty-year-old Rose.*

Feb 5, 1937

Rose Dearest,

I am going to write you a day by day letter. There is'nt enough in my head to make a letter but every little bit, I think of something I want to say to you. The letter will be like the dictionary "fine reading, but the subject changes too often."

Looking through my desk yesterday, I found a book Ma made of writing paper. When I put it there I couldn't bear to read it, but I am having to live over those days with Pa and Ma anyway, so I did.

Ma had written some of her own poetry in it and copied some that she liked.

And Pa had written two songs.

"The Blue Jaece Juniata" and "Mary of the Wild Moor." Any time you want them, I'll send you copies.

He signed the songs and the date is 1860.

The whole songs are there. Blue Juniata is not much like the printed one we had when I used it, but is as I remember hearing it. So is the other but I have never seen or heard it anywhere else. "Oh father, dear father, come down and open the door. But the watch dogs did howl and the village bells tolled and the winds blew across the wild moor"

I am going to write to Grace about the wild flowers there and refresh our memories I'll be able, I think, to sort out the later imported ones from the old timers. I'll send them to you when I get them.

Bruce was over yesterday. Drove over after his day's work was done, to see if we were all right and if we needed anything.

Only stayed a minute for he had to hurry back to do his chores.

He asked if we knew Al was here. Said he hadn't seen him, but Mrs B. saw him go up to the house. She thought she was sure it was Al. I have not heard anything from him and sort of hate to phone anyone and ask. I'd have to ask Hoovers.

Just wondered how come if true.

You remember the old saying that "A man who wont steal from the R. R. Co aint honest."

————

I am at present working on the R. R.

And here is something, I can't use in a child's story, but you could use it if you have a place for it.

On Uncle Hi's first contract he lost money. He had tried to his best to make a profit, been careful of expense, worked three of his own teams for which he could draw no pay. In the settlement the R.R. cheated him in measuring the yards of dirt moved. Their surveyors measured the finished grade and did the figuring. All goods for the camp, in the store, feed for the horses tools etc. were furnished by the R.R. but charged to the contractor. The Co. over-charged Uncle Hi on those.

He was broke and more, but the Co was good and kind and would give him another contract. I remember hearing him say, the only way to make anything was to go behind on a contract. The farther behind a man went, the more he would make.

So he took another contract. He worked his own teams but under other men's names so he could draw pay for them. The R.R. paid the men and charged the wages to the contractor. Uncle Hi kept a team hauling oats out of the feed store away somewhere and selling them. They took them away at night. Contractors had the right to take goods out of their stores but one had to be a little careful. The family took more than they could use of dry groceries and dry goods. When camp broke up, Aunt Docia took the three teams, she drove one, Lena drove one and Gene drove the other. The wagons were loaded with goods and tools. They went before the camp broke and Uncle Hi stayed for the settlement. He was a way behind on the contract, but his pockets were full of money.

All the contractors did that way.

"Old Steffins" kept three teams hauling oats, 100 lbs. to a load, for a month. The oats were unloaded into a feed room 12 x 16 and after they had hauled for a month, there were only a few oats in the room. Manly was one of the teamsters. I don't know where feed was hauled to sell. Perhaps sold to the R.R. to furnish another contractor. Must have been there was no other market.

The letter from Grace came. She said—"flowers that used to grow here, some are here yet, but lots of kinds we don't see any more. The crocus came first in the spring"—and the prairie used to be white with the blossoms of wild onions in the spring.

"Then there were violets, purple and yellow and such a lot of sheep sorrel with its pinkish blossoms.

There were no sunflowers, golden rod nor dandelions until much later. "There were yellow buttercups and white anemone, common name is wind flower." "There were two kinds of wild peas blue and purple and wild parsley and wild clover bean. There were tiger lillies in low places."

"Forty years ago there were wild geraniums (white + red) around Manchester. Never saw them around DeSmet."

To think that I could have forgotten all this which comes back to me now. That's why the sooner I write my stuff the better.

You remember the roses of course and have heard us tell about them.

Well my dear I must get to work. It is nearly dinner time.

Every year, I think, I will remember Valentine's day and be nice to people, but every year I forget until it is too late.

Christmas and birthdays seem to be all I can manage. But it was delightful to have you remember us.

Don't you love the styles this spring? Had a cat. from Bellas Hess Kas. City and the Oh all the clothes are the prettiest for years and years. The only fault is that most of them have short sleeves. Likely I am predjudiced because my arms are not pretty any more, but there should be more long sleeves. I think they are beautiful, princess and swing skirts

I am re-reading Tross of Samathrace and Manly is reading it. Whoever gets it first in the evening reads it. The other has to put up with something else.

I can't work on my book in the evening, because, if I do, I can't sleep. My brain goes right on remembering and it's H——

Lots and lots of love my dear

Mama Bess

N. C. WYETH TO ANDREW WYETH

*"How stimulating is the company
of generous minds . . ."*

An exceptional letter writer, N. C. Wyeth had a great range of interests and broad enthusiasm for the creative mind. Consistently guiding and challenging his five children, Wyeth made certain that life for them was full of wonder, imagination, principle, and productivity.

Here he writes to his son, the distinguished artist Andrew Wyeth. N. C. Wyeth educated his youngest child at home and was the only teacher Andrew Wyeth ever had.

Studio
Chadds Ford, Pennsylvania
February 16, 1944

Dear Andy,

There's a slow billowy wind coming down the valley. It comes in great round intermittent puffs and piles up about the studio ever so like some engulfing and invisible surf. One can almost hear it pouring off the back roof, cascades of spume spending itself in foamy eddies among the orchard trees and tangled grass.

The day is somber and gray, and I am reminded of Thoreau who found the drab days of winter so inspiring. These dreary winter colors which depressed other people suggested to him the high spiritual traits that constituted his concept of beauty.

The week has been, to me, a singular mix of ineffable sadness and inspiration—two moods that often happen together. But there is a persistent melancholy which I seem unable to shake off.

To circumvent these feelings I have devoted most of my spare time to reading, especially at night when sleep eludes me.—Thoreau, Goethe, Emerson, Tolstoy—all have struck me, as always, with incisive vitality and freshness. My ruminations have again been vividly stirred.

These great men forever radiate a sharp sense of that profound requirement of the artist, to fully understand that *consequences* of what he creates are unimportant. "Let the motive for action be in the action itself and not in the event."

I know from my own experience that when I create with any degree of strength and beauty I have had no thought of consequences. Anyone who creates for *effect*—to score a hit—does not know what he is missing!

This period of unprecedented distractions and overstimulation constitutes a fierce antagonist to the accomplishments of the spirit. Whatever is worth discovery in one's heart and mind can only rise to the surface among quiet conditions, in which one thought grows beside another and one has time to compare and reflect. Periods of bleak thinking and austere feeling, that kind that cuts to the bone, are imperative. Experiences which so often masquerade for cultural influences are so often merely cozy and sociable.

I was struck with a quotation from Michelangelo: "It is only well with me when I have a chisel in my hand."

How stimulating is the company of generous minds (I am thinking of the four masters named above) who overlook trifles and keep their minds instinctively fixed on whatever is good and positive in the world about them. Truly magnanimous people have no vanity, no jealousy; they have no reserves and they feed on the true and solid wherever they find it. What is more, they find it everywhere.

There is little doubt that the modern mind is opposed to the romantic mind. The modern mind is mainly content to ask and seek causes and consequences—whereas the romantic mind seeks the *significance* of things. The romantic mind must be restored to its necessary place of leadership. If things have no *significance* things are hollow!

The greats in all the arts have been primarily romanticists and realists (the two canot be separated). They interpreted life as they saw it, but, "through every line's being" soaked in the consciousness of an object, one is bound to feel, beside life as it is, the life that ought to be, and it is *that* that captivates us! All great painting is something that enriches and enhances life, something that makes it higher, wider, and deeper.

"A great painter is a great man painting."

Sound feeling can only exist in a man who is living on all sides the life that is natural to man. Only through this experience can he sense his times and avoid that ever-lurking pitfall of egocentricism. Someone, uncommonly wise, said, "Nothing is so poor and melancholy as art that is interested in itself and not its subject."

To live, to keep one's eyes wide open in wonder, to be surprised by things!

Here's a quote which I think will interest you—"Great painting like Bach's music, in texture closely woven, subdued like the early Gobelin tapestries, no emphasis, no climaxes, no beginnings or endings, merely resumptions and transitions, a design so sustained that there is no effort in starting and every casual statement is equally great."

But of course such depth presupposes another mode of feeling. One has to be a Bach before one can paint in his power and richness. Depth of style can only spring from a deepening of our emotional life. *That* is what we really demand and look for!

There's a real task on our hands, Andy. Modern art critics and their supine followers *like* the flat and the shallow. They like it as they like soft drinks and factory-made bread.

Intensity, distinction, fire—those elements of mature sincerity, these they loathe. They fear disturbance!

Ma's very well; we all are. Remember me to everybody, warmly—and give little Nicholas a special pat for me.

Monday, 7:30 a.m.

P.S. In reading this over I am impressed by the fact that none of the thoughts expressed are new to you. We have, together, gone over these matters again and again. But it is good, I think, to repeat fundamental truths and, if possible, bring them into new and fresh focus.

A great truth is like a mountain that one walks around, and the changes of its contour as one moves his position only emphasize and revivify its majesty.

GEORGE PATTON, JR., TO
GEORGE PATTON, III

"I am sure that if every leader who goes into battle will promise himself that he will come out either a conqueror or a corpse he is sure to win."

On the morning of June 6, 1944, American troops landed on the beach at Normandy, France. The invasion had been planned for the day before but was delayed by bad weather. General George Patton, like the rest of the world, learned of the invasion from a radio announcer. A controversial man but a brilliant military tactician, he would have loved to lead troops into the battle himself, but instead remained in England, training the United States Third Army for the battle that would follow the initial invasion.

In 1944, Patton's only son, George, was a twenty-year-old cadet at West Point. Here, on D-day itself, the general writes to his son.

APO 403, N.Y.

"D" Day

Dear George:

At 0700 this morning the BBC announced that the German radio had just come out with an announcement of the landing of Allied paratroops and of large numbers of assault craft near shore. So that is it.

This group of unconquerable heroes whom I command are not in yet but we will be soon—I wish I was there now as it is a lovley sunny day for a battle and I am fed up with just sitting.

I have no immediate idea of being killed but one can never tell and none of us can live for ever so if I should go don't worry but set yourself to do better than I have.

All men are timid on entering any fight whether it is the first fight or the last fight all of us are timid. Cowards are those who let their timidity get the better of their manhood. You will never do that because of your blood lines on both sides. I think I have told you the story of Marshal Touraine who fought under Louis XIV. On the morning of one of his last battles—he had been fighting for forty years—he was mounting his horse when a young ADC who had just come from the court and had never missed a meal or heard a hostile shot said: "M. de Touraine it amazes me that a man of your supposed courage should permit his knees to tremble as he walks out to mount." Touraine replied, "My lord duke I admit that my knees do tremble but should they know where I shall this day take them they would shake even more." That is it. Your knees may shake but they will always take you toward the enemy. Well so much for that.

There are apparently two types of successful soldiers. Those who get on by being unobtrusive and those who get on by being obtrusive. I am of the latter type and seem to be rare and unpopular: but it is my method. One has to choose a system and stick to it. People who are not themselves are nobody.

To be a successful soldier you must know history. Read it objectively, dates and even the minute details of tactics are useless. What you must know is how man reacts. Weapons change but man who uses them changes not at all. To win battles you do not beat weapons, you beat the soul of man of the enemy man. To do that you have to destroy his weapons but that is only incidental. You must read biography and especially autobiography. If you will do it you will find that war is simple. Decide what will hurt the enemy most within the limits of your capabilities to harm him and do it. TAKE CALCULATED RISKS. That is quite different from being rash. My personal belief is that if you have a 50% chance take it because the superior fighting qualities of American soldiers lead by me will surely give you the extra 1% necessary.

In Sicily I decided as a result of my information, observations, and a sixth sense that I have, that the enemy did not have another large scale attack in his system. I bet my shirt on that and I was right. You cannot make war safely but no dead general has ever been criticised so you have that way out always.

I am sure that if every leader who goes into battle will promise himself that he will come out either a conqueror or a corpse he is sure to win. There is no doubt of that. Defeat is not due to losses but to the destruction of the soul of the leaders. The "Live to fight another day" doctrine.

The most vital quality a soldier can possess is SELF CONFIDENCE, utter, complete and bumptious. You can have doubts about your good looks, about your intelligence, about your selfcontrol but to win in a war you must have NO doubts about your ability as a soldier.

What success I have had results from the fact that I have always been certain that my military reactions were correct. Many people do not agree with me; they are wrong. The unerring jury of history written long after both of us are dead will prove me correct.

Note that I speak of "Military reactions" no one is borne with them any more than any one is borne with muscles. You can be borne with the soul capable of correct military reactions or the body capable of having big muscles but both qualities must be developed by hard work.

The intensity of your desire to acquire any special ability depends on character, on ambition. I think that your decision to study this summer instead of enjoying yourself shows that you have character and ambition— they are wonderful possessions.

Soldiers, all men in fact, are natural hero worshippers. Officers with a flare for command realize this and emphasize in their conduct, dress and deportment the qualities they seek to produce in their men. When I was a second lieutenant I had a captain who was very sloppy and usually late, yet he got after the men for just those faults; he was a failure.

The troops I have commanded have always been well dressed, been smart saluters, been prompt and bold in action because I have personally set the example in these qualities. The influence one man can have on thousands is a never ending source of wonder to me. You are always on parade. Officers who through lazyness or a foolish desire to be popular fail to enforce discipline and the proper wearing of uniforms and equipment not in the presence of the enemy will also fail in battle and if they fail in battle they are potential murderers. There is no such thing as: "A good field soldier" you are either a good soldier or a bad soldier.

Well this has been quite a sermon but don't get the idea that it is my swan song because it is not. I have not finished my job yet.

Your affectionate father.

Woody Guthrie and children (Arlo far right)

General John J. Pershing and
son Warren Pershing

John Steinbeck (center), John Steinbeck IV,
and President Lyndon Johnson

Struggle

Thomas Jefferson to
Martha "Patsy" Jefferson

*"Be assured that it gives much more pain to the mind
to be in debt, than to do without any article
whatever which we may seem to want."*

Standing a lean six feet, two inches tall, Thomas Jefferson was distinguished and elegant. He was also extravagant. In the way of material acquisitions it seems he denied himself not at all. In Philadelphia, Paris, London, and New York, he bought and bought—silver, wine, tablecloths, clothes, candlesticks, a chariot, paintings, sculpture; in Paris alone he purchased approximately two thousand books. Wherever he lived, he did so in grand style, renovating and remodeling houses he rented and always improving and expanding his own Monticello. Debt was a way of life for him, as it was for most Southern planters of the day, debt having been passed down to him, along with his land and his slaves. Throughout his life he increased his debt, incessantly borrowing from creditors in both America and Europe.

At the time of his death, Thomas Jefferson owed more than $100,000 ($1.8 million in today's money), which exceeded in value all that he owned, including Monticello. It was his dutiful and self-reliant daughter, Martha, the only child to survive him, who lived to endure the pain as everything was auctioned away.

Paris June 14. 1787.

I send you, my dear Patsy, the 15 livres you desired. You propose this to me as an anticipation of five weeks allowance. But do you not see my dear how imprudent it is to lay out in one moment what should accomodate you for five weeks? That this is a departure from that rule which I wish to see you governed by, thro' your whole life, of never buying anything which you have not money in your pocket to pay for? Be assured that it gives much more pain to the mind to be in debt, than to do without any article whatever which we may seem to want. The purchase you have made is one of those I am always ready to make for you, because it is my wish to see you dressed always cleanly and a little more than decently. But apply to me first for the money before you make a purchase, were it only to avoid breaking thro' your rule. Learn yourself the habit of adhering vigorously to the rules you lay down for yourself. I will come for you about eleven o'clock on Saturday. Hurry the making your gown, and also your redingcote. You will go with me some day next week to dine at the Marquis Fayette's. Adieu my dear daughter. Your's affectionately,

TH: JEFFERSON

ABIGAIL ADAMS TO THOMAS BOYLSTON ADAMS

"I have in the various stages of Life, been call'd to endure afflictions, and dangers of many kinds, but this was something so new, so unexpected, that I could scarcely realize it."

Abigail Adams was accustomed to making ends meet. With an eye for economy, she churned her own butter, did her own sewing, fed the chickens, skimmed the milk, and wove her own cloth. Raising young children and managing the Adams farm, Stoneyfield, she supported the family during the Revolutionary War and during those years her husband was serving the country in Philadelphia and Europe. She was never afraid of hard work, nor of scrimping and saving. Debt was something she was always determined to avoid.

By the early 1800s, through years of effort, the Adamses had acquired additional properties to increase their Braintree, Massachusetts, farm to more than six-

hundred acres. They had also managed to save a goodly sum of money, some $13,000, which they had put in the London bank, Bird, Savage & Bird. Then in 1803, catastrophic news came that Bird, Savage & Bird had collapsed and their money, nearly all of their savings, was gone. Abigail was fifty-nine years old, John Adams, the former president of the United States, sixty-eight.

Their eldest son, John Quincy Adams, who had initially suggested the bank in London, was determined to "share in the suffering." He sold his own home, used his savings and borrowed. Slowly he bought his parents' real estate holdings (they held title for life) and eventually replenished their depleted savings.

Here Abigail Adams illuminates the family predicament for the youngest son, Thomas, a thirty-one-year-old lawyer in Philadelphia.

Quincy April 26th 1803

My dear Son

A very bad whitloe upon the finger of my right Hand has prevented my holding a pen; or useing my hand for a long time, or I should not have been so long silent. Altho my communications will give you more pain than pleasure, it may relieve your mind respecting the loss your Brother has sustaind; but it will be only shifting the Burden upon older Shoulders. You know your Father had some Money in Holland, which since your Brothers return, he concluded to draw out, and vest in the Farm which belonged to your Great Grandfather Quincy. Mr. Tufts after keeping his part a year, made an offer of it to your Father and he concluded to take it; relying upon the property he had abroad to pay for it. Your Brother undertook the management of the buisness abroad and as the exchange was more in favour of England than Holand, the money was drawn from thence, and placed in the Hands of the House which has lately faild, Bird Savage & Bird. A Catastrophe so unexpected to us, and at a time when we had become responsible for so large a sum, has indeed distrest us. At no other time of our lives could we have been equally affected by it. The cloud is not however so black as it first appeard; the Bill which past through your Hands, and upon which such heavey damages would arise if returned, the House inform your Brother that Mr. King kindly agreed to take up, upon honour; if this should be true as I sincerely hope it may, it will save us from such sacrifice of property as at first appeard necessary to us. Your Brother tho no way to blame in the Buisness, having conducted it with as much circumspection as possible, still insists upon selling some property which he has in Boston; a House which he lately purchased in order to aid in raising the money necessary upon this occasion: we shall endeavour to make him secure so that he shall not finally be a looser any further than in common with the rest of the family. At first my phylosophy was put to a trial, different from any I had ever before experienced. I have in the various stages of Life, been call'd to endure afflictions, and dangers of many kinds, but this was something so new, so unexpected, that I could scarcely realize it. Your Father bears it as well and better than I could have expected, but as yet we hardly know what we may call our own. There is the Farm, that has not vanished, and will fetch as much as we agreed to give for it, but what the damages will finally amount to, upon the Bills we cannot yet determine: let it not depress your Spirits, it is one of the unfortunate incidents in human affairs to which no remedy but patience and Submission applies. It was not dissipation, extravagance or lack of Judgement which on our part produced the event. I hope we may yet be able to obtain some part of the property in time. In the mean time, the sacrifices we must make shall on my part be cheerfully borne. If I cannot keep a carriage, I will ride in a chaise. If we cannot pay our labourers upon our Farms, we will let them to the halves, and live upon a part. To know how to a bond and to suffer want is a new lesson, but I will bring my mind to my circumstances. I do not dread want, but I dread debt, and for that reason I would contract no debt which I do not see a way clear to pay.

I shall upon the next arrivals from England be able to let you know further respecting the State of this Busness.

I have not had a letter from you for a long time. Adieu my dear Son. My anxiety is chiefly upon my childrens account. Neither your Father or I can have a much longer lease. We should have been rejoiced to have left our children with better prospects. Your affectionate Mother

A A

GEORGE CATLIN TO LOUISE CATLIN

"My conduct has broken your hearts . . .
I have done the best I could under
cruel and painful circumstances."

As white settlers moved increasingly westward, artist George Catlin feared that Native Americans and their way of life would be forever destroyed. Concerned for

the wildlife and wilderness of the West, he is credited for first envisioning the national park system, and he himself worked from 1829 to 1837 to make a pictorial record of the tribes and their people. Traveling by steamboat, horseback, and canoe, he created some six hundred paintings in all—of chiefs and tribal leaders, men, women, and children in their customary clothing and scenes of village life, spiritual ceremonies, and domestic routines. His depictions of the Native American were neither the idealized "noble savage," nor the threatening beast. Instead Catlin's was a portrayal of individuals living in vibrant cultures all their own.

His hope was that the United States government would purchase his complete body of work, the "Indian Gallery" as it was known, as a permanent record for the nation of a vanishing world. He drummed up interest by staging exhibitions in eastern cities, and when Congress refused to buy his paintings, he angrily took the entire collection, in 1839, to Europe. There he exhibited the paintings and then went on to produce an expensive and extravagant "Wild West Show" that was to be the beginning of his personal ruin. First, his wife and young son caught pneumonia and died in France, and then he lost his money and his honor to creditors and wound up in debtors' prison. His surviving family returned to America. The entire "Indian Gallery" was sold in 1852 to Philadelphia businessman Joseph Harrison, who stored the paintings in his factory's boiler room for the next twenty-seven years.

In 1861, George Catlin was deaf and nearly crippled. It had been nearly a decade since he had seen his three daughters. For the previous nine years he had wandered Europe like a vagrant and then, attempting to recapture his days in the American West, he traveled the world painting native peoples. Here, from his small apartment in Belgium, he writes to twenty-year-old Louise.

Ostende, Belgium
April 22nd 1861

My Dear, Sweet little Louise,

Your affectionate and beautiful letter came to me yesterday, and I lose no time in answering it, to tell you what pleasure it has brought me: this I shall scarely be able to do for there are many things which language was not made perfect enough to express or explain.

One of these things is the paternal and filial affections which connects parents and children together—when like cords, they are stretched, but not snapped, by distance and long absence.

My dear child, I have read your affectionate letter over and over, with tears in my eyes, and I thank you for every line of it. It is so tender—so loving—so devotional. My conduct has broken your hearts, but my lovely children I pray to God that He may help you to forgive me. He is my witness that I have done the best I could under cruel and painful circumstances. You can imagine somewhat of the shame, the pain, the anguish of an affectionate and loving parent so long separated from those that he most loves— that he idolizes, but you can never know the whole of it. The labours and fatigues I have been through since we parted have been many, as well as my successes and misfortunes. I made a fortune for you since I saw you, but I lost it again. I have seen much and I have done much—I have traveled much, and for the last year and a half I have suffered much—I have stood upon the crater of the two volcanos in the Koriak Mountains of Siberia. I have been to the Aleutian Islands, & Kamchatka, traced the Pacific Coast to the mouth of Columbia—ascended that and crossed the Rocky Mountains to Santa Fe—from that to Matamoras, by the Rio Colorado—from that to Cuba—to the Amazon, (the second time) to Venezuela to Bolivia—to Perou—to Equador—to Central Ama—to Yucatan—Palenque to Uxmal &c &c. The expenses of traveling in foreign lands are enormous, & I have had nothing but my own hands with the talent which the Almighty gave me (perhaps for that purpose) to pay my way. You can imagine, my dear child that I have travelled to a disadvantage—that my life has been a rough one, & that I have had to labour hard and constantly, to go through what I have done. I have had no time for pleasure or enjoyment, save those which my labours and the thoughts of my dear little children have afforded me. If my life had been thrown away in idleness or dissipations during these long years of absence there would be no excuse for me. I would be a monster, and I should have no right to ask forgiveness of my dear little angels, but I have been constantly at work, and still am so, even when lying on my back, or hobbling about on Crutches.

I know by my recollections of your early taste as well as by the graceful and prettily formed lines in your letter that you have a talent for the Art; and I believe (yes, that you *can* "help me") I think I am preparing enough for your delicate little fingers to work on for a long time, if you are disposed to do so, and for the benefit of yourself and your dear sisters, when I shall be dead and gone. These things I intend to bring to you before long, if our Country is not deluged in blood which I am any day afraid to hear of.

Your sweet and pretty little postcard came safe in your letter, as well as one from Clara, & one from Libby in her letter from Cincinnati. Oh how pretty they look to me—and how they accuse me. Clara told me in her last letter that both you and she had written me before, but I never have rec*d* those letters, nor can I account for them. I have now but two traces from your little fingers on earth—the one is your composition in French, on La Morgue—and the other, the affectionate letter which I recd yesterday. I came to Ostende about 10 days since, having been in London for a few days, hobbling about on one Crutch. I have now no appearance of any further volcanic affairs in my knee, but I am still a cripple. And such I fear I shall be for the remainder of my days. I suffer considerable pain at times, and mostly in the night, when one should suppose I should be most at ease. While I hobble about in the open air, and keep in motion, I get along tolerably well; but after sitting for a while it is hard starting. I am *giving myself pain* in walking, in order to prevent a crooked leg.

Libby wrote me that Mr. Dudley Gregory had been very ill—this I am sorry to hear, but I hope he has greatly recovered. I shall always sympathize deeply and tenderly with such any afflictions amongst those who have been so kind to my little daughters. How long I shall be in Ostende I know not—it matters little where I am now, as I require but a small space and am solely occupied in writing. And there is such a splendid promenade here on the parapet between the town and the beach—in the sea air, that I believe it may be the best place I could be in. Letters addressed to me at present, to *Porte Restard, Ostende, Belgique* will be sure to reach me. Give my love to dear, *dear* little Clara, and tell her that I will answer her letter in a few days. Remember me affectionately to all those so kind to you and rest assured that I have never for a moment lost that love that I always had for my dear little girls.

Your affectionate parent
Geo. Catlin.

I send a kiss.

George Catlin was reunited with his daughters in 1870, but he did not live to know that his "Indian Gallery" was, in 1879, donated to the United States government by the family of Joseph Harrison. The collection is now at the Smithsonian Institution.

WILLIAM JAMES TO MARGARET MARY JAMES

*"The disease makes you think of yourself all the time;
and the way out of it is to keep as busy as we can
thinking of things and of other people."*

Philosopher, writer, scientist, and psychologist, William James was a towering figure in America's intellectual golden age. In 1872, at the age of thirty, he was recruited to teach at Harvard, just as it was being transformed into a vigorous modern university. Through his teaching and writing, he came to be known as the father of modern psychology. A member of the esteemed James family (his brother was the novelist Henry James), William James was brilliant, apprehensive, intellectually irreverent, and often insecure.

Plagued most of his adult life by various ailments and debilitating depression, he and his wife, Alice, spent 1899 and 1900 traveling about Europe in search of treatment for his seriously diseased heart. Their thirteen-year-old daughter, Peggy, stayed in England with family friends. Feeling lonely and isolated and fearing for her father's health, Peggy was overwhelmed with anxiety. Here psychologist James, a man who had firsthand experience with emotional breakdown and once described himself as his children's "half-cracked neurotic daddy," writes to his distressed daughter. The letter was written fifteen years before Sigmund Freud published his first essay on depression.

Villa Luise, Bad-Nauheim, | May 26, 1900.

Darling Peg,

Your letter came last night & explained sufficiently the cause of your long silence. You have evidently been in a bad state of spirits again, and dissatisfied with your environment; and I judge that you have been still more dissatisfied with the inner state of trying to consume your own smoke, and grin and bear it, so as to carry out your mother's behests made after the time when you scared us so by your inexplicable tragic outcries in those earlier letters. Well! I believe you have been trying to do the manly thing under difficult circumstances, but one learns only gradually to do the *best* thing, and the best thing for you would be to write at least weekly, if only a post-card, and say just how things are going. If you are in bad spirits, there is no harm whatever in communicating that fact, and defining the character of it, or describing it as exactly as you like. The bad thing is to pour out the *contents* of ones bad spirits on others and leave them with it, as it were, on their hands, as if it was for them to do something about it. That was what you did in your other letter which alarmed us so, for your shrieks of anguish were so excessive and so unexplained by anything you told us in the way of facts, that we didn't know but what you had suddenly gone crazy. That is the *worst* sort of thing you can do. The *middle* sort of thing is what you do this time—namely keep silent for more than a fortnight, and when you do write, still write rather mysteriously about your sorrows, not being quite open enough. Now, my dear little girl, you have come to an age when the inward life developes, and when some people (and on the whole those who have most of a destiny) find that all is not a bed of roses. Among other things there will be waves of terrible sadness, which last sometimes for days; and dissatisfaction with one's self, and irritation at others, and anger at circumstances and stony insensibility, etc., etc, which taken together form a melancholy. Now, painful as it is, this is sent to us for an enlightenment. It always passes off, and we learn about life from it, and we ought to learn a great many good things if we react on it rightly.* Many persons take a kind of sickly delight in hugging it; and some sentimental ones may even be proud of it, as showing a fine sorrowful kind of sensibility. Such persons make a regular habit of the luxury of woe. That is the worst possible reaction on it. It is usually a sort of disease, when we get it strong; arising from the organism having generated some poison in the blood; and we mustn't submit to it an hour longer than we can help, but jump at every chance to attend to anything cheerful or comic, or take part in any thing active that will divert us from our mean pining inward state of feeling. When it passes off, as I said, we know more than we did before. And we must try to make it last as short a time as possible. The worst of it often is that while we are in it, we don't *want* to get out of it. We hate it, & yet we prefer staying in it—that is a part of the disease. If we find ourselves like that, we must make ourselves *do* something different, go with people, speak cheerfully, set ourselves to some hard work, make ourselves sweat, etc.; and that is the good way of reacting that makes of us a valuable character. The disease makes you think of *yourself* all the time; and the way out of it is to keep as busy as we can thinking of *things* and of *other people*—no matter what's the matter with our Self. I have no doubt you are doing as well as you know how, darling little Peg; but we have to learn everything, and I also have no doubt that you'll manage it better and better if you ever have any more of it, and soon it will fade away, simply leaving you with more experience. The great thing for you *now*, I should suppose, would be to enter as friendlily as possible into the interests of the Clark children. If you like them, or acted as if you liked them, you needn't trouble about the question of whether they like *you* or not. They probably will, fast enough; and if they don't, it will be their funeral, not yours. But this is a great lecture, so I will stop. The great thing about it is that it is all true.

The baths are threatening to disagree with me again, so I may stop them soon. Will let you know as quick as anything is decided. Good news from home: the Merrimans have taken the Irving street house for another year, and the Wambaughs (of the Law School) have taken Chocorua, though at a reduced rent. The weather here is almost continuously cold & sunless. Your mother is sleeping, and will doubtless add a word to this when she wakes. Keep a merry heart—"time & the hour run through the roughest day." And believe me ever your most loving

W.J.

* For instance, you learn how good a thing your home is, and your country, & your brothers; and you may learn to be more considerate of other people, who, you now learn, may have their inner weaknesses, and sufferings too.

JOHN J. PERSHING TO
F. WARREN PERSHING

"I especially miss you at night."

Straight, stern, a stickler for manners and courtesy, General John J. Pershing commanded respect. He was the hero of the Great War and the only American since George Washington ever to reach the highest military rank of all, General of the Armies. Those in his command knew him to be impressive, yet cold, stubborn, and inflexible. And they knew, too, what personal tragedy he had endured. On the night of August 27, 1915, General Pershing's wife, Frankie, and their three daughters, Helen, Anne, and Mary Margaret, were killed in a fire that swept through their San Francisco Presidio home. For Pershing all was lost, all except his little blond-haired boy, Warren.

Not quite two years after the catastrophic fire, General Pershing was named commander-in-chief of the American Expeditionary Forces in Europe. He worked determinedly to build an independent American army, but by the early spring of

1918 Germany was forcefully on the offensive. "Extreme pessimism prevailed" as the French and British lost ground and troops lost heart. In March 1918, it seemed France might be lost, and in a dramatic move, Pershing temporarily laid aside American plans and quickly offered U.S. troops to replenish the ranks of the French and British militaries. At the time he was in command of 500,000 men in Europe; the number would swell to nearly 2.5 million by war's end.

Here, on May 9, 1918, in the midst of war, the commander-in-chief writes a kind and longing letter to his only surviving child, eight-year-old Warren, across the ocean nearly five thousand miles away. The boy, who had lost his mother and all his sisters and who sent his adored father "one million kisses," was now living a quiet life in Lincoln, Nebraska, cared for by the general's maiden sister, May Pershing.

France, May 9, 1918.
Master Warren Pershing,
1748 B Street,
Lincoln, Nebraska.

My dear Warren:

I have just had a very pretty horseback ride along the Marne. You know the Marne River rises in Eastern France and flows into the Seine just east of Paris. It is a beautiful river and has a canal along its entire course. The banks of the canal are level and grassy and, usually, lined with trees. We frequently take horseback rides along this canal because it is so lovely and because the banks are soft for the horses' feet.

This morning I rode along the banks for about two miles and came to a point where the canal runs across the river and into a tunnel through a mountain. The bridge that carries the canal is very deep of course and is made of iron—simply an iron trough made like a bridge, and right after the canal crosses the river it flows into the mountain, through a tunnel of course. I thought you would be interested to know about this.

I have a very good horse, a bay which I brought from San Antonio. He has a splendid trot, a nice canter and gallops well when you want him to.

The only thing that was lacking this morning in making my ride a complete joy was that you were not here to go with me. I often wish you were with me when I see beautiful things as I travel around the country. I would also like to have you with me always under all circumstances. I especially miss you at night.

I am just dictating this short note while I am eating breakfast, so goodbye. Write me very often.

CARL SANDBURG TO MARGARET SANDBURG

". . . we are going to go on slowly, quietly,
hand in hand, the three of us, never giving up."

Carl Sandburg, with his signature lock of straight white hair, wrote in the language of the American vernacular. A poet, historian, and folksinger, he was a man who had faith in the people, the land, the cities, and in the American dream. He was a devoted husband and the father of three daughters, the eldest of whom was diagnosed with epilepsy in the days before there were seizure-suppressing medications. Here, forty-three-year-old Sandburg writes to his ten-year-old daughter, a patient at the Battle Creek Sanatorium.

[Elmhurst, Illinois]
[November 1921]

Dear Margaret:

This is only a little letter from your daddy to say he thinks about you hours and hours and he knows there was never a princess nor a fairy worth so much love. We are starting on a long journey and a hard fight—you and mother and daddy—and we are going to go on slowly, quietly, hand in hand, the three of us, never giving up. And so we are going to win. Slowly, quietly, never giving up, we are going to win.

Daddy

WILLIAM CARLOS WILLIAMS TO
WILLIAM ERIC WILLIAMS

". . . I had to fight to keep myself as I wanted to be."

Medicine and literature were a vital combination for William Carlos Williams. "One feeds off the other in a manner of speaking; both seem necessary to me," he said. A major poet of the twentieth century who strived to establish an American style of verse all its own, Williams was also a physician who, during the course of

his medical career, delivered two thousand babies in and around his native Ruther-
ford, New Jersey.

In 1942, he was especially hard at work in his general practice. Most of the
younger doctors were off serving in World War II, and Williams knew that "as the
younger men go, we older men must do their work—there's no question about
that." At the same time, he was just beginning his epic poem Paterson, *but it*
wasn't going well. He felt he was laboring and not writing as confidently as usual.
And as a father, he was struggling with the absence of both his children. Paul was
on a destroyer patrolling the Atlantic and Bill was a naval medical officer in the Pa-
cific. Here fifty-nine-year-old Williams writes to his son and fellow doctor, twenty-
eight-year-old Bill.

Sept. 25, 1942

Dear Bill:

Your letters recently have shown me the changes that are taking place
in you, a maturity which I want to salute and acknowledge. Generally
speaking, your present experience has been of decided benefit, something
you could not achieve, at least not so quickly, in any other way. Part of it
has been the enforced separation from any protecting influence I may still
have had on you, a very good thing. What you're facing is your world, a
world in which I haven't the slightest part. We are now two individuals,
two men, closely bound by mutual beliefs and interests but completely independent as to the future. Strangely enough, this separation has brought
me much closer to you. I'm glad that early phase is at an end.

That relationship between father and son is one of the toughest things
in the world to break down. It seems so natural and it is natural—in fact
it's inevitable—but it separates as much as it joins. A man wants to protect
his son, wants to teach him the things he, the father, has learned or thinks
he has learned. But it's exactly that which a child resents. He wants to
know but he wants to know on his own—and the longer the paternal influence lasts the harder it is to break down and the more two individuals
who should have much in common are pushed apart. Only a sudden enforced break can get through that one.

But I've sweated over wanting to do and say the right thing concerning you boys. Certain things stick in my mind—I just didn't do the right
thing and I suffered for it. Once when you were a little kid some question
of veracity came up between you and Elsie, that goofy girl we had here. I

should have known that you were just a baby but I lost my temper, insisting that one of you was lying when I should have known, if I had thought for a moment, that it wasn't you. Or if it was, then what the hell anyway? It might have been from fear—no doubt of me. Then one day at the close of Watty's camp in Maine you were in some sort of a canoe race and were about to win when someone quite unfairly cut you out and you cried. I like a God damned fool laughed at you. Why? Just to hide my own embarrassment. You looked at me and said, "It was my only chance to win anything!" I tell you that hurt. I've never forgotten it. Such are a father's inner regrets. Stupid enough. And what in the hell is a parent to do when an older child is tormented by a younger child, finally smears his younger tormentor and then comes up for punishment? I've never solved that one. I've done many more seriously stupid things than those mentioned—but I wanted so hard to give you the best.

On the other hand, when you say you've got so much more in the bank than some of the men you have to deal with, I feel that what we did for you wasn't too bad. The same for what you say about the kitten and the spiders. That you can get the good out of such trivia is a tribute to your mind which I have always respected and which I'm glad to see maintaining itself with distinction in the situation in which you are placed. I don't know what kind of a father I was but in things like that at least something "took" of what I intended and that it wasn't all beside the point.

You say you'd like to see my book of poems. What the hell? Let 'em go. They are things I wrote because to maintain myself in a world much of which I didn't love I had to fight to keep myself as I wanted to be. The poems are me, in much of the faulty perspective in which I have existed in my own sight—and nothing to copy, not for anyone even so much as to admire. I have wanted to link myself up with a traditional art, to feel that I was developing individually it might be, but along with that, developing still in the true evolving tradition of the art. I wonder how much I have succeeded there. I haven't been recognized and I much doubt that my technical influence is good or even adequate.

However, this is just one more instance of the benefits to be gained by breaking entirely with the father-son hook-up. It was logical for you not to have looked at my poems—or only casually to look at them. You had me in my own person too strongly before you to need that added emphasis. You did the right thing and I never cared a damn. Now, separated from me by distance and circumstance, it may after all be permissible for you to look at the poems. Not to do anything more than to enjoy them, man to man, if you can get any enjoyment out of them. I'll send them. I have a gold-edged copy reserved for you, one of the de luxe copies, but I'll not send that. Look, if you care to, at whatever I have done as if you had never known me. That's the only way for a father and son to behave toward each other after the son's majority has been reached. Then, if you still find something to cherish, it will be something worthwhile.

You in your recent letters have shown that you have a style of your own—another testimonial to your own character and a tribute to your parents for not trying, really, to press themselves upon you. You have an interesting prose style that everyone who reads your letters admires. It's really comical. Some say, "A chip off the old block"; others say, "He writes better than you do," and so it goes. You are entirely different from me in your approach, and yet we are alike in our interests. . . .

They finished insulating the attic today and are putting storm windows all along the front of the house. Better to be prepared for what may happen the coming winter.

Love,
DAD

Both of Williams's sons returned from World War II intact.

WOODY GUTHRIE TO ARLO GUTHRIE

". . . all of us when you come right down to it all of us
are just every bit as weakened here in
some way or the other . . ."

Stricken with a horrific disease of the nervous system, Woody Guthrie, on a visit home from the hospital, once took his young son, Arlo, out into the backyard alone. He was hardly able to hold his guitar anymore, but he knew the random, jerky movements and mental imbalance caused by Huntington's chorea would only grow worse. There wasn't much time left and the "Father of Folk Music," the writer of more than a thousand songs for the people, wanted to be sure his son knew and would never forget the last verses of "This Land Is Your Land." It begins with the "ribbon of highway," the "endless skyway," and the "sparkling sands of her diamond deserts," but Woody Guthrie feared the world would forget his ending, and his original intent.

One bright sunny morning in the shadow of the steeple
By the relief office I saw my people—
As they stood there hungry, I stood there wondering if
This land was made for you and me.

Guthrie was a man who knew hardship. His early childhood was spent in Dust Bowl Oklahoma, where his father's business went bankrupt, his sister was killed in a freak explosion, and his mother was institutionalized with the same hereditary disease with which Guthrie himself was later afflicted. He had lived in poverty, had troubles with alcohol, three times failed at marriage, and suffered the death of his four-year-old daughter, Cathy. And yet there was always an enduring optimism to Woody Guthrie and his work. To the wage earner, to the laborer, and to the ordinary American he said, "I am out to sing the songs that make you take pride in yourself and your work."

Here forty-four-year-old Woody Guthrie writes from a state institution to nine-year-old Arlo, who was born with a weak eye. The letter was written in September. By December Guthrie had sent his last piece of correspondence. He survived in the hospital for another eleven years, suffering the rampages of the disease that eventually rendered him immobile, unable to speak, read, or use his hands.

Deary Arlo Davy

Of course now concerning you and that weakerly nearly blinded eye of yours all that I or all that anybody cood tell you is for you just to pray your very head off for god your heavenly father your maker and your creator to heal you to heal you the same as I do pray every minnit here for god to heal me of all my bad wrongs I've done in my lifetime for god to heal me of all my sicknesses I have here just as bad as you have there god hits us all god makes us all every living man and woman among us all just every bit as baddy sick as you are with your weakedy blinded eye you're not the only only one god has knocked down sick with your weaky eye all of us when you come right down to it all of us are just every bit as weakened here in some way or the other maybe lots lots blindeyer sicker weaklyer than you are no person living is ever perfect we are all as weakledy sickedy as you are so don't feel like you're the only sicky one here on god's earth Don't whine to god Don't even complain one little bitsy word back to god Be silent Be quiet Be thankyful Be faithyful Be grateful Be gaylyful Be Joydyful Be thankenful to god for giving you your very very life on gods earthy here anyhow I do lovey you all just the same if you are halfways blind halfways dead I do love you all the same no matter how good nor how bad you do or you don't do in all your sports in alla your schools in alla your activities in alla your colleges in alla your jobs in alla your works in alla your labors goody baddy up or down I love you all the very same Richy poory I love you all the very samey sicker Well I love you just the very same in and out I love you all the very very same I lovey lovey lovey you Arlo Davy Arlo Barlow just because you're my boy because you're my son because you're my own pore ½ways blinded humanly flesh all my humanky fleshedy folkes I see around me here are all of us so blinded we have only one wee smallyful hope to be cured one little halffa chancey to all or any of us all to be wholy and permantly healer a here If we all love and all pray all just believey in god like Jesus died to tell us to tell you

lovey me
daddy   Woody Guthrie

September 1956
Ward forty
Graystone Park N.J.

HUME CRONYN TO TANDY CRONYN

*"The barbarian lies miserably close
under the skin of all of us."*

"The son of a bitch would fix the damn lights if they'd let him," said Spencer Tracy when he was asked what it was like to work with Hume Cronyn. Small and wiry, Hume Cronyn was a professional obsessed with detail. In a career that spanned nearly sixty years, he wrote, directed, produced, and acted. His talent and drive earned him an Oscar nomination, a Tony, an Emmy, and the National Medal of Arts. He performed for television and the movies, but it was in the theater where he felt he most belonged, and never more so than when he was acting with his wife Jessica Tandy. As a professional team they were legendary, but offstage Cronyn "never felt [he] was much of a success as a parent." He thought his standards may have been too exacting and that he had been overly rigid with his stepdaughter, son, and daughter. His letters, however, especially those to youngest daughter, Tandy, are exceptional—straightforward, challenging, respectful, and affectionate.

In 1961, sixteen-year-old Tandy was enamored with the experience of study-ing in Germany. In an enthusiastic and essentially thoughtful letter, she told her parents of her fascination with the German people and went on to say that "we have to forgive them sometime" for the Nazi atrocities of World War II. "If a race of people has to be blamed, why not admit that the humans in general are guilty," she wrote. "Every nation has its black side." Here, with clarity and humanity, Hume Cronyn responds to his adolescent daughter.

May 26th, 1961

Tandy dear,

This letter is confidential, something between you and me alone, so I urge you not to leave it and certain of the enclosures lying around. It's merely a matter of discretion, certainly not of shame or apology. You are a guest in Germany and I think it's stupid to risk hurting feelings and, as you've wisely pointed out, it's hardly fair to blame your contemporaries for the injustices of another generation.

In all probability, few of your friends can read English and few of the faculty, too, perhaps, but it would not take a very astute individual whose eye might fall on the words, Auschwitz or Ravensbrueck, to conclude that your reading matter was rather particular in nature. I sound rather like I'm pussy-footing, don't I? The essence of what I'm getting at is this. I'm no less willing to introduce you to the influences of anti-Germanism than I am to those of anti-Semitism. Your personal and political feelings must be based on your own judgment and your own experience. You are liberal and tolerant by instinct and I hope by upbringing. These attitudes would seem to be reflected in the long letter you wrote to us from Italy. It was a copy of this letter that I sent to Eleanor Wolquitt. Do you remember her? A very pretty, very clever young woman, a great linguist who is a reader at 20th Century-Fox. Eleanor is a great and respected friend of mine. She is also Jewish. As she says herself, her feelings in regard to anti-Semitism, the Nazi persecution of the Jews and the Eichmann trial are visceral . . . if you don't know that word, it has to do with guts, your insides. It's an emotion so deep that it cannot honestly be considered objective, and yet Eleanor's "visceral" feelings are buttressed by great intelligence and sensitivity.

It seems to me that you are old enough and wise enough to be exposed to both sides of an appaling controversy, and that you may be safely exposed to the conflict and arguments no matter how ugly nor how frightening.

It's a great temptation to me to express my own viewpoint in regard to your Italian letter, the Eichmann trial and Eleanor's letters, but I'm going to resist this because I want you to come to your own conclusions and I would like to be able to discuss those with you when you're at home again. "Conclusions" is, perhaps, a bad word. While you may strive for absolute opinions with regard to moral issues, I doubt that you can come to absolute conclusions in regard to history and politics. And I doubt that it's possible to be absolute in an opinion of a nation. The barbarian lies miserably close under the skin of all of us. I *do* think that we are inclined to have national traits and characteristics, some of them pretty frightening, just as we have them in families. Our last best hope may be that, as the world grows smaller and we become one community of human beings, our good and our bad may counter-balance one another and that between all families, there may emerge a universal morality and a universal human characteristic superior to any of those in existence today.

Coming back to Eleanor's letters and the piece in the Saturday Review, *please bring these home with you.* I have no copies.

I was fascinated to hear that you'd written something on the Eichmann trial and I'm most curious about the point of view which you expressed. I would have thought it might have been a difficult subject to tackle in your present surroundings. However, I don't know them and you do.

I can't continue with this letter, my darling, as I promised to go and watch Mummie run through MACBETH. Dr. Gott promises you a very warm welcome at l'Arcadie. Chris seems to have his job on a boat for the latter part of the summer and both Mummie and I await your homecoming with great eagerness. I shall send Brenda a check for your traveling expenses. I'd already written to Mr. Hansen—before I knew you were going to spend a holiday with them—and I'm sure you will acknowledge their hospitality.

Much love, dear one.

P.S. If you feel you must discuss any of the enclosed material with someone at Stein, then of course you are free to do so, but be careful about it, darling, and I would avoid discussing it with your young German friends unless they are both wise and tolerant beyond their years. They may feel that you are somehow accusing them in that very fashion that you yourself seem to consider unfair.

JOHN STEINBECK TO JOHN STEINBECK IV

"I had deep down convictions that I was a coward."

*"He always wanted to be where the action was," said John Steinbeck's wife
Elaine. So eager was he to witness World War II firsthand, that the Pulitzer
Prize–winning author of* The Grapes of Wrath *became a war correspondent in
England, Italy, and Northern Africa for the* New York Herald-Tribune. *The
following letter was written decades later, just months after Steinbeck's twenty-year-
old son had gone overseas to fight the war in Vietnam with the United States
Army. Five months later, in December of the same year, the sixty-four-year-old
John Steinbeck himself flew to Southeast Asia to cover the war for* Newsday.

Sag Harbor
July 16, 1966

Dear John:

I do know what you mean. I remember the same feeling when there
were areas of trouble. "What the hell am I doing here? Nobody made me
come." On the other hand, when it was over, I was usually glad I had gone.
And one other thing. Once it started the blind panic went away and another dimension took its place. Thinking about it afterward I became convinced that there is some kind of built in anaesthesia that balances and sets
the terror back. Another thing that helps is the fact that you aren't alone.
And everybody feels just as lousy when it is about to be. I don't know
whether or not you took the Sneaky with you—that little leather flask. Fill
it with whiskey—brandy is better. It can be a great comfort to you. There's
no law against false courage. It's better than none at all.

Now let me discuss what you call your compulsion to be miserable.
You think you had a choice—that you could just as well be in S.F. with all
the amenities, comfort, ease and a certain immunity from gunfire. Well,
the fact of the matter with you as well as with me is that there wasn't really
any choice. You did and will do what you are. If you had forced yourself
to make the opposite choice you would have been in violation of yourself,
and I truly believe you would have been much more miserable than you
are. Of course I am worried about you, just terribly worried, but I am
proud too that you have not violated what you are.

Also check with yourself on this. I know it was true of me. I had deep down convictions that I was a coward. I think everyone has. If I had broken or gone to pieces, I wouldn't have been surprised. But when it came and I didn't go haywire, when I was scared but no more scared than those around me, the sense of relief was like a flood of compensation. Because I think a good part of this particular fear is a fear of how you will behave. And no one knows for sure, until he has gone through it.

I was horrified when you asked me to get you orders to go out, but I couldn't have failed you there. Do you know, that is the only request I have ever made of the President. The only one. And I was not happy about making it. But if I had had to request that you *not* be sent, I think I would have been far more unhappy.

Please keep in touch. I love you.

Fa

ANNE SEXTON TO LINDA SEXTON

"Live to the HILT!"

That in the end Anne Sexton would take her own life was of little surprise to those close to her. Preoccupied with death, fascinated by suicide, for years she went about with a pocketbook equipped with pills, prepared at any time to end it all. A poet, a playwright, a wife and the mother of two daughters, Sexton was tall, beautiful, privileged, glamorous, promiscuous, quick-minded, and shaken to the core. Her daughter Linda said, "I ALWAYS lived on that brink of fear that she was going to fall apart and really kill herself."

In her late twenties Anne Sexton was incapacitated and sent into a psychological tailspin by the trials of managing a household and caring for her two small daughters. Hospitalized and suicidal, she was set to the task of writing poetry by her psychiatrist. In a sense, she was broken by motherhood and saved by poetry. Her writing and her growing daughters held her from the world of the insane. In a poem for her younger daughter, Joy, Sexton concludes, "I made you to find me."

In 1969 Anne Sexton was at her professional peak. For the first time a play she had written was to be staged Off-Broadway. She was a sought-after and well-paid performer, reading her poetry for audiences around the country. Her latest book, Live or Die, *was about to win the Pulitzer Prize. It seemed, too, that her suicidal fantasies were being held at bay. Here, five years before her final day, Anne Sexton writes to her fifteen-year-old daughter, Linda.*

[April 1969]
Wed—2:45 pm

Dear Linda,

I am in the middle of a flight to St. Louis to give a reading. I was reading a *New Yorker* story that made me think of my mother and all alone in the seat I whispered to her "I know, Mother, I know." (Found a pen!) And I thought of you—someday flying somewhere all alone and me dead perhaps and you wishing to speak to me.

And I want to speak back. (Linda, maybe it won't be flying, maybe it will be at your *own* kitchen table drinking tea some afternoon when you are 40. *Anytime.*)—I want to say back.

1st I love you.

2. You *never* let me down.

3. I know. I was there once. I *too*, was 40 with a dead mother who I needed still. . . .

This is my message to the 40 year old Linda. No matter what happens you were always my bobolink, my special Linda Gray. Life is not easy. It is awfully lonely. *I* know that. Now you too know it—wherever you are, Linda, talking to me. But I've had a good life—I wrote unhappy—but I lived to the hilt. You too, Linda—Live to the HILT! To the top. I love you 40 year old, Linda, and I love what you do, what you find, what you are!—Be your own woman. Belong to those you love. Talk to my poems, and talk to your heart—I'm in both: if you need me. I lied, Linda. I did love my mother and she loved me. She never held me but I miss her, so that I have to deny I ever loved her—or she me! Silly Anne! So there!

XOXOXO
Mom

Yolande Du Bois

Theodore Roosevelt

John O'Hara and daughter Wylie

Strength of
Character

JONATHAN EDWARDS TO MARY EDWARDS

"But yet my greatest concern is for your soul's good."

Jonathan Edwards, theologian, revivalist, and philosopher, was colonial America's most prominent religious thinker. He led eighteenth-century New Englanders into the "Great Awakening" by preaching a classic Puritanism that incorporated the new ideas of the Age of Reason.

During the summer of 1749, fifteen-year-old Mary Edwards was more than 150 miles from her Massachusetts home, visiting family friends in Portsmouth, New Hampshire, while her father was embroiled in a furious battle with his congregation over the requirements for church membership. Edwards argued—contrary to the current acceptance of laxed standards—that membership should be granted only to those who provided evidence of an experience of "Saving Grace." The following year his ardent position cost him his church.

Northampton, July 26, 1749

Dear Child,

You may well think that it is natural for a parent to be concerned for a child at so great a distance, so far out of view, and so far out of the reach of communication; where, if you should be taken with any dangerous sickness that should issue in death, you might probably be in your grave before we could hear of your danger.

But yet my greatest concern is for your soul's good. Though you are at so great a distance from us, yet God is everywhere. You are much out of the reach of our care, but you are every moment in his hands. We have not the comfort of seeing you, but he sees you. His eye is always upon you. And if you may but be sensibly nigh to him, and have his gracious presence, 'tis no matter though you are far distant from us. I had rather you should remain hundreds of miles distant from us and have God nigh to you by his Spirit, than to have you always with us, and live at a distance from God. And if the next news we should hear of you should be of your death (though that would be very melancholy), yet if withal we should hear of that which should give great grounds to hope that you had died in the Lord, how much more comfortable would this be (though we should have no opportunity to see you, or take our leave of you in your sickness), than if we should be with you all in your sickness, and have much opportunity to tend to you, and converse and pray with you, and take an affectionate leave of you, and after all have reason to apprehend that you died without God's grace and favor! 'Tis comfortable to have the presence of earthly friends, especially in sickness and on a deathbed; but the great thing is to have God our friend, and to be united to Christ, who can never die anymore, and whom even death can't separate us from.

My desire and daily prayer is that you may, if it may consist with the holy will of God, meet with God where you be, and have much of his divine influences on your heart wherever you may be, and that in God's due time you may be returned to us again in all respects under the smiles of heaven, and especially in prosperous circumstances in your soul; and that you may find all us alive. But that is uncertain; for you know what a dying time it has been with us in this town, about this time of year, in years past. There is not much sickness prevailing among us as yet, but we fear whether mortal sickness is not beginning among us. Yesterday Eliphaz Clap's remaining only son died of the fever and bloody flux, and is to be buried today. May God fit us all for his will.

I hope you will maintain a strict and constant watch over yourself and against all temptations: that you don't forget and forsake God; and particularly that you don't grow slack in secret religion. Retire often from this vain world, and all its bubbles, empty shadows, and vain amusements, and converse with God alone; and seek that divine grace and comfort, the least drop of which is more worth than all the riches, gaiety, pleasures and entertainments of the whole world.

If Madam Stoddard of Boston, or any of that family, should send to you to invite you to come and remain there on your return from Portsmouth, till there is opportunity for you to come home, I would have you accept the invitation. I think it probable that they will invite you. But if otherwise, I would have you go to Mr. Bromfield's. He and Madam both told me you should be welcome. After you are come to Boston, I would have you send us word of it. Try the first opportunity, that we may send for you without delay.

We are all through divine goodness in a tolerable state of health. The ferment in town runs very high concerning my opinion about the sacrament: but I am no better able to foretell the issue than when I last saw you. But the whole family has indeed much to put us in mind and make us sensible of our dependence on God's care and kindness, and of the vanity of all human dependences. And we are very loudly called to seek his face, trust in him, and walk closely with him. Commending you to the care and special favor of an heavenly Father, I am

Your very affectionate father,
Jonathan Edwards.

Your mother and all the family give their love to you.

ABIGAIL ADAMS TO JOHN QUINCY ADAMS

"It is not in the still calm of life, or the repose of a pacific station, that great characters are formed."

With his education in mind, Abigail Adams strongly encouraged her son, John Quincy Adams, to cross the wintery Atlantic for the second time with his father. The year was 1779, America was furiously engaged in the War of Independence, and John Adams once again responded to the call of his countrymen to serve as

Minister to France. With him aboard the French warship Sensible, *John Adams took his boys, twelve-year-old John Quincy and nine-year-old Charles. Had the* Sensible *been captured by a British ship on the crossing, all 350 people on board would have been taken as prisoners of war.*

They were spared a British assault, but the trip was harrowing still. Just two days off the coast of Massachusetts, the Sensible *sprang a leak that continually grew worse and for the rest of the voyage the ship required constant pumping. Then, encountering a fierce storm, they were sent barely afloat into the nearest port at El Ferrol, Spain. One thousand miles from Paris, John Adams decided to make the rest of the journey with his boys by land, crossing the Pyrenees on mules in the middle of winter.*

Nearly two months after John Quincy, Charles, and John Adams departed from America, Abigail Adams, at home in charge of the family farm in the midst of war, wrote the following letter to her eldest son. What the travelers had encountered on the high seas, whether they had arrived safely in Europe or that they were now crossing the Pyrenees, she had no way of knowing.

It would be well over four years before Abigail Adams saw her son John Quincy again.

Janry. 19 1780

My dear Son

I hope you have had no occasion either from Enemies or the Dangers of the Sea to repent your second voyage to France. If I had thought your reluctance arose from proper deliberation, or that you was capable of judgeing what was most for your own benifit, I should not have urged you to have accompanied your Father and Brother when you appeared so averse to the voyage.

You however readily submitted to my advice, and I hope will never have occasion yourself, nor give me reason to Lament it. Your knowledge of the Language must give you greater advantages now, than you could possibly have reaped whilst Ignorant of it, and as you increase in years you will find your understanding opening and daily improveing.

Some Author that I have met with compares a judicious traveler, to a river that increases its stream the farther it flows from its source, or to certain springs which running through rich veins of minerals improve their qualities as they pass along. It will be expected of you my son that as you are favourd with superiour advantages under the instructive Eye of a tender parent, that your improvements should bear some proportion to your advantages. Nothing is wanting with you, but attention, diligence and steady application. Nature has not been deficient.

These are times in which a Genious would wish to live. It is not in the still calm of life, or the repose of a pacific station, that great characters are formed. Would Cicero have shone so distinguished an orater, if he had not been roused, kindled and enflamed by the Tyranny of Catiline, Millo, Verres and Mark Anthony. The Habits of a vigorous mind are formed in contending with difficulties. All History will convince you of this, and that wisdom and penetration are the fruits of experience, not the Lessons of retirement and leisure.

Great necessities call out great virtues. When a mind is raised, and animated by scenes that engage the Heart, then those qualities which would otherways lay dormant, wake into Life, and form the Character of the Hero and the Statesman.

War, Tyrrany and Desolation are the Scourges of the Almighty, and ought no doubt be deprecated. Yet it is your Lot my Son to be an Eye witness of these Calimities in your own Native land, and at the same time to owe your existance among a people who have made a glorious defence of their invaded Liberties, and who, aided by a generous and powerfull Ally, with the blessing of heaven will transmit this inheritance to ages yet unborn.

Nor ought it to be one of the least of your excitements toward exerting every power and faculty of your mind, that you have a parent who has taken so large and active a share in this contest, and discharged the trust reposed in him with so much satisfaction as to be honourd with the important Embassy, which at present calls him abroad.

I cannot fulfill the whole of my duty toward you, if I close this Letter, without reminding you of a failing which calls for a strict attention and watchful care to correct. You must do it for yourself. You must curb that impetuosity of temper, for which I have frequently chid you, but which properly directed may be productive of great good. I know you capable of these exertions, with pleasure I observed my advice was not lost upon you. If you indulge yourself in the practise of any foible or vice in youth, it will gain strength with your years and become your conquerer.

The strict and inviolable regard you have ever paid to truth, gives me pleasing hopes that you will not swerve from her dictates, but add justice, fortitude, and every Manly Virtue which can adorn a good citizen, do Honor to your Country, and render your parents supreemly happy, particuliarly your ever affectionate Mother,

AA

THOMAS JEFFERSON TO
MARTHA "PATSY" JEFFERSON

*". . . do what is right and you will
find it the easiest way . . ."*

*In 1787 the Minister to France, Thomas Jefferson, toured southern France and
northern Italy for three months. He was a forty-four-year-old widower, and of his
six children, only two were still living. Here he writes to fifteen-year-old "Patsy"
about the impending arrival from Virginia of her only remaining sibling, nine-year-
old Maria, or "Polly." It had been more than two years since the girls had seen
each other.*

Toulon April 7. 1787.

My Dear Patsy

I received yesterday at Marseilles your letter of March 25. and I received it with pleasure because it announced to me that you were well.
Experience learns us to be always anxious about the health of those whom
we love. I have not been able to write to you so often as I expected, because I am generally on the road; and when I stop any where, I am occupied in seeing what is to be seen. It will be some time now, perhaps three
weeks before I shall be able to write to you again. But this need not slacken
your writing to me, because you have leisure, and your letters come regularly to me. I have received letters which inform me that our dear Polly
will certainly come to us this summer. By the time I return it will be time
to expect her. When she arrives, she will become a precious charge on
your hands. The difference of your age, and your common loss of a
mother, will put that office on you. Teach her above all things to be good:
because without that we can neither be valued by others, nor set any value
on ourselves. Teach her to be always true. No vice is so mean as the want
of truth, and at the same time so useless. Teach her never to be angry.
Anger only serves to torment ourselves, to divert others, and alienate their
esteem. And teach her industry and application to useful pursuits. I will
venture to assure you that if you inculcate this in her mind you will make
her a happy being in herself, a most inestimable friend to you, and precious to all the world. In teaching her these dispositions of mind, you will
be more fixed in them yourself, and render yourself dear to all your ac-

quaintance. Practice them then, my dear, without ceasing. If ever you find yourself in difficulty and doubt how to extricate yourself, do what is right, and you will find it the easiest way of getting out of the difficulty. Do it for the additional incitement of increasing the happiness of him who loves you infinitely, and who is my dear Patsy your's affectionately,

TH: JEFFERSON

DANIEL WEBSTER TO EDWARD WEBSTER

"All that can be done for you by others will amount to nothing unless you do much for yourself."

Daniel Webster, statesman and distinguished lawyer, was known as the "Defender of the Constitution." His total devotion to the Union and fear that slavery might one day tear the country apart led him, more than thirty years before the Civil War, to deliver the now famous line "Liberty and Union, one and inseparable, now and forever."

Here he writes to his thirteen-year-old son, Edward, who was just beginning at Phillips Exeter Academy. Webster had planned to take his son to Exeter himself, but a lengthy congressional session on banking kept the senator in Washington longer than expected. Edward's twenty-year-old brother, Fletcher, escorted him instead.

Washington, June 23, 1834.

My Dear Son:

Fletcher wrote me from Exeter the next day after your arrival, and informed me that you had been so fortunate as to be received at Colonel Chadwick's, and was commencing your studies. I am glad you are so well situated, and trust you will make progress in your studies.

You are now at a most important period of your life, my dear son, soon growing up to be a young man and a boy no longer, and I feel a great anxiety for your success and happiness.

I beseech you to be attentive to all your duties, and to fulfill every obligation with cheerfulness and punctuality. Above all, remember your moral and religious concerns. Be constant at church, and prayers, and every opportunity for worship. There can be no solid character and no true happiness which are not founded on a sense of religious duty. Avoid all evil company and every temptation, and consider that you have now left your father's house and gone forth to improve your own character,—to prepare your own mind for the part you are to lead in life. All that can be done for you by others will amount to nothing unless you do much for yourself. Cherish all the good counsel which your dear mother used to give you, and let those of us who are yet alive have the pleasure of seeing you come forward as one who gives promise of virtue, usefulness, and distinction. I fervently commend you to the blessing of our Heavenly Father.

.   .   .   .   .

I wish you to make my best respects to Dr. Abbot, and remember me to Colonel and Mrs Chadwick and their family. If I do not hear from you sooner, I shall expect to find a letter from you when I reach Boston.

> Your affectionate father,
> Daniel Webster

P.S. Since writing this I have received your letter, and am very glad to hear from you.

Give my love to your friend Upham. I remember the great tree, and know exactly where your room is. Charles sends love.

WILLIAM LLOYD GARRISON TO WILLIAM LLOYD GARRISON, JR.

"May you never go with the multitude to do evil, but be willing to stand alone, if need be . . ."

"I do not wish to think, or speak, or write with moderation . . . I am in earnest—I will not equivocate—I will not excuse—I will not retreat a single inch—and I WILL BE HEARD," wrote William Lloyd Garrison in the 1831 inaugural issue of his antislavery periodical The Liberator. *Controversial, self-righteous, impractical, he was a reformer in the extreme with an ability to antagonize even his supporters. Yet his position as the courageous and steadfast early leader of the American antislavery movement is secure.*

He was the father of seven children, two of whom died in infancy. Here, at the age of fifty-three and thirty years into his battle for emancipation, Garrison writes to his son, who is about to turn twenty-two years old.

Boston, Dec. 31, 1858.

Dear William:

Though it is the last day of the year, there is no reason why I, and your mother, and Fanny and Franky, should not wish you a happy new year. May you be happily preserved from all "the ills that flesh is heir to," and continue daily to "grow in knowledge and in grace." May you ever keep in the right path, shun the very appearance of evil, be superior to every evil temptation, and reverently seek to know and do the will of God. May your moral vision ever be clear to discern the right from the wrong, your conscience ever clean and vital, your heart ever tender and affectionate, your spirit ever pure and elevated. May you be prudent and economical without being parsimonious, and generous and philanthropic without being credulous and inconsiderate. May your interest in all the reforms of the day,—especially in the cause of the imbruted slave,—grow more and more vital, impelling you to the performance of high moral achievements in behalf of suffering humanity, and making your life a blessing to the world. May you be delivered from "that fear of man which bringeth a snare," in sustaining what is just, following what is good, and adhering to what is right. May you never go with the multitude to do evil, but be willing to stand alone, if need be, with God and the truth, even if it bring you to the cross or the stake. May you be known for your integrity of character, and aim at perfection in all noble qualities. My heart-felt benediction, mingled with your mother's, is upon you; and may the benediction of "our Father in heaven" be added thereto!

Thus far, my happiness in my children has been without alloy. George has always been circumspect and exemplary in his conduct, to a remarkable degree; and I feel that he may be safely trusted, even at the far West, where great temptations beset young men, though I would much prefer to have him with us at home. Wendell has always been a model boy, mature beyond his years, unexceptionable in deportment, amiable and affectionate in spirit, and full of promise for the future. Fanny is a dear child, specially dear because she is the only daughter, of a most generous and loving nature, full of sensibility, and promising to make a noble woman. Franky is the Benjamin of the flock, around whom my heartstrings very closely twine, gentle, conscientious, most affectionate, laudably ambitious, studious and thoughtful, sensitive to blame, with a large brain and a large heart for a little boy. As for yourself, I am delighted with your ingenuousness, kindness of heart, self-forgetfulness, loving disposition, and generous regard for every member of the family. In a few days you will complete your twenty-first year, and take upon yourself the responsibilities of manhood. Let us have a little celebration of the event, at home, that evening, if you can leave seasonably, or on the subsequent evening, (Saturday,) remaining with us till Monday. Do not fail to come.

I send the accompanying volume to Mr. Mudge, with a letter accompanying it, to which no written reply is needed.

Your loving father,

Wm. Lloyd Garrison.

SIDNEY LANIER TO CHARLES D. LANIER

". . . I admire the sight of a man fighting his own small failings, as a good knight who never ceases to watch, and war against, the least blemish or evil . . ."

Confederate soldier, prisoner of war, accomplished musician and poet, Sidney Lanier spent his entire creative life fighting poverty and illness. That music and poetry were his calling he was completely sure. "Psalm of the West," "Evening Song," and "Sunrise" are today among his most well-known poems.

By July 1881 Lanier was thirty-nine years old. He was the father of four young boys and he was losing his long battle with tuberculosis. He struggled through his final summer moving about the North Carolina mountains from one "tent-camp" to another in hopes of benefiting from the pure, high-altitude air. Determined to continue with his work, Lanier dictated poetry from his sickbed when he had breath enough to speak. The following letter, to his eldest son, twelve-year-old Charley, was one of only two letters he managed to write in his own hand during that last summer.

Asheville, N.C.
July 20, 1881.

My dear Son Charley:

I have been for several weeks lying at the very gates of death—so close that I could almost peep in upon the marvels of that mysterious country—and it has been long since I could write a letter with my own hand; but your mother has read me Mrs. Maxwell's report of your ever-increasing manfulness and of your gentle disposition toward your brothers, and this has brought me such deep gratification that I cannot help devoting a part of my very little strength this morning to the pleasant work of sending you this brief line of thanks and love which will enable you to share my pleasure with me. It would require a great many more pages than I can now write for me to tell you how earnestly I admire the sight of a man fighting his own small failings, as a good knight who never ceases to watch, and war against, the least blemish or evil: you may therefore fancy how my heart warms with loving pride in you and for you as I learn from Miss Mary the patience and generosity and large conduct which you daily exhibit toward your brothers, the gentlemanly thoughtfulness which you show for the comfort of all about you, and the general advance and growth which your whole nature appears to be achieving.

This makes me much more easy in mind when I think of the possibility that death may at any time compel me to leave my dear wife and my three beautiful boys (you should see Robin at this moment! with his great shining blue eyes and his milk-and-roses complexion, and magnificent limbs, he is like a young inhabitant of a morning-star just caught among the rhododendrons of these mountains) in your charge as head of the family; for I well know that as long as you behave like a man you will never lack men for your friends.

But,—over and above all this,—I take the gravest pleasure in seeing you unfold what I know to be your natural qualities; I have always known that your character is strong and fine, but I have feared that your beautifully-sympathetic disposition would sometimes be apt to persuade you that you liked people or things which were really unworthy of you, and that you might have trouble with entanglements or stains thus arising, even after you had yourself perceived the unworthiness: but I rejoice to find in you a reasonableness and good judgment which I think will always bring you out safely at the end.

This is but a dry and didactic letter: nor will you know how much pleasure, how much hope, and how much affection go with it, until you yourself, my dear, dear boy, shall have a son who seems as fine as my Charley and whom you love as loves

your own
father.

THEODORE ROOSEVELT TO
KERMIT ROOSEVELT

"I would rather have a boy of mine stand high in his studies than high in athletics, but I could a great deal rather have him show true manliness of character than show either intellectual or physical prowess . . ."

A dedicated sportsman, the young and vigorous President Theodore Roosevelt boxed in the White House, played football on the lawn, led groups of children on Sunday "scrambles" through Rock Creek Park, and rode horseback at every opportunity. In the fall of 1903, his second and somewhat frail son, fourteen-year-old Kermit, had just made the Groton football team and the president was leading a very difficult fight to gain full rights for America to build a canal on the Colombian isthmus at Panama.

The White House
Washington, DC
October 2, 1903.

Dear Kermit:

I was very glad to get your letter. Am glad you are playing foot ball. I should be very sorry to see either you or Ted devoting most of your attention to athletics, and I haven't got any special ambition to see you shine overmuch in athletics in college, at least (if you go there), because I think it tends to take up too much time; but I do like to feel that you are manly and able to hold your own in rough, hardy sports. I would rather have a boy of mine stand high in his studies than high in athletics, but I could a great deal rather have him show true manliness of character than show either intellectual or physical prowess; and I believe you and Ted both bid fair to develop just such character.

There! You will think this a dreadfully preaching letter! I suppose I have a natural tendency to preach just at present because I am overwhelmed with my work. I enjoy being President, and I like to do the work and have my hand on the lever. But it is very worrying and puzzling, and I have to make up my mind to accept every kind of attack and misrepresentation. It is a great comfort to me to read the life and letters of Abraham Lincoln. I am more and more impressed every day, not only with the man's wonderful power and sagacity, but with his literally endless patience, and at the same time unflinching resolution.

Mother and I had a nice ride yesterday, Yagenka behaved well, but upon my word Renown is more nervous and given to shying than ever. "Age cannot still nor custom wither" the infinite variety of that particular fool's folly. He is worse about automobiles than he ever was, and as they swarm in and around Washington a ride upon him is a live experience.

Allan has gone to be trained. Ronald has won golden opinions of all the people around here, as he is very well trained. He sits up beside the driver in the wagon, and follows every one obediently round. He seems to be an excellent city dog.

Quentin is the proud possessor of two white rabbits with pink eyes, in which he and Archie revel. Ethel and Archie played tennis yesterday.

Your loving father,
Theodore Roosevelt

W. E. B. Du Bois to Yolande Du Bois

"The main thing is the YOU beneath the clothes and skin—the ability to do, the will to conquer, the determination to understand and know this great, wonderful, curious world."

At thirty-five years old, W. E. B. Du Bois soared to prominence with the 1903 publication of The Souls of Black Folk, *a collection of essays exposing the extent of racial prejudice in America. His challenge of the undisputed African-American leader of the time, Booker T. Washington, caused particular sensation. Du Bois criticized Washington especially for shifting "the burden of the Negro problem to the Negro's shoulders . . . when in fact the burden belongs to the nation."*

As a founder of the NAACP, historian, professor, and the first African Amer-

ican to earn a Ph.D. from Harvard, Du Bois knew the opportunity afforded by vigorous study. Here he writes to his only daughter, Yolande, a nearly fourteen-year-old student at the Besales School in England.

New York, October 29, 1914

Dear Little Daughter:

I have waited for you to get well settled before writing. By this time I hope some of the strangeness has worn off and that my little girl is working hard and regularly.

Of course, everything is new and unusual. You miss the newness and smartness of America. Gradually, however, you are going to sense the beauty of the old world: its calm and eternity and you will grow to love it.

Above all remember, dear, that you have a great opportunity. You are in one of the world's best schools, in one of the world's greatest modern empires. Millions of boys and girls all over this world would give almost anything they possess to be where you are. You are there by no desert or merit of yours, but only by lucky chance.

Deserve it, then. Study, do your work. Be honest, frank and fearless and get some grasp of the real values of life. You will meet, of course, curious little annoyances. People will wonder at your dear brown and the sweet crinkley hair. But that simply is of no importance and will be soon forgotten. Remember that most folk laugh at anything unusual, whether it is beautiful, fine or not. You, however, must not laugh at yourself. You must know that brown is as pretty as white or prettier and crinkley hair as straight even though it is harder to comb. The main thing is the YOU beneath the clothes and skin—the ability to do, the will to conquer, the determination to understand and know this great, wonderful, curious world. Don't shrink from new experiences and custom. Take the cold bath bravely. Enter into the spirit of your big bed-room. Enjoy what is and not pine for what is not. Read some good, heavy, serious books just for discipline: Take yourself in hand and master yourself. Make yourself do unpleasant things, so as to gain the upper hand of your soul.

Above all remember: your father loves you and believes in you and expects you to be a wonderful woman.

I shall write each week and expect a weekly letter from you.

Lovingly yours,
Papa

John O'Hara to Wylie O'Hara

"Beginning with the day you read this
you cease to be a child."

John O'Hara was not a darling of the critics, nor was he the recipient of major literary honors—and it bothered him. Yet, beginning with his first novel in 1934, Appointment in Samarra, *through thirty-five subsequent books, including* Pal Joey *and* From the Terrace, *John O'Hara consistently enjoyed the attention and financial rewards of a large readership. He had a plain and old-fashioned style, combining masterful dialogue and precise, accurate details, and always his mission was to show clearly "the way it was." He wrote mostly in the hours after midnight, usually short stories in the summers and novels in the winters, and he considered himself a "pro"—one who was at his work day after day, making it "look easy," when of course it was not.*

In 1959, O'Hara was in the decade that would be his most prolific. His work had made him a wealthy man and he spent summers on Long Island, took pride in his Rolls-Royce, traveled often to England, joined clubs, and passed winters at his French manor house in Princeton, New Jersey. Yet, despite all of his commercial success and popularity, O'Hara's commitment to his writing never dwindled. His only daughter, Wylie, was fourteen years old in September 1959 and was just beginning her first year at her deceased mother's alma mater, the St. Timothy's School in Maryland.

22 Sept. 59

My dear:

Welcome to St. Tim's! I am writing this on Tuesday afternoon. You are upstairs, I am in my study, unable to leave because I am expecting two telephone calls. Hot out, isn't it?

By the time you read this you will have spent your first night in your new room, or so I imagine, and I am also imagining what your first day will be like. You will be doing and seeing so many new things and meeting so many new faces that you will wonder how so much could be crowded into one day, and you won't have a chance to think about it until you go to bed, the second night. That's the way it will be for a week—you must have had much the same experience at Interlaken and Ralston Creek. Then, almost without realizing it, you will find yourself a member of a new community.

And that's something I would like to talk about. Just as I am going on a voyage, so are you embarking on a journey that is much more important than my quick trip. Mine will be over in a month, and the real purpose of my trip is to get away from my typewriter and my habits of work in order to get a new perspective and come back, I hope, the better for my holiday. But your journey is more important because you are entering into a new phase of your life. Beginning with the day you read this you cease to be a child. Your memories, naturally, will all be memories of childhood, the life you have led so far. But each day will be part of the future that you have been looking forward to all your childhood days. You will be assuming new responsibilities but you will also find that responsibility does not necessarily mean something irksome. Responsibility, and responsibilities, can be a pleasure. The greatest pleasure I have in life is the responsibility of being your father. It is a greater pleasure than my work, which is saying a lot because I love my work. But a man is not born with a love of his work, and he *is* born with the nucleus of a love for his children, and his responsibility toward them, or toward her, in my case, is only the practical side of that love.

In the Catholic Church you are taught to start each day by dedicating everything you do that day toward the greater honor and glory of God. Most Catholics forget that, and none of them remembers it every day, throughout the day. We are all human. But it is possible to copy something from the Catholics that is helpful: as I wrote you two years ago, "to thine own self be true," and if you do that every day you'll be all right. When I stopped drinking I did not say to myself "Quit for a year." I did it a day at a time; get through one day, then repeat it the next. Well, that's more than six years ago. And quite frankly, I still do it day by day. I take those damned exercises every day, not with the thought that I will be taking them for the rest of my life, but with the thought that I will do them today—and let tomorrow's temptation to skip them take care of itself tomorrow.

I hope you will write me while I am abroad. The address is at the bottom of this page so you can tear it off. After the 15th of October write me at home, as letters sent abroad will not reach me after that date.

I wish you happiness in this new phase of your life. You have come through childhood as a fine person, with wonderful prospects for a wonderful future. You have made Sister love you as though you were her own. And I was born loving you.

Dad

Care of Cresset Press,
    11, Fitzroy Square—London, W.1, England

*"Life is tough, Wylie. But you don't
have to be tough to enjoy it."*

*One week later, on September 29, 1959, O'Hara again wrote to Wylie. The
following morning he departed by ship to join his third wife, Katharine "Sister"
Barnes Bryan, in London.*

Tuesday p.m.

My dear:

The Outerbridges very thoughtfully, very kindly had me to dinner
tonight, otherwise I'd have been alone at home. They also invited Mr. and
Mrs. Bramwell. We watched the Braves lose to the Dodgers until five minutes of nine, when I excused myself to telephone you. I wanted to speak
to you again after you and Patience had your chat, but I guess she misun-
derstood me and the connection was broken. So I am writing you to finish up what I wanted to say—and probably will say it a little better here
than on the phone.

You and I are really very close, I think. I think we understand each
other because we are both sensitive people. I'm sure, for instance, that you
understand what I mean when I say that I have misgivings about my trip,
somewhat the way you felt when you were getting ready to go to the
ranch last June. We are both shy people, and yet are fond of other people.
For instance I had a good time with Mr. and Mrs. Outerbridge and Mr.
and Mrs. Bramwell tonight because I know them and am relaxed with
them. When I get on the ship tomorrow I will not know a soul, and even
though there is quite a good chance that I will run into people I know, I
am prepared to spend the entire time alone. The Cunard Line has put a
typewriter in my room, and I have a book I want to read (The Education
of Henry Adams) and a double-crostic to do, so I will be able to occupy
myself until I meet Sister in London.

It would have been a lot easier for me just to stay home and not to take
this trip. But because it would have been easier is precisely the reason I am
going. I love my work, I am happy when I have work to do, but if I sit
here in my study in Princeton I am really pampering myself, even though
I may justify it by saying I am working. It is a dangerous thing for a writer
to do, to bury himself in his work and never stir away from it. I know that
is true, because I will confess to you that I am *afraid* to be alone in England,
etc. I would not make the trip if I were not going to meet Sister. Now that

is proof of the danger of sitting here and burying myself in my work. My life has become you and Sister, and even my friends don't count as much as they should. What remains is my work, with which, as I say, I pamper myself and make excuses for not participating in life.

What I am leading up to is that life is or should be full of doing things you would prefer not to do. The best recent example of that was the ranch experience, which you didn't want to do, but ended up being glad you did it. Believe me, it is easier to learn self-discipline when you are young than when you are older. By self-discipline I mean obeying your parents and your teachers. Yes, that may seem contradictory. You may think of it only as discipline and not self-discipline, but it is *self*-discipline if you follow advice in the proper spirit. It is discipline when you obey because you have no other choice.

Life is tough, Wylie. But you don't have to be tough to enjoy it. However, you do need some toughening, and the best toughening is that which you give yourself. In fact it may be the only kind that has lasting value. It becomes part of you and not something that originated with someone else.

You have only to look at the faces of men and women who have not learned to discipline themselves. Then look at those who have. Whom do you trust? Whom would you count on? Your Grandmother O'Hara is a case in point. She was strictly brought up in a family who were in comfortable circumstances, able to send her away to boarding school. Soon after that she married my father and she began to have children, eight of them, with all the problems of a large family. Then when my father died and there was practically no money and none of us old enough to make a decent living, she had to struggle somehow to keep a family going, giving up things she had been accustomed to, unable to provide what she wanted to provide. But I never heard her complain, and neither did anyone else. Sometimes I would come home and find her doing household arithmetic, trying to figure out how to pay taxes, grocery bills, etc., but there would be no complaints, although God knows she must have stayed awake many nights wondering and worrying. Now she is over 80, as enthusiastic and loving about you as though you were her first-born, and if you study her face you will see that it is remarkably unlined. There are women, and men, many years younger, who do not have her serenity, and the reason is that they do not have her character. And the character was something she acquired through self-discipline.

Already you have shown me that you have some of the same qualities. Honesty. Kindness. Sweetness. Courage. Understanding. You have all of these to a degree that is extraordinary in a girl your age. There are unlucky girls who grow into womanhood without any of them. You have something else: humility. And it is your humility that keeps you from realizing that you have the other qualities. Humility is a quality that the possessor of it does not enjoy, but that makes her or him easier to live with. Sometimes it is seen as shyness and sometimes as sensitivity. Whatever it appears to be, it is a gracious quality, a warm quality that is particularly attractive when it is accompanied by the five other qualities I mentioned. I'm very glad you have it now, because you are also going to become a handsome woman, and it is as a handsome woman that you will live the greater part of your life, not merely as a pretty teen-ager.

Please do me a favor. Save this letter and read it when you have time to give it some thought. There are things in it that will guide you and that you may overlook in a quick, first reading.

As I told you, we'll be on our way home before you will get my later communications. We sail from England a month from today and will be home on the 3d of November, and I will make plans to go see you. Do write me, all that you want to tell me. Once again the address: Care of Cresset Press; 11 Fitzroy Square; London, W.1; England. But letters mailed after about the middle of October will probably not reach me.

All my love
Dad

William James and daughter Margaret

Mark Twain and family (Clara far left, wife, Olivia, second from left,
Jean center, and Susie far right)

The Pleasures
of Life

JOHN ADAMS TO
JOHN QUINCY ADAMS

"You will never be alone with a Poet in your Poket."

John Adams was one of the most learned Americans of his time and his eldest son, John Quincy, was his pride and joy. The following letter was written while the father was serving as Minister to the Netherlands and the son was a student at Leyden. The fourteen-year-old John Quincy was himself already one of the most well-traveled and well-read Americans of the day.

Amsterdam, May 14. 1781

My dear Son

I received yours of 13 this morning.

If you have not found a convenient Place to remove into, you may continue your present Lodgings another Month.

I am glad you have finished Phaedrus, and made Such Progress in Nepos, and in Greek.

Amidst your Ardour for Greek and Latin I hope you will not forget your mother Tongue. Read Somewhat in the English Poets every day. You will find them elegant, entertaining and instructive Companions, through your whole Life. In all the Disquisitions you have heard concerning the Happiness of Life, has it ever been recommended to you to read Poetry?

To one who has a Taste, the Poets serve to fill up Time which would otherwise pass in Idleness, Languor, or Vice. You will never be alone with a Poet in your Poket. You will never have an idle Hour.

How many weary hours have been made alert, how many melancholy ones gay, how many vacant ones useful, to me, in the course of my Life, by this means?

Your brother grows daily better but is still weak and pale. He shall write to you, Soon.

Your affectionate Father,

J. Adams

MARK TWAIN (SAMUEL CLEMENS) AS SANTA CLAUS TO SUSIE CLEMENS

"I will call at your kitchen door about nine oclock this morning to inquire. But I must not see anybody, & I must not speak to anybody but you."

In the mid-1870s, Christmas at the Clemens's Hartford, Connecticut, home was a grand affair. Mrs. Clemens spent hours on end in the "mahogany room" wrapping gifts and the children later remembered riding over the countryside in a horse-drawn sleigh delivering Christmas baskets and turkeys to less fortunate neighbors. *Samuel Clemens himself dressed as Santa Claus and delighted in the family rituals, yet he also referred to the elaborate holiday production as Mrs. Clemens's "infernal Christmas-suicide."*

On Christmas morning 1875 the following letter from "Santa Claus" was left for Clemens's three-year-old daughter, Susie.

Palace of St. Nicholas
In the Moon
Christmas Morning, [1875]

My dear Susie Clemens:

I have received & read all the letters which you & your little sister have written me by the hand of your mother & your nurses; & I have also read those which you little people have written me with your own hands—for although you did not use any characters that are in grown people's alphabets, you used the characters which *all* children in all lands on earth & in the twinkling stars use; & as all my subjects in the moon are children & use no character but that, you will easily understand that I can read your & your baby sister's jagged & fantastic marks without any trouble at all. But I had trouble with those letters which you dictated through your mother & the nurses, for I am a foreigner & cannot read English writing well. You will find that I made no mistakes about the things which you & the baby ordered in your *own* letters—I went down your chimney at midnight when you were asleep, & delivered them all myself—& kissed both of you, too, because you are good children, well trained, nice mannered, & about the most obedient little people I ever saw. But in the letters which you dictated there were some words which I could not make out, for certain, & one or two small orders which I could not fill because we ran out of stock. Our last lot of kitchen furniture for dolls has just gone to a very poor little child in the North Star, away up in the cold country above the Big Dipper. Your mama can show you that star & you will say: "Little Snow Flake (for that is the child's name) I'm glad you got that furniture, for you need it more than I." That is, you must *write* that, with your own hand, & Snow Flake will write you an answer. If you only spoke it, she wouldn't hear you. Make your letter light & thin, for the distance is great and the postage very heavy.

There was a word or two in your mama's letter which I couldn't be certain of. I took it to be "trunk full of doll's clothes"? Is that it? I will call at your kitchen door about nine oclock this morning to inquire. But I must not see anybody, & I must not speak to anybody but you. When the kitchen door-bell rings, George must be blindfolded & sent to open the door. Then he must go back to the dining room or the china closet & take the cook with him. You must tell George he must walk on tip-toe & not speak—otherwise he will die some day. Then you must go up to the nursery & stand on a chair or the nurse's bed, & put your ear to the speaking-tube that leads down to the kitchen, & when I whistle through it you must speak in the tube and say, "Welcome, Santa Claus!" Then I will ask whether it was a trunk you ordered or not? If you say it was, I shall ask you what *color* you want the trunk to be. Your mama will help you to name a nice color, & then you must tell me every single thing in detail which you want the trunk to contain. Then when I say "Good bye & a Merry Christmas to my little Susie Clemens," you must say "Good bye, good old Santa Claus, & I thank you very much—& please tell that little Snow Flake I will look at her star tonight and she must look down here— I will be right in the west bay-window; & every fine night I will look at her star & say, "I know somebody up there, & *like* her, too." Then you must go down in the library & make George close all the doors that open into the main hall, & everybody must keep still for a little while. I will go to the moon and get those things, in a few minutes I will come down the chimney which belongs to the fire-place that is in the hall—if it is a trunk you want, because I couldn't get such a thing as a trunk down the nursery-chimney, you know.

People may talk if they want, until they hear my footsteps in the hall— then you tell them to keep quiet a little while till I go back up the chimney. Maybe you will not hear my footsteps at all—so you may go now & then & peep through the dining-room doors, & by & by you will see that thing which you want, right under the piano in the drawing room—for I shall put it there. If I should leave any snow in the hall, you must tell George to sweep it into the fireplace, for I haven't time to do such things. George must not use a broom, but a rag—else he will die some day. You must watch George, & not let him run into danger. If my boot should leave a stain on the marble, George must not holy-stone it away. Leave it there always in memory of my visit; & whenever you look at it or show it to anybody you must let it remind you to be a good little girl. Whenever you are naughty, & somebody points to that mark which your good old Santa Claus's boot made on the marble, what will you say, little Sweetheart?

Goodbye for a few minutes, till I come down to the world and ring the kitchen door-bell.

> Your loving
> SANTA CLAUS
> Whom people sometimes call
> "The Man in the Moon."

FREDERICK LAW OLMSTED TO HENRY PERKINS OLMSTED

"A pile of 5000 cats and kittens, some of them black ones, in front of my window would make my office so dark I should not be able to write in it."

On a "fine day" in May 1875, Frederick Law Olmsted wrote to his youngest child, Henry (whose name was later changed to Frederick Law Olmsted, Jr.). The four-year-old boy was likely with his mother visiting family friends, the Knapps, in Plymouth, Massachusetts. Olmsted is apparently responding to Henry's request to send the family dog, Quiz, to Plymouth.

This letter illustrates clearly what Olmsted once wrote to a friend: "I enjoy my children. They are the center of my life."

13th May, 1875

Dear Henry:

The cats keep coming into the yard, six of them every day, and Quiz drives them out. If I should send Quiz to you to drive the cows away from your rhubarb he would not be here to drive the cats out of the yard. If six cats should keep coming into the yard every day and not go out, in a week there would be 42 of them and in a month 180 and before you came back next November 1260. Then if there should be 1260 cats in the yard before next November half of them at least would have kittens and if half of them should have 6 kittens apiece, there would be more than 5000 cats and kittens in the yard. There would not be any place for Rosanna to spread the clothes unless she drove them all off the grass plot, and if she did they would have to crowd at the end of the yard nearest the house, and if they did that they would make a great pile as high as the top of my windows. A pile of 5000 cats and kittens, some of them black ones, in front of my window would make my office so dark I should not be able to write in it. Besides that those underneath, particularly the kittens, would be hurt by those standing on top of them and I expect they would make such a great squalling all the time that I should not be able to sleep, and if I was not able to sleep, I should not be able to work, and if I did not work I should not have any money, and if I had not any money, I could not send any to Plymouth to pay your fare back on the Fall River boat, and I could not pay my fare to go to Plymouth and so you and I would not ever see each other any more. No, Sir. I can't spare Quiz and you will have to watch for the cows and drive them off yourself or you will raise no rhubarb.

Your affectionate father.

SIDNEY LANIER TO CHARLES D. LANIER

"A young man came to our house yesterday morning who claims that he is a brother of yours and Sidney's and Harry's, and that he is entitled to all the rights and privileges appertaining unto that honorable connection."

In an unusual and creative fashion, musician and poet Sidney Lanier makes an important announcement to his eleven-year-old son, Charley.

West Chester, Pa.
August 15, 1880

My dear Charley:

A young man came to our house yesterday morning who claims that he is a brother of yours and Sidney's and Harry's, and that he is entitled to all the rights and privileges appertaining unto that honorable connection. You will be surprised to learn that both your mother and I are disposed to allow his pretensions, from the fact that he looks a great deal like Sidney,— and from several other circumstances which I need not detail. Indeed your mother has already gone so far as to take him on her breast and nurse him exactly as she did you three young scamps somewhere between twelve and seven years ago. I write therefore to ask whether you and Sidney and Harry are willing to accept our opinion of this young person's genuine kinship to you, or whether you will require him to employ a number of lawyers, like the Tichborne Claimant in England, to assert his rights in due form before the courts of the United States. If the latter, you had best give him early notice of your intention; for the fact is he has taken such a hold upon our affections here, by the quietness and modesty of his demeanor and by the beauty of his person, that if we were summoned into Court as witnesses in the case of

Robert Sampson Lanier Jr (so called), Plaintiff Action on a Bond (of brotherhood),

Versus

Charles Day Lanier
Sidney   "   Jr.   Defendants
and
Henry   "

we would be obliged to testify that we feel almost as sure—if not quite—that he is your brother as that you are our son.

As I have said, he is a most exemplary young man. He never stays out late at night; neither chews, smokes, nor uses snuff; abstains from all intoxicating liquors, and does not touch even tea or coffee; however much preserves and fruit-cake there may be on the supper-table, he never asks for any; he does no kind of work on the Sabbath; he honors his father and mother, particularly his mother; he plays no games of hazard, not even marbles for winnance; and I am positively certain that in the whole course of his life he has never uttered a single angry or ungentlemanly word. I am bound to admit that he has his shortcomings: he *isn't* as particular about his clothes as I would like to see him; he has a way of trying to get both fists in his mouth which certainly does look odd in company; and he wants his breakfast in the morning at four o'clock—an hour at which it is very inconvenient, with *our* household arrangements, to furnish it to him. But we hope that perhaps he will amend in these particulars, as time rolls on, and that he will become as perfect a gentleman as his three brothers. In fact we attribute these little faults of his to the fact that he appears to have been in a Far Country—like the Tichborne Claimant—, and the manners and customs of peoples are so different that we really don't know whether it may not be considered a sign of good breeding *There* to cram one's fists into one's mouth, and perhaps the very highest circles of the nobility and gentry in that Region take their breakfasts before daylight.

Earnestly hoping that this lovely little (for I omitted to mention that he is small of stature) brother Rob may find a good warm place in your three hearts without being obliged to resort to extreme measures, and with a hundred embraces for you, me dear big Charley,

I am
Your &c &c &c.

WILLIAM JAMES TO MARGARET MARY JAMES

". . . the beautifullest sight you ever saw."

With ingenuity and grace, William James solved a problem for a tiny trapped hummingbird. Here he describes the scene to his eight-year-old daughter.

Swanswick—June 19th. [18]95

Sweet Peg.

I am very happy here, and fear that you may already have gone up to Chocorua with your Mamma. Yesterday a beautiful humming bird came into the library and spent two hours without resting, trying to find his way out by the skylight in the ceiling. You never saw such untiring strength. Filled with pity for his fatigue, I went into the garden and culled a beautiful rose. The moment I held it up in my hand under the skylight, the angelic bird flew down into it and rested there as in a nest—the beautifullest sight you ever saw.

Your loving
Dad.

ALEXANDER GRAHAM BELL TO
MARIAN "DAISY" BELL

"Never take a 12.50 train, for it is
ten to one if you catch it."

Alexander Graham Bell's lifelong interest in and study of the deaf led him to re-
search the possibility of a hereditary component to hearing loss. He had worked with
families and communities in New England, studied genealogical records, and by 1901
he was evaluating vast quantities of statistics from the United States census of 1900.
It was an enormous undertaking and he felt the pull to get back to his laboratory as
never before. Even his normally supportive wife, Mabel, deaf herself, complained, "I
hate this census with a personal hatred," because of the time it was consuming.

Here, taking a break from his work, he writes to twenty-one-year-old Daisy
from the Washington, D.C., Volta Bureau. The Volta Bureau was a facility es-
tablished by Bell that was soon to be one of the leading centers of information on
the deaf and deafness in the world.

Volta Bureau, May 4, 1901.

Dear Daidums:—

I was very much interested in your Pompeiian letter. You are evidently
having a fine time in Italy and Sicily. Wish I could be with you. IF THE
TEMPERATURE IS NOT TOO HIGH. Haven't time to write you a
proper letter. I am stealing ten minutes from other matters to send you a
few—

Jokes

An Italian Count, the other day introduced his American heiress to a
friend as his "financee." A very appropriate term by the by.

_____

The Queen of Holland's latest remark to her husband:—
"Is my crown on straight?"

_____

Never take a 12.50 train, for it is ten to one if you catch it.

_____

Why is a pretty girl like a mirror?
Because she is a good looking lass.

—————

Heat travels faster than cold, because you can easily catch cold.

—————

Why is a stick of candy like a horse?
The more you lick it the faster it goes.

—————

When a girl faints, why should you always bring more than one doctor?
If she is not brought two she will die.

—————

Why is an empty room like a room completely full of married people.
Because there is not a single one in it.

—————

Theatrical.—The best seats in the house?—the receipts.

—————

What is the longest word in the English language?
The word "smiles," because there is a mile between the first and last letters.

—————

Why is it impossible for a fisherman to be generous?
Because his business makes him sell fish.

—————

The following are items from my note book culled from the newspapers. They are not exactly jokes, but purport to be true occurrences;—

There was a flood in one of the rivers out west the other day, and the young school teacher had to wade through a foot of water to get to her school where she found thirteen little children assembled. She noticed that the water was rising and remembered that the school house was in a hollow, and determined at once to get assistance. She made the children promise not to leave the building, and then started for the neighboring farm house. She found the water, however, up to her waist and feared the school would be gone before she could get assistance. There was no one at the farm house, and the barn was empty excepting for a horse. Without a moment's delay she seized the horse and a long rope and started for the school, which was then afloat. She swam the horse to the building—tied the rope to the door—and started the horse back to shore with the school house in tow. After a desperate struggle she reached the shore and tied the other end of the rope to a tree. Having tethered the school house she started off again for assistance and brought back the farmer and saved the children. People out west are wild over her now, and she can have as many husbands as she wants.

———

I have just sent a suicide item to Mr. Kennan, for I doubt whether he has in his collection a more curious cause of suicide.

The man concerned was shot in the Civil War, and had lost both legs beneath the knee. When he recovered consciousness after the amputation he was concerned about the disposal of his feet, but was unable to trace them. He could feel, he said, that something improper was being done with his feet. One heel was cold and the ball of the foot was hot and itching, but he could not relieve the sensation, for his foot was gone. Little by little the extraordinary sensations experienced—apparently in the missing feet—drove him distracted and he committed suicide. He labored under the common delusion of ignorant people that he could feel what was done to his dead feet. The sensations, of course were real, but his friends thought him insane and did nothing to relieve him. They thought he was subject to delusions, whereas any doctor would have known that the sensations simply indicated pressure upon the nerves that had formerly led to the feet.

Probably some small abcess had formed somewhere in the stump of his leg and had his friends been more intelligent they would have placed him again in the Surgeon's care, and a slight operation would have relieved him of the difficulty. But ignorance coupled with superstition made his case seem a hopeless one and the poor fellow ended his misery by suicide.

———

Elsie has not been very well lately but seems better now. The doctor is keeping her in bed for a few days, more as a precaution than anything else.

I am going to take a cottage at Atlantic City for a month, and Bert and Elsie and my father and mother will come with me and stay with me there.

I understand that my father has presented you with some stock or bonds that will bring you in an income—according to Bert—of about fifteen hundred dollars a year. He has given Elsie the same and has also presented property to others, to Aileen, Bobbie, Ralf Ker and others. I am seriously concerned about it. It is all right to give away the property, but it is not right that he should deprive himself of the income. Elsie, at suggestion, wrote to him accepting the stock, but wishing him to have the income during his life. This he has declined to accept. She has now written to Mrs. Bell asking her to accept the income during my father's life and expend it upon him. I think this is the best plan to do, and if your mother approves I should like you to do the same.

Your loving father,
Alexander Graham Bell

THEODORE ROOSEVELT TO KERMIT ROOSEVELT AND THEODORE ROOSEVELT, JR.

". . . they have taught me three new throws that are perfect corkers."

When Theodore Roosevelt was a child, frail and asthmatic, his father told him, "You have the mind but you have not the body, and without the help of the body the mind cannot go as far as it should. You must make *your body."*

Here, the president of the United States writes with hilarious effect to his two eldest sons, Ted and Kermit, about his latest form of exercise.

White House, March 5, 1904

Dear Kermit:

It does not look as if Renown would ever be worth anything, and I am afraid that Wyoming is gone too. Bleistein probably, and Yagenka, almost certainly will come out all right. Allan is back here now and very cunning, so you will see him on your return.

I am wrestling with two Japanese wrestlers three times a week. I am not the age or the build, one would think, to be whirled lightly over an opponent's head and batted down on a mattress without damage; but they are so skillful that I have not been hurt at all. My throat is a little sore because once when one of them had a strangle hold I also got hold of his windpipe and thought I could perhaps choke him off before he could choke me. However he got ahead!

Your loving father,
Theodore Roosevelt

White House, April 9, 1904

Dear Ted:

I am very glad I have been doing this Japanese wrestling, but when I am through with it this time I am not sure I will ever try it again while I am so busy with other work as I am now. Often by the time I get to five o'clock in the afternoon I will be feeling like a stewed owl, after an eight hours grapple with Senators, Congressman, etc.; then I find the wrestling a trifle too vehement for mere rest. My right ankle and my left wrist and one thumb and both great toes are swollen sufficiently to more or less impair their usefulness, and I am well mottled with bruises elsewhere. Still I have made good progress, and since you left they have taught me three new throws that are perfect corkers.

I hope that Congress will only be here a fortnight more. I have gotten on with them very well, and I do not want to take any chances for something wrong happening. I am all at sea as yet as to whom to have for Chairman of the National Committee, which is a very important office. We shall have a hard campaign this year; and if the result depends upon New York State no one can tell how it will come out, so that I want to get as many chances on my side as possible.

Your loving father,
Theodore Roosevelt

P.S. Since writing the above, yours and Kermit's letters about the mumps have arrived. Well, we did play it in bad luck! I am afraid you can not come home at present. Mother starts for Groton this afternoon, and will reach you before this letter.

THEODORE ROOSEVELT TO QUENTIN ROOSEVELT

". . . lippity lippity lippity . . ."

Theodore Roosevelt adored reading to his children. The family was particularly fond of Joel Chandler Harris's Uncle Remus stories. Here the president of the United States writes to his six-year-old son, Quentin.

[White House]
June 21, 1904

Dear Quentyquee:

The other day when out riding what should I see in the road ahead of me but a real B'rer Terrapin and B'rer Rabbit. They were sitting solemnly beside one another and looked just as if they had come out of a book; but as my horse walked along B'rer Rabbit went lippity lippity lippity off into the bushes and B'rer Terrapin drew in his head and legs till I passed.

Your loving father,
Theodore Roosevelt

JOHN D. ROCKEFELLER TO JOHN D. ROCKFELLER, JR.

"Respecting your kind offer of the Rolls-Royce . . . if it would be your pleasure to give me this value in cash, in place of the car . . ."

In celebration of John D. Rockefeller's ninetieth birthday, John D. Rockefeller, Jr., wanted to give his father a Rolls-Royce. At first, the elder Rockefeller gratefully protested, claiming that he had enough cars and was reluctant to set an extravagant example for "all our young people coming along, and our neighbors and others." Then the old man had second thoughts.

Golf House
Lakewood, NJ
June 13, 1929

Dear Son:

After reflection in the night, last night, I am emboldened to say, re-specting your kind offer of the Rolls-Royce in yours of the 10th, and my answer of yesterday, that if it would be your pleasure to give me this value in cash, in place of the car, I would be glad to make judicious use of it in connection with my most needy charity cases, thus making the investment of the greatest value to us both.

This is only a suggestion, and you must exercise your own good judge-ment, with which, be assured, I shall be perfectly satisfied.

> With tenderest affection,
> Father

On July 5, the son sent the father "$19,000 being the cost of a Rolls-Royce car which I offered you, and instead of which you said you'd prefer to have cash."

MOE HOWARD TO JOAN SALLY HOWARD

"And well behaved I'm telling you . . ."

Creator and star of the vaudeville, movie, and television act "The Three Stooges," Moe Howard, along with his cohorts, delighted generations of Americans with outrageous antics. Howard was best known as the comedian who got laughs by banging his costars' heads together, poking them in the eyes, and kicking their shins. However, his daughter, Joan, described "Moe without mayhem" as a loving father and husband who spent many lonely hours on the road. Howard filled the time between acts by making hook rugs and crocheting afghan blankets. The fol-lowing poem was written by Moe Howard from a hotel room in Toronto to his eight-year-old daughter at home in California.

[circa 1936]

To my little Pal

I miss and love a little girl,
She's awfully cute and sweet,
To me she's precious as a pearl,
So sweet and hard to beat.

She has red curls and freckles too,
The sweetest loving Pal,
And well behaved I'm telling you,
I call her Joanie-Sal.

I'm waiting patiently to see,
My Joanie doll and all,
I know they're waiting home for me,
with my little Skipper Paul!

Daddy Dear

GROUCHO MARX TO ARTHUR MARX

*"I've often wondered why people drink.
It's gradually beginning to dawn on me."*

Julius Henry "Groucho" Marx was twentieth-century America's wiseguy. First, with his brothers Chico, Harpo, and Zeppo and then as a solo act, he elevated in-nuendo to the level of an art form. He was known for his cigar and his grease-paint mustache and for so many memorable slapstick lines like "Remember we're fighting for her honor—which is probably more than she ever did." Making fun of middle-class America, he struck at people's vulnerabilities, yet he himself described his hu-mor as being the kind "that made people laugh at themselves."

In 1940 his marriage to the socially ambitious Ruth Johnson, the mother of his two children, was nearing its end. Away from the discontented Beverly Hills house-hold on a tennis tournament tour was Marx's son, nineteen-year-old Arthur. "My tennis was so-so," wrote Arthur, "but the letters I received from Father . . . made the tours worthwhile."

Summer of 1940

Dear Art:

For a tennis bum, you're certainly leading a luxurious life and I only hope you can keep it up. I see by the papers that it rained in St. Louis yesterday, so that gave you time to eat six meals at the hotel instead of the customary five.

We just came back from Lake Arrowhead. It's a wonderful spot and we had a fine time sailing on the lake. With the wind on my back, I was Sir Thomas Lipton, Sir Francis Drake and Captain Kidd. However, when I tried to tack against it and sail into home plate, I botched it up completely and finally had to suffer the humiliation of being towed back to port by a small boy in an outboard motor. This made Miriam very happy, for during the entire voyage she kept telling me that I didn't know how to manipulate a sailboat and predicted that it was only a question of time before I'd be towed back to shore. Despite my inadequacies as commander, I would spend a good part of my declining years on the bounding waves. That's really the life. You need no golf ball, no caddy, no racket or busted gut. All you need is a stout heart, a strong back, plenty of wind and a cast-iron stomach. Avast, mates! Yo-ho and a bottle of rum! Tonight I'll listen to "Pinafore" on the record player.

We expect to start shooting around July first, so for the next eight weeks you can reach me on the back lot at MGM. Please bring ice packs and menthol and a portable air conditioner.

I'm brushing up on all the current movies. I saw "Strange Cargo" and was having a pretty good time until the head usher at the Marquis tapped me on the shoulder and sharply told me that no smoking was allowed.

He walked away and I began smoking again. Again he tapped me on the shoulder. This time he didn't walk away—he just stood there, arms folded, and glared at the back of my head. Then my cigar went out: and then I went out. Sometime, I wish you'd let me know what happened to the nature girl in the last four reels.

Last night, I saw "Waterloo Bridge" at the Westwood Theater. It's quite a bit different from the old version. MGM, being a more leisurely studio, didn't make the girl a streetwalker until the fourth reel. In the original version, they opened up in the first reel with the little lady hustling on Waterloo Bridge. It was better that way—I could get home earlier.

I can't write any more at this time as I have to take dancing lessons for the next three days. Our friends, the Arthur Murrays, have bestowed the lessons upon us, which, you may be sure, is the only reason I am submitting to them.

Love,
Padre

P.S. Saturday night, the Beverly Hills Tennis and Bad Food club is throwing a barn dance and it's going to be a sensation. How surprised we'll all be when we gather there that evening to see all the new faces that we had left only an hour before on the tennis court.

The food won't be served until midnight, so I've arranged with your mother to pay for the privilege of eating stale delicatessen food and listening to Dave's wife, who used to be a showgirl, sing a medley of airs from "The Chocolate Soldier." If this keeps up, I may take to drinking in a serious way. I've often wondered why people drink. It's gradually beginning to dawn on me.

"I don't know whether you have ever been a dog—
I know you look like one—but it has certain
advantages and disadvantages."

Five years later Groucho Marx's dog, Duke, writes to twenty-three-year-old Arthur, who was serving in the United States Coast Guard in the Philippines.

Beverly Hills, California,
February 16, 1945

Dear Art,

Irene was telling me that in the letters you receive nobody mentions my name. This is not unusual; it happens to many dogs. You know, it's a strange thing, but once you walk around on four legs, instead of the orthodox two, people begin to suspect that you don't know what's going on. I don't know whether you have ever been a dog—I know you look like one—but it has certain advantages and disadvantages. Your father, as you know, and I both live under the same roof. He is not a bad guy, despite the fact that he kicks me occasionally, especially those days when the market goes down. When he strokes me affectionately, I know then that the stocks are on the upswing. I watch your old man very closely, although I don't imagine he thinks I do, and he is quite a character. He reads the paper every morning, worries about the war, the position of the Jews in this country, and all the other problems that the morning paper presents. I don't know whether I ever told you this, Arthur, but I am also partly Jewish. As you know, I originally came from the Schulberg family. Ben, who used to be the head of

Paramount, was my father. My mother was Rin-Tin-Tin's stand-in, a beautiful red-headed airedale. I worry a good deal, too, about the Jews, and when I go out in the morning with your old man, many of the dogs I meet won't permit me within smelling distance. There is one dog, on Lomitas near Foothill who despises me. She's an Irish setter and goes to early mass every Sunday morning. She's a real anti-Semite and I have frequently seen her with a copy of Father Coughlin's Social Justice tied to her tail.

Your father and I have many run-ins these days. You see, he can't get it into his thick skull that I have come of age and that sex is just as necessary to me as it is to him. There's a beautiful collie in the 500 block on Palm Drive that thinks I'm a pretty hot dog. I'm crazy about her and, although it isn't good for my social prestige to be seen around with a bitch from the 500 block, I try to be broadminded about it and not too dogmatic in my views. I've done considerable running away in recent months—sometimes for days. It isn't that I don't like your father but my freedom is terribly important to me and I am not going to relinquish it for that mangy pound and a half of horse meat that he tosses at me each evening. I may not even go with him when he moves to Westwood. The backyard is exceedingly small and there is a hell of a high steel picket fence surrounding it. I am convinced that if I try to scale this enclosure I will probably be disemboweled, so I may solve the whole think by just remaining in Beverly, feeding out of garbage cans and living a dog's life with my collie.

Well, I could go on and tell you many tales of my adventures in the hills of Beverly but I don't want to bore you. The only reason I wrote you at all was because I didn't want you to think that I was an out-of-sight out-of-mind dog. As a matter of fact, I miss you a lot and if you could send me a few bones, even those of a Jap, I certainly would appreciate it.

By the way, when you write to your father again, remember, not a word about this letter—he doesn't know I can write, in fact, he thinks I'm a complete schmuck.

Well, take care of yourself. That's the leash you can do.

Your old pal,
Duke Marx

F. Scott Fitzgerald and daughter Scottie

Jack London and daughter Joan

Thomas Edison (center) and Thomas Edison, Jr. (far right)

Brace-Up

THOMAS JEFFERSON TO
MARTHA "PATSY" JEFFERSON

*"Of all the cankers of human happiness, none corrodes
it with so silent, yet so baneful a tooth, as indolence."*

Indolence, a dissatisfaction resulting from a lack of interest, and ennui, a disinclination to work, were intolerable to Thomas Jefferson. He was fascinated by almost all that was around him—history, philosophy, the law, design, architecture, agriculture, painting, sculpture, music, horses, fossils, antiquities. And his interest was not passive. As an architect he designed Monticello, the Virginia state capitol, and the original campus of the University of Virginia. He performed horticultural experiments. He played the violin. And he wrote—political pamphlets, the Declaration of Independence, a book about Virginia, and it is estimated nearly fifty thousand letters. Neither indolence nor ennui were manifest in Thomas Jefferson.

Here he responds to his fifteen-year-old daughter, Martha, who had complained slightly about her reading of the Roman historian Livy.

Aix en Provence March. 28. 1787.

I was happy, my dear Patsy, to receive, on my arrival here, your letter informing me of your health and occupations. I have not written to you sooner because I have been almost constantly on the road. My journey hitherto has been a very pleasing one. It was undertaken with the hope that the mineral waters of this place might restore strength to my wrist. Other considerations also concurred. Instruction, amusement, and abstraction from business, of which I had too much at Paris. I am glad to learn that you are employed in things new and good in your music and drawing. You know what have been my fears for some time past; that you do not employ yourself so closely as I could wish. You have promised me a more assiduous attention, and I have great confidence in what you promise. It is your future happiness which interests me, and nothing can contribute more to it (moral rectitude always excepted) than the contracting a habit of industry and activity. Of all the cankers of human happiness, none corrodes it with so silent, yet so baneful a tooth, as indolence. Body and mind both unemployed, our being becomes a burthen, and every object about us loathsome, even the dearest. Idleness begets ennui, ennui the hypochondria, and that a diseased body. No laborious person was ever yet hysterical. Exercise and application produce order in our affairs, health of body, chearfulness of mind, and these make us precious to our friends. It is while we are young that the habit of industry is formed. If not then, it never is afterward. The fortune of our lives therefore depends on employing well the short period of youth. If at any moment, my dear, you catch yourself in idleness, start from it as you would from the precipice of a gulph. You are not however to consider yourself as unemployed while taking exercise. That is necessary for your health, and health is the first of all objects. For this reason if you leave your dancing master for the summer, you must increase your other exercise. I do not like your saying that you are unable to read the antient print of your Livy, but with the aid of your master. We are always equal to what we undertake with resolution. A little degree of this will enable you to decypher your Livy. If you always lean on your master, you will never be able to proceed without him. It is a part of the American character to consider nothing as desperate; to surmount every difficulty by resolution and contrivance. In Europe there are shops for every want. Its inhabitants therefore have no idea that their wants can be furnished otherwise. Remote from all other aid, we are obliged to invent and to execute; to find means within ourselves, and not to lean on others. Consider therefore the conquering of your Livy as an exercise in the habit of surmounting difficulties, a habit which will be necessary to you in the country where you are to live, and without which you will be thought a very helpless animal, and less esteemed. Music, drawing, books, invention and exercise will be so many resources to you against ennui. But there are others which to this object add that of utility. These are the needle, and domestic oeconomy. The latter you cannot learn here, but the former you may. In the country life of America there are many moments when a woman can have recourse to nothing but her needle for employment. In a dull company and in dull weather for instance. It is ill manners to read; it is ill manners to leave them; no card playing there among genteel people; that is abandoned to blackguards. The needle is then a valuable resource. Besides without knowing to use it herself, how can the mistress of a family direct the works of her servants? You ask me to write you long letters. I will do it my dear, on condition you will read them from time to time, and practice what they will inculcate. Their precepts will be dictated by experience, by a perfect knowledge of the situation in which you will be placed, and by the fondest love for you. This it is which makes me wish to see you more qualified than common. My expectations from you are high: yet not higher than you may attain. Industry and resolution are all that are wanting. No body in this world can make me so happy, or so miserable as you. Retirement from public life will ere long become necessary for me. To your sister and yourself I look to render the evening of my life serene and contented. Its morning has been clouded by loss after loss till I have nothing left but you. I do not doubt either your affection or dispositions. But great exertions are necessary, and you have little time left to make them. Be industrious then, my dear child. Think nothing unsurmountable by resolution and application, and you will be all that I wish you to be. You ask me if it is my desire you should dine at the abbess's table? It is. Propose it as such to Madame de Traubenheim with my respectful compliments and thanks for her care of you. Continue to love me with all the warmth with which you are beloved by, my dear Patsy, yours affectionately.

TH: JEFFERSON

MARY TODD LINCOLN TO
ROBERT TODD LINCOLN

"You have injured yourself, not me,
by your wicked conduct."

Mary Todd Lincoln could turn from tenderness to rage in an instant and wherever money was concerned she was usually irrational. Acquisitive beyond reason, she lavished upon herself extravagant gifts of elegant clothing, jewels, lace, china, silver, crystal, watches, and gloves. Thrilled by and obsessed with the act of making a purchase, she left many of the things she bought unused and unopened even, and with the credit extended her she often incurred enormous debt.

Her life was tragic in the extreme and she was destroyed by the experience. The loss of her husband to an assassin and the deaths of three of her four sons of fever, one after another over the course of twenty-one years, led in 1875 to a moment of deep crisis. Her actions—she was hallucinating, shopping irrationally, carrying $57,000 worth of securities in her skirt pocket, and wandering the halls of her Chicago hotel half-dressed—led her only remaining child, firstborn Robert, to commit her to Bellevue Place sanitarium on the basis of insanity.

One year after she was institutionalized, Mary Todd Lincoln, aged fifty-eight, was released to the care of her sister and brother-in-law. She wrote the following letter to Robert just three days after her departure from Bellevue. (It is important to note that only a few years earlier she wrote affectionately to Robert's wife, "Anything and everything is yours . . . it will be such a relief to me to know that articles can be used and enjoyed by you.")

Springfield, Illinois
June 19th—1876

Robert T. Lincoln

Do not fail to send me without *the least* delay, *all* my paintings, Moses in the bullrushes included—also the fruit picture, which hung in your dining room—my silver set with large silver waiter presented me by my New York friends, my silver tete-a-tete set also other articles your wife appropriated & which are *well known* to you, must be sent, without a day's delay. Two lawyers and myself, have just been together and their list, coincides with my own & will be published in a few days. Trust not to the belief, that Mrs Edward's tongue, has not been *rancorous* against you all winter & she has maintained to the very last, that you dared not venture into her house & our presence. Send me my laces, my diamonds, my jewelry—My unmade silks, white lace dress—double lace shawl and flounce, lace scarf—2 blk lace shawls—one blk lace deep flounce, white lace sets 1/2 yd in width and eleven yards in length. I am now in constant receipt of letters, from my friends denouncing you in the bitterest terms, six letters from prominent, *respectable*, Chicago people such as you do not associate with. No John Forsythe's & such scamps, including Scamman. As to Mr. Harlan—you are not worthy to wipe the dust, from his feet. Two prominent clergy men have written me, since I saw you—and mention in their letters, that they think it advisable to offer up prayers for you in Church, on account of your wickedness against me and High Heaven. In reference to Chicago you have the enemies, & I chance to have the friends there. Send me all that I have written for, you have tried your game of robbery long enough. On yesterday, I received two telegrams from prominent Eastern lawyers. You have injured yourself, not me, by your wicked conduct.

Mrs. A. Lincoln

My engravings too send me. M. L. Send me Whittier Pope, Agnes Strickland's Queens of England, other books, you have of mine—

In 1881, one year before her death, Mary Todd Lincoln was visited by her son, Robert, who had just become Secretary of War under President James Garfield.

Thomas Edison to Thomas Edison, Jr.

". . . it would be impossible to connect you with any of the business projects of mine."

Thomas Edison, the "Wizard," was an inventor and entrepreneur for the ages. At the time of his death he held more patents than any American before or since. With his team of researchers and assistants he invented the electric lightbulb, made valuable improvements to the telegraph and telephone, and contributed significantly to the founding of new industries, including telephone, recorded sound, motion picture, and electrical utilities. His Edison General Electric Company became General Electric.

Working eighteen hours a day, he seemed inconvenienced by the necessities of life—eating, bathing and sleeping. It seemed, too, that his six children were mere distractions.

In 1903 Edison employed hundreds of people in his vast and prolific inventing laboratory and business ventures. His troubled eldest son, twenty-seven-year-old Tom, Jr., had already been fired from a lowly laboring job at his father's mining company. Of his father he was both reverent and resentful, and their correspondence with each other was normally conducted through Edison's assistant, John Randolph. But here Edison himself responds to a pathetic four-page letter in which Tom, Jr., begs for a job, any job, or even a note to help him get a job, and pleads with his father to "answer this letter personally."

[1903]

Tom—

You must know that with your record of passing bad checks and use of liquor all of which is known to every one having business connection with my concerns that it would be impossible to connect you with any of the business projects of mine. It is strange that with your income you cant go into some small business—there are more than 10 000 such little businesses, William seems to be doing well.

TAE

THEODORE ROOSEVELT TO ALICE LEE ROOSEVELT

". . . when you do foolish things, you make it certain that worse than foolish things will be ascribed to you."

Alice Roosevelt was a joy to her father—and a handful. It was reported that Theodore Roosevelt once told a friend, "I can be President of the United States— or—I can attend to Alice." Here Roosevelt writes to his eldest child, his twenty-year-old daughter, about her unladylike behavior—betting at the racetrack and circulating stories about her pet snake, "Emily Spinach."

Sagamore Hill
August 28, 1904

Dear Alice:

Do you know how much talk there has been recently in the newspapers about your betting and courting notoriety with that unfortunate snake. I gave you permission to keep the snake because I thought you liked it as children like their pets. But you used it in a way that seems to show that you did as a matter of fact court notoriety . . . You must not get a snake or anything like it, and do try to remember that to court notoriety by bizarre actions is underbred and unladylike. You should not bet at all, and never in public. I wish you had some little sense of responsibility towards others. In your present position your example might be one for good; but at least you need not make it one for evil. The effect is unfortunate in many ways. Remember that when you do foolish things, you make it certain that worse than foolish things will be ascribed to you. To run into debt and be extravagant as to your clothes—such pointless extravagance, too—is not only foolish, but wicked.

Your father
Theodore Roosevelt

Jack London to Joan London

"Am I dirt under your feet?"

"My face changed forever in that year of 1913. It has never been the same since," Jack London told his second wife. The year was a downward spiral for the author of The Call of the Wild *and* "To Build a Fire," *arguably the most widely read American short story ever. Someone had shot his prized mare in the head, he was losing crops on his ranch, his finances were in trouble, he was fatally ill with diseased kidneys, and, during the summer, a dream of his lifetime literally went up in smoke. On his 1,500-acre Beauty Ranch in California, London was building a grand stone mansion which, on August 22, burned to the ground. So devastated was he by the loss of the house that those close to him felt he never fully recovered.*

Just two days after the fire, he wrote to his twelve-year-old daughter, Joan, from whom he felt he deserved a letter. Joan lived with her mother, who had been divorced from Jack London for eight years.

Glen Ellen
August 24, 1913

Dear Joan:—

I feel too miserable to write this at my desk. I am sitting up in bed to write it.

First, please remember that I am your father, I have fed you, clothed you, and housed you, and *loved* you since the moment you first drew breath. I have all of a father's heart of love for you.

And now we come to brass tacks. What have you done for me in all the days of your life? What do you *feel* for me? Am I merely your meal-ticket? Do you look upon me as merely a creature with a *whim*, or *fancy*, or *fantasy*, that compels him to care for you and to take care of you?—because he is a fool who gives much and receives . . . well, receives nothing?

Please answer the foregoing questions. I want to know how I stand with you.

You have your dreams of education. I try to give you the best of my wisdom. You write me about the demands of the U.C. in relation to selection of high school courses. I reply by (1) telegram, (2) by letter. And I receive no word from you. Am I dirt under your feet? Am I beneath your contempt in every way save as a meal-ticket? Do you love me at all? What do I *mean* to you?

Answer the above queries of mine.

My home, as yet unoccupied, burns down—and I receive no word from you. When you were sick I came to see you. I gave you flowers and canary birds.

Now I am sick—and you are silent. My home—one of my dreams—is destroyed. You have no word to say.

Your education is mixed up by conflict between high school and university. You write me. I reply by telegram and letter. I spring to help you with my wisdom in your trouble, in the realization of your dream.

I say, very sadly, that when my dream is ruined, I do not notice that you spring to me.

Joan, my daughter, please know that the world belongs to the honest ones, to the true ones, to the right ones, to the ones who talk right out; and that the world does not belong to the ones who remain silent, who, by their very silence lie and cheat and make a mock of love and a meal ticket of their father.

Don't you think it is about time I heard from you? Or do you want me to cease forever from caring to hear from you?

Daddy

*"If . . . you . . . elect for yourself to become
a little person in a little place in a little portion
of the world, it will be a great misfortune
for which there will be no help."*

Rising from poverty through his own hard work and determination, London grew to hate polite society and anything that hinted at what he felt was mediocrity. Under the roof and influence of his first wife, he was certain his daughters were living just such a disdainful existence.

In October 1913 London asked twelve-year-old Joan to choose a new way of life by coming to live with him and his second wife. He was asking his daughter to make a choice between her mother and father.

[Glen Ellen]
October 11, 1913

Dear Joan:

I am in a great hurry. Find inclosed check for $4.00 to pay the Whitaker boy for the work he did on the back-yard. The $80 for the front steps, and the $185 for the back-yard is too extortionate to be considered by me if I did have the money, and at the present time I haven't any such sum of money. I have inclosed your letter describing the front and back yards to Uncle Ernest, and asked him to go up and take a look at what is needed. I have told him I haven't the money for the back-yard improvement, and have told him I have no such sum as $80 for the front steps. Also, I have told Uncle Ernest to show the letter I have written him to your mother, so she may know it is all right for him to go ahead and do his best with the least amount of money I can spare at the present time for the front steps alone.

The estimate for the awning comes to $11.50. Do I understand this means canvas alone? Please give me details. What does this $11.50 pay for? Does it pay for the mere canvas, or does it pay for the canvas, for the wood, for the nails, for the ropes, pulleys, etc., etc. Also, you failed to tell me what your friend Mr. Thoms will do the work for. How do I know what his work will amount to? Please give me full details about the total cost of this canvas, and of the labor involved in putting the canvas in place, and about what sort of guaranty this Mr. Thoms will give that the thing will work after he has put it up. Give me this clearly and immediately, so I may be able to tell you to go ahead and work on it.

In your excitement, you forgot, or did not hear me tell you, that I had sent the order for $3 for renewal of the *St. Nicholas* directly to The Century Co. That was done before I came out to Piedmont and saw you.

And now to other things. Please know that silence on your part and a sore hand on your mother's part, means satisfaction on your part and on your mother's part with your mother's present policy and attitude concerning the matter I talked over with you on Sunday evening.

And please, please remember what I told you on Sunday evening, concerning the fact that the less I see of you and Bess, the less I would be bound to be interested in you. Just as a token of this state of mind, which is common to all human beings, namely, to be interested in the things one sees and is in some sort of contact with, let me tell you an incident that happened last night: I was thinking over this matter at table. Nakata, my Japanese boy, was waiting on the table; and the thought so suddenly came to me, and came to me with such strength, that I immediately said to Nakata: "Nakata, you know that I have two daughters. When I knew these daughters they were little babies and did not count. I know scarcely anything about them since. Nakata, for six or seven years you have been with me night and day. You have been with me through every danger over the whole world. Storm and violent death have been common in your and my experience. I remember the times in storms when you have stood nobly by. I remember the time when the cannibals assailed us 1500-strong, when you stood on the wreck of our vessel, dashing to pieces on the reef, a rifle in either hand ready to pass me whenever I wanted to use it. I remember the hours of sickness when you nursed me. I remember the hours of fun when you laughed with me and I laughed with you. I remember so many, many of these hours of all sorts, of contact with you, that I know that I know you ten thousand times better than I know my two daughters."

Now, Joan. Remember that the world is populated by big people and by little people. Almost the entire population of the world consists of little people. Here and there are a few of the big people. It is a hard proposition to put up to you at your age, and the chances are that in deciding on this proposition that I put up to you on Sunday night, you will make the mistake of deciding to be a little person in a little place in a little part of the world. You will make this mistake because you listened to your mother, who is a little person in a little place in little part of the world, and who, out of her female sex jealousy against another woman, has sacrificed your future for you. If you join with your mother in this little sex jealousy of a thwarted female, you will doom yourself to grow up in the little environment of the little place called Piedmont, which is populated by little people. On the other hand, I offer you the big things of the world; the big things that the big people live and know and think and act. You are now a little woman. You will grow into a mature woman. In the next four or five years your entire future life, so far as your development be concerned, will be determined. The chances are since you know more about Jim Whitaker, or Jim Whitaker's boys, or your mother, or Uncle Ernest, or Aunt Florrie, or all the other persons about you, than you do know about me, your Daddy—the chances are that you will decide to follow your mother's policy which, as I have already told you, is based upon sex jealousy of a thwarted female. The result will be that when you are a mature woman of eighteen or twenty, you will be merely the little person in the little place in a little portion of the world.

This will be too bad for you, for at about that time you will begin to read with understanding all the books I have written, and you will come to realize the smallness of yourself and of your place. Unfortunately, it will then be too late. You will not then be able to change yourself. You will have been already developed. The developing time is now. From now until you are eighteen years of age. Having developed, you cannot change yourself any more than the leopard can change its spots. You will know your tragedy, you will know what you missed, but you will be unable to remedy it, and so shall I be unable to remedy it for you.

And this also will be my tragedy: The thing will have happened to you. You will be as small as the persons around you are small, and it will then be too late for me to lend you a helping hand, because you will have already been fully developed. Also, what will you mean to me when you are eighteen or twenty years old, developed in such an environment? I will know as a matter of fact, that you are my daughter. But I shall also know that you are a strange sort of wizened, pinched, human female creature of eighteen or twenty years, and that it is too late to change you into anything bigger.

Well, anyway, I gave you on last Sunday night several problems. I referred you to the New Testament and the study of Christ. Christ was a big man. He was not a little person in a little place in a little portion of the world. If you do not study out these problems, or if in studying out these simple problems I gave you, you come to the wrong conclusion and elect for yourself to become a little person in a little place in a little portion of the world, it will be a great misfortune for which there will be no help. Although it will not avail you any to do so, you will then be able to charge this malformation of you in your developmental period, this wizening and pinching of you into the little person—you may be able to charge this directly to your mother's conduct in influencing your conduct, because your mother is so small, so primitive, so savage, that she cherishes a sex hatred for a woman who is bigger than she to such an extent that her face is distorted with passion while she talks about it, as it was distorted last Sunday night.

Now, Joan, remember the silence so far has been on your part. If this silence continues, I shall not break it. Any time you want to break it, I shall be here or somewhere in the world. In the meantime, carry my warnings and my problems closely to your heart and head.

Affectionately yours,
Daddy

*"Unless I should accidentally meet you on the street,
I doubt if I shall ever see you again."*

Joan chose her mother. Four months later, her father responded.

[Glen Ellen]
February 24, 1914

Dear Joan:—

In reply to yours of February 10th, 1914. I have just got back from the East, and am taking hold of my business. Please find herewith check for the $4.50, according to account presented by you. When I tell you that this leaves me a balance in the bank of $3.46, you will understand how thin the ice is upon which I am skating.

I note by your letter that you have been charging schoolbooks in my account at Smith's. Never again do a thing like this. Never be guilty of charging to anybody's account when you have not received permission from that person to charge to their account. I shall make a point of sending you the money for your schoolbooks when you write to me for same, or, if I have not the money, of giving you permission to charge to my account. If I am away, and if Mrs. Eliza Shepard has not the money, she may also give you permission to charge to my account. Under no other circumstances except those of permission, may you in the future charge anything to any account of mine anywhere. This is only clean, straight, simple business, Joan.

Now I have what most persons would deem a difficult letter to write; but I have always found that by being frank and true, no thing is difficult to say. All one has to say is all that he feels or thinks.

Let me tell you a little something about myself: All my life has been marked by what, in lack of any other term, I must call "disgust." When I grow tired or disinterested in anything, I experience a disgust which settles for me that thing forever. I turn the page down there and then. When a colt on the ranch, early in its training, shows that it is a kicker or a bucker or a bolter or a balker, I try patiently and for a long time to remove, by my training, such deleterious traits; and then at the end of a long time if I find that these vicious traits continue, suddenly there comes to me a disgust, and I say Let the colt go. Kill it, sell it, give it away. So far as I'm concerned I am finished with the colt. So it has been with all things in my whole life from the very first time that I can remember anything of myself. I have been infatuated with many things, I have worked through many things, have become disgusted with those many things, and have turned down the pages forever and irrevocably on those many things. Please believe me—I am not stating to you my strength, but my weakness. These colossal disgusts that compel me to turn down pages are weaknesses of mine, and I know them; but they are there. They are part of me. I am so made.

Years ago I warned your mother that if I were denied the opportunity of forming you, sooner or later I would grow disinterested in you, I would develop a disgust, and that I would turn down the page. Of course, your mother, who is deaf to all things spiritual, and appreciative, and understanding, smiled to herself and discounted what I told her. Your mother today understands me no more than she has ever understood me—which is no understanding at all.

Now, do not make the mistake of thinking that I am now running away from all filial duties and responsibilities. I am not. I shall take care of you; I shall take care of Baby B., I shall take care of your mother. I shall take care of the three of you. You shall have food and shelter always. But, unfortunately, I have turned the page down, and I shall no longer be interested in the three of you.

I do not imagine that I shall ever care to send you to the University of California, unless you should develop some tremendous desire to do specific things in the world that only a course in the University of California will fit you for. I certainly shall never send you to the University of California merely in recognition of the bourgeois valuation put upon the University pigskin.

I should like to see you marry for love when you grow up. That way lies the best and sweetest of human happiness. On the other hand, if you want a career instead, I'll help you to pursue whatever career you elect. When you were small, I fought for years the idea of your going on the stage. I now withdraw my opposition. If you desire the stage with its consequent (from my point of view) falseness, artificiality, sterility and unhappiness, why go ahead, and I will do what I can to help you to it.

But please, please remember that in whatever you do from now on, I am uninterested. I desire to know neither your failures nor your successes; wherefore please no more tell me of your markings in High School, and no longer send me your compositions.

When you want money, within reason, I shall send it to you if I have it. Under any and all circumstances, so long as I live, you shall receive from me food in your stomach, a roof that does not leak, warm blankets, and clothing to cover you.

A year from now I expect to have a little money. At the present moment, if I died, I should die One hundred thousand dollars in debt. Therefore, a year from now I may be more easy with you in money matters than I am capable of being now.

I should like to say a few words further about the pages I turn down because of the disgusts that come upon me. I was ever a lover of fatherhood. I loved fatherhood over love of woman, I have been jealous of my seed, and I have never wantonly scattered my seed. I gave you well (we'll say my share at least) a good body and a good brain. I had a father's fondest love and hope for you. But you know, in bringing up colts, colts may be brought up good and bad, all according to the horseman who brings up the colts. You were a colt. Time and fate and mischance, and a stupid mother, prevented me from having a guiding hand in your upbringing. I waited until you, who can dramatize "Sohrab and Rustum," could say for yourself what you wanted. Alas, as the colt, you were already ruined by your trainer. You were lied to, you were cheated. I am sorry; it was not

your fault. But when the time came for you to decide (not absolutely between your mother and me)—to decide whether or not I might have a little hand in showing and training you to your paces in the big world, you
were already so ruined by your trainer, that you declined. It's not your
fault. You were trained. It is not your mother's fault—she was born stupid,
stupid she will live, and stupid she will die. It was nobody's fault—except
God's fault, if you believe in God. It is a sad mischance, that is all. In connection therewith I can only quote to you Kipling's "Toolungala Stock-
yard Chorus":

> *"And some are sulky, while some will plunge.*
> (So ho! Steady! Stand still, you!)
> *Some you must be gentle, and some you must lunge.*
> (There! There! Who wants to kill you?)
> *Some—there are losses in every trade—*
> *Will break their hearts ere bitted and made,*
> *Will fight like fiends as the rope cuts hard,*
> *And die dumb-mad in the breaking yard."*

Whether or not you may die dumb-mad, I know not. I do know that
you have shown, up to the present time, only docility to your trainer. You
may cheat and fool your trainer, and be ruined by your trainer. I only think
that I know that you are too much of a diplomat to die over anything—
result of your reaction over your training, plus your inherent impulse to
avoid trouble, kick-up, and smashing of carts and harnesses.

You cannot realize all this letter. You may when you are older. Save it
for that time. But I have lost too many colts not to be philosophical in losing you. It might be thought that I am unfair to your youthfulness—yet
you dramatized "Sohrab and Rustum," and calmly state to me narrow-
minded, bourgeois prejudices (instilled into your mind by your mother),
such as: My present wife, my Love Woman, is all that is awful and horrible in that I do truly love her, and in that she does truly love me.

All my life I have been overcome by disgust, which has led me to turn
pages down, and those pages have been turned down forever. It is my
weakness, as I said before. Unless I should accidentally meet you on the
street, I doubt if I shall ever see you again. If you should be dying, and
should ask for me at your bedside, I should surely come; on the other
hand, if I were dying I should not care to have you at my bedside. A ruined
colt is a ruined colt, and I do not like ruined colts.

Please let me know that you have read this letter in its entirety. You will not understand it entirely. Not for years, and perhaps never, will you understand. But, being a colt breaker, I realize that a colt is ruined by poor training, even though the colt never so realizes.

Whenever you want money, within reason, for clothes, books, spending, etc., write me for it, and if I have it at the time, I shall send it to you.

Jack London

By the time of his death, less than three years later, Jack London had forgiven his daughter.

JOHN J. PERSHING TO F. WARREN PERSHING

"As the boy, so is the man."

General Pershing felt that, after a year at Phillips Exeter Academy in New Hampshire, his son had "gotten in with a crowd of triflers, loafers, very much to the detriment of his studies," so he sent the boy to far-off Switzerland. Warren's academic results at the Swiss Institut Carnal were not much better. Here the recently retired sixty-four-year-old general aboard the USS Utah on a South American goodwill mission writes to his fifteen-year-old son.

At Sea
On board U.S.S. "Utah,"
February 28, 1925.

IMPORTANT
READ THIS LETTER OVER SEVERAL TIMES AND PUT IT AWAY
AND READ IT OVER AGAIN AT FREQUENT INTERVALS.

My dear Warren:
Your letter of January 11th reached me the other day at Caracas, so it was nearly two months in reaching me, a long time to await news of you.

We have now but one more stop to make and that is in Cuba. We arrive at Guantanamo tomorrow, go to Santiago the next day, reaching Havana on March 3rd. I anticipate a rather busy program during the next few days and shall be quite delighted when it is all over.

It will be necessary for me to remain for a week or so in Washington, after which I want to go out to Lincoln for a week or two, and shall then decide what to do for the summer and thereafter, at least while you are in school abroad. It is rather difficult to forecast just what the decision will be, but of course you know how much I wish to be near you, as far as possible shall arrange my affairs to that end.

I am very glad you liked the Christmas presents and that you had a good time during the holidays. I note that your Tuxedo has arrived and that you have already had occasion to wear it.

In your letter you did not say anything about your studies, which is very surprising and indicates that you have not been doing very well, not nearly as well as you are capable of doing. In the same mail with your letter came one from Monsieur Carnal giving your marks for December, and I was very much surprised and altogether disappointed to see how badly you are doing in Latin, and with the exception of English none of your marks are up to what I had reasonably expected they would be.

I wrote you a letter about your studies some time ago when your October marks were not satisfactory, but possibly you had not received that particular letter or, of course, you would have undertook to do better.

Now, Warren, there is only one conclusion that I can reach in this matter, and that is that you are again loafing your time away. It seems to be a repetition of last year at Exeter. What can you be thinking about to allow yourself to drop back into these slothful, indolent habits? What can you expect to amount to if at your age you do not take your work seriously? Remember that you are creating an impression for good or bad upon everybody that knows you, and the impression so far is one that is not very flattering. As the boy, so is the man. If you are lazy and no-account in your school work, you will be lazy and no-account after you grow up.

This seems to settle the question of your going to West Point. I thought that you were up against a rather hard proposition last year at Exeter and was inclined to make excuses for you, but I am not inclined nor do I make any excuses for you this year at Carnal. You have the brains; you have the background, and you have the duty, all of which should stimulate you to the greatest kind of effort from now on. Otherwise, it may as well be determined now as at any future time you cannot go to West Point. I make this as a positive statement because it would only mean your failure and dismissal from that institution, which would be a disgrace to us all, and I am not willing to take a chance on it based on the showing you are making.

You are too much inclined to play and to trifle your time away during study hours. Your mark on Application was only 8, which was only four-fifths of what it ought to be. With an Application of 10 and some extra time taken from your recreation hours, you can undoubtedly equal any student in the institution. For heaven's sake do not allow yourself to be led away by trifling boys and establish in Carnal Institut, as you have already established at Exeter, a reputation for general worthlessness.

Warren, this is a very serious matter, although you do not seem to take it so. It simply means that you will not be prepared to meet the problems of life, either through a desire to achieve or through preparation in school. At West Point, of course, discipline is very rigid and you will be required to study if you would hold any sort of standing. Now you know what discipline is, because you have had it. Warren, why can you not discipline yourself? Please imagine yourself as your own boss, as arbiter of your own fate, as responsible for your own success, and rule yourself with an iron hand. This is the only way that you will ever amount to a hill of beans.

What I am saying is very, very serious and should be taken deeply to heart. Please read this letter a number of times and see if you cannot take hold of yourself and make yourself do the things that you know you ought to do. Whatever resolutions you make you should follow up and not allow yourself to be led astray like a weakling by every wind that blows and every worthless boy who wants you to neglect your work. You are a man and must take a man's attitude in this matter. It is your life work you are now doing.

Remember that you will be left nothing in this world in all probability, and that you are liable to be thrown at any time on your own resources and be compelled to make your own living. There is no assurance whatever that you will ever fall heir to a dot, and anyway you ought to have pride enough to prepare yourself to make your own living and take a stand among men of your generation.

You were practically dismissed last year from Exeter, and I suppose that that will be your fate this year. Perhaps Mr. Carnal will likely say that he does not think you are studious enough to go on further. Think of what this will mean to me. Think of the disgrace that I have already suffered and that I would more than ever suffer with such an outcome as this. Mr. Carnal told me that if boys did not do well that they did not want them, and that is so with everybody. If men are not worthwhile, people do not want them. If you have not a reputation for doing things honestly, faithfully, and industriously, people do not want you.

What I have said above, Warren, is entirely for your own good, as I see it, from the standpoint of a father who is interested in the future of his son. Don't be a quitter; don't be a failure.

Yours affectionately,

Warren Pershing never went to West Point. Instead, he graduated from Yale University and was named Most Likely to Succeed by his class of 1931. He went on to found Pershing & Company, a Wall Street investment firm, and until General Pershing's last days, Warren was his father's greatest source of pleasure.

Eugene O'Neill to Shane O'Neill

"But if you show no friendship toward me, if you prove by your actions you are indifferent whether I live or die, except when you want something from me, then you must admit I would be a poor sap and sucker to waste my friendship on you, simply because you happen to be my son."

At the end of 1936, having just won the Nobel Prize, forty-nine-year-old Eugene O'Neill was admitted to the hospital with acute appendicitis and nearly died from complications. He remained hospitalized for months, battling depression all the while. From his two younger children, twelve-year-old Oona and eighteen-year-old Shane, he heard not a word.

Below is Eugene O'Neill's bitter first letter to Shane following the illness.

(Shane later convinced O'Neill that both he and Oona had written during his struggle, but that the correspondence never reached their father. Apparently, and for reasons unknown, O'Neill's third wife, Carlotta, seized and destroyed the children's letters while O'Neill was in the hospital.)

[Fall 1937]

Dear Shane:

Your letter arrived a few days ago. Yes, I received the letter you sent to Sea Island last spring. I did not answer it because I was sore at you. And I still am sore—and with good reason. You may not remember it but for nearly three months last winter I was in a hospital seriously ill and during all that time I did not receive one damned line from either you or Oona. You can't have the excuse that you did not know. The news of my illness was sent out by the Associated Press, United Press, etc. to papers all over the country. So, later on, was the fact that the Nobel Prize medal had to be presented to me in the hospital at Oakland. I received letters and wires of sympathy from all over, even from strangers. From my own children— except Eugene—nothing. And yet you knew, even if you didn't get the Oakland address from the papers, that you could always reach me care of Harry Weinberger.

Now if you think that is any way to act, or that I am going to stand for your acting like that and still feel any affection for you, you are badly mistaken. Oona has some excuse. She is still only a kid. But you are old enough to be responsible for your actions—or lack of them—and I hold you responsible. I expect the same sort of respect and consideration from you that I received from Eugene when he was your age. If you give it, there is no reason why the relationship between you and me should not develop into as fine a one as that between Eugene and me has been for years and still is. Quite outside of our being father and son, Eugene and I are friends, as man to man, which is a thing few fathers and sons manage to achieve. And that's what I want to be to you—a friend. But if you show no friendship toward me, if you prove by your actions you are indifferent whether I live or die, except when you want something from me, then you must admit I would be a poor sap and sucker to waste my friendship on you, simply because you happen to be my son.

I am giving you this straight from the shoulder because it is time you and I came to a frank understanding. It is time you realize that in this life you are going to get from others exactly the same treatment you give to others. If you take me for granted, and think you can treat me as no friend of mine would dare to treat me without losing my friendship forever, why then I warn you you must be prepared to lose my friendship forever, too.

So think it over. It is up to you. If you want to be my son more than in name, you will have to act with a little more decent consideration and gratitude—not to add, respect. It isn't difficult, you know. Eugene has done it without breaking his back. All you have to do is get it in your head that you can't expect something for nothing, even from fathers.

Well, that's that. If you are the boy I still hope you are, despite evidence to the contrary, then this letter should make you think, and so much good will come of it for us both. If you are not—well, then it's just too bad.

Carlotta is glad you liked the Japanese robe. And we are both happy that you are so pleased with the new school. It sounds grand. And it's your luck to be away from that damned hookworm Florida joint. That country, with its rotten debilitating climate did more than anything else to wreck my health and lead to the long stretch of hospital and illness I went through last winter and spring. I am feeling fine again now and will be able to start hard work again, I hope, by the first of next year—or when we move into the new home we are building in the San Ramon Valley (near Oakland) which will be finished sometime in January. At present, we are living in a small rented house. I like California immensely. Carlotta joins in love to you.

F. SCOTT FITZGERALD TO
FRANCES SCOTT "SCOTTIE" FITZGERALD

"I never wanted to see again in this world women who were brought up as idlers."

In July 1938 F. Scott Fitzgerald was forty-one years old. Five years had passed since his last novel was published and he was having trouble financially, so he took a job writing screenplays in Hollywood. With his wife, Zelda, institutionalized for schizophrenia, he felt the responsibility of raising Scottie was his alone. The following letter was written to sixteen-year-old Scottie after a series of episodes of bad behavior, including her expulsion from the Ethel Walker School, a Connecticut boarding school, for sneaking away from campus to hitchhike to Yale. Less than two years later Fitzgerald was dead from a heart attack following years of heavy drinking.

July 7th, 1938

Dearest Scottie:

I don't think I will be writing letters many more years and I wish you would read this letter twice—bitter as it may seem. You will reject it now, but at a later period some of it may come back to you as truth. When I'm talking to you, you think of me as an older person, an "authority," and when I speak of my own youth what I say becomes unreal to you—for the young can't believe in the youth of their fathers. But perhaps this little bit will be understandable if I put it in writing.

When I was your age I lived with a great dream. The dream grew and

I learned how to speak of it and make people listen. Then the dream divided and one day when I decided to marry your mother after all, even though I knew she was spoiled and meant no good to me. I was sorry immediately I had married her, but being patient in those days, made the best of it and got to love her in another way. You came along and for a long time we made quite a lot of happiness out of our lives. But I was a man divided—she wanted me to work too much for *her* and not enough for my dream. She realized too late that work was dignity and the only dignity and tried to atone for it by working herself but it was too late and she broke and is broken forever.

It was too late for me to recoup the damage—I had spent most of my resources, spiritual and material, on her, but I struggled on for five years until my health collapsed, and all I cared about was drink and forgetting.

The mistake I made was in marrying her. We belonged to different worlds—she might have been happy with a kind simple man in a southern garden. She didn't have the strength for the big stage—sometimes she pretended, and she pretended beautifully, but she didn't have it. She was soft when she should have been hard, and hard when she should have been yielding. She never knew how to use her energy—she passed that failing on to you.

For a long time I hated *her* mother for giving her nothing in the line of good habit—nothing but "getting by" and conceit. I never wanted to see again in this world women who were brought up as idlers. And one of my chief desires in life was to keep you from being that kind of person, one who brings ruin to themselves and others. When you began to show disturbing signs at about fourteen, I comforted myself with the idea that you were too precocious socially and a strict school would fix things. But sometimes I think that idlers seem to be a special class for whom nothing can be planned, plead as one will with them—their only contribution to the human family is to warm a seat at the common table.

My reforming days are over, and if you are that way I don't want to change you. But I don't want to be upset by idlers inside my family or out. I want my energy and my earnings for people who talk my language.

I have begun to fear that you don't. You don't realize that what I am doing here is the last tired effort of a man who once did something finer and better. There is not enough energy, or call it money, to carry anyone who is dead weight and I am angry and resentful in my soul when I feel that I am doing this. People like Rosalind and your mother must be carried because their illness makes them useless. But it is a different story that *you* have spent two years doing no useful work at all, improving neither your body nor your mind, but only writing reams and reams of dreary letters to dreary people, with no possible object except obtaining invitations which you could not accept. Those letters go on, even in your sleep, so that I know your whole trip now is one long waiting for the post. It is like an old gossip who cannot still her tongue.

You have reached the age when one is of interest to an adult only insofar as one seems to have a future. The mind of a little child is fascinating, for it looks at old things with new eyes—but at about twelve this changes. The adolescent offers nothing, can do nothing, say nothing that the adult cannot do better. Living with you in Baltimore—(and you have told Harold that I alternated between strictness and neglect, by which I suppose you mean the times I was so inconsiderate as to have T.B., or to retire into myself to write, for I had little social life apart from you)—represented a rather too domestic duty forced on me by your mother's illness. But I endured your Top Hats and Telephones until the day you snubbed me at dancing school; less willingly after that. There began to be an unsympathetic side to you that alienated first Mrs. Owens, then your teachers at Bryn Mawr. The line of those who felt it runs pretty close to you—adults who saw you every day. Among them you have made *scarcely a single close friend, with all your mastery of exterior arts of friendliness.* All of them have loved you, as I do, but all of them have had reservations, and important ones: they have felt that something in you wasn't willing to pull your weight, to do your part—for more than an hour.

This last year was a succession of information beginning as far back as December that you were being unfair to me, more frankly that you were cheating. The misfortune about your standing in your class, the failure to tutor at the Obers at Christmas, the unwillingness to help with your mother at Easter in golf or tennis, then the dingy outbreak in the infirmary at the people who were "on to you," who knew you had none of the scholar in you but lived in a babyish dream—of the dance favors of a provincial school. Finally the catastrophe which, as far as I am able to determine, had no effect except to scare you because you knew I wouldn't maintain you in the East without some purpose or reason.

If you did not have a charm and companionability, such a blow might have chastened you, but unlike my Uncle Phil you will always be able to find companions who will reassure you of your importance even though your accomplishment is a goose-egg. To the last day of his life Phil was a happy man, though he loafed always and dissipated a quarter of a million of his own and his sister's money and left his wife in poverty and his son as you saw him. He had charm—great charm. He never liked me after I was grown, because once he lost his charm in front of me and I kicked his fat backside. Your charm must have not been in evidence on the day Mrs. Perry Smith figuratively did the same to you.

All this was the long preparation for the despair I experienced ten days ago. That you did or did not know how I felt about Baltimore, that you thought I'd approve of your meeting a boy and driving back with him unchaperoned to New York by night, that you *honestly* thought I would have permitted that—well, tell it to Harold, who seems to be more gullible.

The clerk from the Garden of Allah woke me up with the telegram in which I mistook *Simmons* for *Finney* and I called the *Finneys*—to find them gone. The result was entirely a situation of your own making—if you had any real regret about the Walker episode you'd have respected my wishes for a single week.

To sum up: what you have done to please me or make me proud is practically negligible since the time you made yourself a good diver at camp (and now you are softer than you have ever been.) In your career as a "wild society girl," vintage 1925, I'm not interested. I don't want any of it—it would bore me, like dining with the Ritz Brothers. When I do not feel you are "going somewhere," your company tends to depress me for the silly waste and triviality involved. On the other hand, when occasionally I see signs of life and intention in you, there is no company in the world I prefer. For there is no doubt you have something in your belly, some real gusto for life—a real dream of your own—and my idea was to wed it to something solid before it was too late—as it was too late for your mother to learn anything when she got around to it. Once when you spoke French as a child it was enchanting with your odd bits of knowledge—now your conversation is as commonplace as if you'd spent the last two years in the Corn Hollow High School—what you saw in *Life* and read in *Sexy Romances*.

I shall come East in September to meet your boat—but this letter is a declaration that I am no longer interested in your promissory notes but only in what I see. I love you always but I am only interested by people who think and work as I do and it isn't likely that *I* shall change at my age. Whether you will—or want to—remains to be seen.

Daddy

P.S. If you keep the diary, please don't let it be the dry stuff I could buy in a ten-franc guide book. I'm not interested in dates and places, even the

Battle of New Orleans, unless you have some unusual reaction to them. Don't try to be witty in the writing, unless it's natural—just true and real.

P.P.S. Will you please read this letter a second time—I wrote it over twice.

ELEANOR ROOSEVELT TO JAMES ROOSEVELT

"This is the kind of high-handed, pompous action which loosens family ties . . ."

Likely the most influential woman of the twentieth century, Eleanor Roosevelt was a first lady like no other. She was kind, independent, tough, self-confident, and a sympathetic and effective advocate for those with no voice. After her husband's death in 1945, she remained an active force both nationally and internationally as a columnist and a delegate to the young United Nations. During these years she became known as the First Lady of the World.

As the mother of five and a steadfast and devoted friend, she loved a house to be filled with family and comrades. "The people I love mean more to me than all the public things . . ." she wrote. She held fast to family traditions, admonished her children "never to say anything derogatory about each other," and nothing depressed her emotions more than the troubles of her children, or quarrels among them.

In September 1949, James Roosevelt and his wife, Rommie, sent out a letter asking to be taken off Christmas gift lists as they felt the holiday spirit could "better be fulfilled in other ways." Mrs. Roosevelt was incensed. Here the United States delegate to the United Nations, Eleanor Roosevelt, responds sharply to her eldest son, a forty-two-year-old man preparing to make a run for the governorship of California.

Sept. 22, 1949

Dearest Jimmy:

I am deeply hurt by your letter of the 16th and also frankly I was very angry. Through all the years Christmas at home was a joy to me and I hoped I had given to you all the feeling that it was a time for thinking of others even if we were far apart. It is never a burden to me. If you and

Rommie find the expense too great or the burden too great of thinking beyond each other and the children, I shall accept your decision. In fact now no presents from you would be acceptable but I think it strange that you want to deprive me and others of the pleasure of thinking and showing our thought of you and your children in a tangible way.

This is the kind of high-handed, pompous action which loosens family ties and does not bind them closer. When I was young and could only give little, I made things for family and friends but I gave and if I leave you and yours out of my Christmas thought and giving then I don't want to talk to you on Christmas Day.

Your letter does not sound like you. How could you have dictated it?

Also, how could you have sent it without mention of Sis when you know my deep anxiety and I hope are sharing it.

I have decided to send Rommie a copy of this letter. One must do things for people one loves or love dies and you are moving in the direction of narrowing your affections, one has less to give that way.

> My love to you, dear
> Mother

In November Jimmy Roosevelt acquiesced and asked the family to "forget we ever mentioned the subject."

Berlin, July 25, 1945.

THE WHITE HOUSE
WASHINGTON

Dear Margie:— We went to the British
dinner I night before last—and was _it_ a
show piece too! Mr. Byrnes and I walked
from the Berlin White House (it's still yellow
trimmed in dirty red—dirty yellow too) to Mr.
Churchill's place about three blocks down
the street or up (it's level so either one
is all right.) Churchill had phoned Gen.
Vaughan, my _chief of protocol_, that he would
greatly, very greatly appreciate it if I
would arrive a few minutes late as
I happened to be the senior guest and Uncle
Joe should realize it. Well we arrived a
directed and were recieved by the P. M. and
his nice daughter, Mary. I had to shake hands
with Marshall, now Generalissimo Stalin, Genera

The first page of President Harry Truman's letter
from Potsdam to his daughter Margaret

A Place in Time

GEORGE WASHINGTON TO
JOHN "JACK" PARKE CUSTIS

*"I have been called upon by unanimous voice
of the Colonies to take the command of the
Continental Army . . ."*

On June 16, 1775, at the Second Continental Congress, when George Washington accepted the appointment to command the Continental Army, it was not with false modesty that he said, "I do not think myself equal to the Command I am honored with." He didn't think he was up to the extraordinary task, but he also knew he was the best man for the job. He was forty-three years old, tall, dignified, and both patient and calm by nature. As the master of an eight-thousand-acre plantation he was accustomed to commanding a large enterprise and to making the most of what resources were available to him. In 1775 he was still remembered for his heroism twenty years before in the French and Indian War, but Washington's military experience was comparatively small and he plainly knew that the task now before him was enormous. Armed citizens were fighting the British in Massachusetts, but a Continental Army, as such, did not exist. There were few supplies, no staff, little powder, no money, and it was now Washington's duty to take charge of it all—and fight the most formidable army in the world.

It was several days before he could bring himself to write home to tell of his new position. From Philadelphia on June 19, he wrote three letters, one to his wife, Martha; one to his brother, John Augustine; and one to his twenty-one-year-old stepson, John Parke Custis. Unbeknownst to those in Philadelphia, the first major battle of the American Revolution had just been fought at Bunker Hill and by the twenty-third of June General Washington was on his way to Cambridge, Massachusetts, to take command.

Philadelphia June 19th 1775.

Dear Jack,

I have been called upon by unanimous voice of the Colonies to take the command of the Continental Army—It was an honour I neither sought after, or was by any means fond of accepting, from a consciousness of my own inexperience, and inability to discharge the duties of so important a Trust. However, as the partiality of the Congress have placed me in this distinguished point of view, I can make them no other return but what will flow from close attention, and an upright Intention. For the rest I can say nothing—my great concern on this occasion, is the thoughts of leaving your Mother under the uneasiness which I know this affair will throw her into; I therefore hope, expect, & indeed have no doubt, of your using every means in your power to keep up her Spirits, by doing everything in your power, to promote her quiet—I have I must confess very uneasy feelings on her acct, but as it has been a kind of unavoidable necessity which has led me into this appointment, I shall more readily hope, that success will attend it, & crown our Meetings with happiness.

At any time, I hope it is unnecessary for me to say, that I am always pleased with yours & Nelly's abidance at Mount Vernon, much less upon this occasion, when I think it absolutely necessary for the peace & satisfaction of your Mother; a consideration which I have no doubt will have due weight with you both, & require no arguments to inforce.

As the publick Gazettes will convey every article of Intelligence that I could communicate in this Letter, I shall not repeat them, but with love to Nelly, & sincere regard for yourself I remain Yr Most Affecte

Go: Washington

P.S. Since writing the foregoing I have receiv'd your Letter of the 15th Instt—I am obliged to you for the Intelligence therein containd—and am glad you directed about the Tobacco, for I had really forgot it. You must now take upon yourself the entire management of your own Estate, it will no longer be in my power to assist you, nor is there any occasion for it as you have never discover'd a disposition to put it to a bad use.

During the war Jack Parke Custis and his wife, Nelly, continued to reside at their own Virginia home, but visited Mount Vernon often. Martha Washington periodically joined her husband at Continental Army headquarters. From 1764 to 1785 Mount Vernon was managed by the general's cousin, Lund Washington.

BENJAMIN FRANKLIN TO
WILLIAM FRANKLIN

*". . . nothing has ever hurt me so much and affected
me with such keen Sensations, as to find myself
deserted in my old Age by my only Son; and not
only deserted, but to find him taking up Arms
against me, in a Cause, wherein my good Fame,
Fortune and Life were all at Stake."*

Benjamin Franklin's oldest child, William, was illegitimate, but was raised in his father's household. William was at his father's side assisting with the kite experiment that led to the invention of the lightning rod, and he was the only relative to accompany Benjamin Franklin to London while he served as the American agent to Great Britain. During his years in London, Benjamin Franklin grew to hold genuine affection for England, and in this he was joined by William.

In 1762 King George III appointed thirty-year-old William Franklin to be the Royal Governor of New Jersey and when the young man took the oath of office, Benjamin Franklin was delighted. But as the revolution mounted and the father's commitment to the people of America remained steadfast, a rift developed between them over William's devotion to the crown of England. Their divided loyalties caused an estrangement that lasted for nearly ten years.

In 1784, William made the first overture, writing to his father that he wished to "revive that affectionate intercourse and connexion which till the commencement of the late troubles had been the pride and happiness of my life." He acknowledged that his actions during the war had disappointed his father, yet he did not explicitly apologize for remaining loyal to Great Britian. The following letter is Benjamin Franklin's reply, written from France where he was America's Minister Plenipotentiary.

Passy, Aug. 16, 1784.

Dear Son,

I received your Letter of the 22d past, and am glad to find that you desire to revive the affectionate Intercourse, that formerly existed between us. It will be very agreeable to me; indeed nothing has ever hurt me so much and affected me with such keen Sensations, as to find myself deserted in my old Age by my only Son; and not only deserted, but to find him taking up Arms against me, in a Cause, wherein my good Fame, Fortune and Life were all at Stake. You conceived, you say, that your Duty to your King and Regard for your Country requir'd this. I ought not to blame you for differing in Sentiment with me in Public Affairs. We are Men, all subject to Errors. Our Opinions are not in our own Power; they are form'd and govern'd much by Circumstances, that are often as inexplicable as they are irresistible. Your Situation was such that few would have censured your remaining Neuter, *tho' there are Natural Duties which precede political ones, and cannot be extinguish'd by them.*

This is a disagreable Subject. I drop it. And we will endeavour, as you propose mutually to forget what has happened relating to it, as well as we can. I send your Son over to pay his Duty to you. You will find him much improv'd. He is greatly esteem'd and belov'd in this Country, and will make his Way anywhere. It is my Desire, that he should study the Law, as a necessary Part of Knowledge for a public Man, and profitable if he should have occasion to practise it. I would have you therefore put into his hands those Law-books you have, viz. Blackstone, Coke, Bacon, Viner, & c. He will inform you, that he received the Letter sent him by Mr. Galloway, and the Paper it enclosed, safe.

On my leaving America, I deposited with that Friend for you, a Chest of Papers, among which was a Manuscript of nine or ten Volumes, relating to Manufactures, Agriculture, Commerce, Finance, etc., which cost me in England about 70 Guineas; eight Quire Books, containing the Rough Drafts of all my Letters while I liv'd in London. These are missing. I hope you have got them, if not, they are lost. Mr. Vaughan has publish'd in London a Volume of what he calls my Political Works. He proposes a second Edition; but, as the first was very incompleat, and you had many Things that were omitted, (for I used to send you sometimes the Rough Drafts, and sometimes the printed Pieces I wrote in London,) I have directed him to apply to you for what may be in your Power to furnish him with, or to delay his Publication till I can be at home again, if that may ever happen.

I did intend returning this year; but the Congress, instead of giving me Leave to do so, have sent me another Commission, which will keep me here at least a Year longer; and perhaps I may then be too old and feeble to bear the Voyage. I am here among a People that love and respect me, a most amiable Nation to live with; and perhaps I may conclude to die among them; for my Friends in America are dying off, one after another, and I have been so long abroad, that I should now be almost a Stranger in my own Country.

I shall be glad to see you when convenient, but would not have you come here at present. You may confide to your son the Family Affairs you wished to confer upon with me, for he is discreet. And I trust, that you will prudently avoid introducing him to Company, that it may be improper for him to be seen with. I shall hear from you by him and any letters to me afterward, will come safe under Cover directed to Mr. Ferdinand Grand, Banker at Paris. Wishing you Health, and more Happiness than it seems you have lately experienced, I remain your affectionate father,

B. Franklin.

Herman Melville to Malcolm Melville

". . . the sailors who held the plank tipped it up, and immediately the body slipped into the stormy ocean . . ."

In late May of 1860, in Boston Harbor, Herman Melville boarded the clipper ship Meteor *bound for a trip around the world. His younger brother, Thomas, was the captain; and he himself a passenger, aboard to regain his health and improve his outlook. Fortune had not been good to Melville. He was the author of the once-popular autobiographical adventure books* Typee *and* Omoo, *but his epic novel,* Moby-Dick, *had not been given the attention it deserved, and his subsequent work was savagely reviewed. He was forty-one years old and it now seemed he was unable to make a living at all. Encouraged by his family and financially supported by his understanding and generous father-in-law, Lemuel Shaw, Melville, seasick at first, departed New England leaving behind his wife and four children.*

He wrote that he was bringing along on the voyage "plenty of old periodicals—lazy reading for lazy latitudes," but he also carried with him volumes of poetry for serious study. He had begun, two years earlier, writing poetry in secret and before he sailed, he left with his brother Allan poems and explicit instructions for getting them published. He expected that a fresh volume of Poems *by Herman Melville would be waiting for him when he arrived in San Francisco.*

On September 1, 1860, headed north through the Pacific, Melville wrote to his eldest child, eleven-year-old Malcolm. He had been at sea for ninety-five days.

Pacific Ocean
(Off the coast of South America
On the Tropic of Capricorn)
Saturday September 1st 1860

My Dear Malcolm:

It is now three months exactly since the ship "Meteor" sailed from Boston—a quarter of a year. During this long period, she has been continually moving, and has only seen land on two days. I suppose you have followed out on the map (or my *globe* were better—so you get Mama to clean it off for you) the route from Boston to San Francisco. The distance, by the straight track, is about 16000 miles; but the ship will have sailed before she gets there nearer 18 or 20000 miles. So you see it is further than from the apple-tree to the big rock. When we crossed the Line in the Atlantic Ocean it was very warm; & we had warm weather for some weeks; but as we kept getting to the Southward it began to grow less warm, and then coolish, and cold and colder, till at last it was winter. I wore two flannel shirts, and big mittens & overcoat, and a great Russia cap, a very thick leather cap, so called by sailors. At last we came in sight of land all covered with snow—uninhabited land, where no one ever lived, and no one ever will live—it is so barren, cold and desolate. This was Staten Land—an island. Near it, is the big island of Terra del Fuego. We passed through between these islands, and had a good view of both. There are some "wild people" living on Terra del Fuego; but it being the depth of winter there, I suppose they kept in their caves. At any rate we saw none of them. The next day we were off Cape Horn, the Southernmost point of all America. Now it was very bad weather, and was dark at about three o'clock in the afternoon. The wind blew terribly. We had hailstorms, and snow and sleet, and often the spray froze as it touched the deck. The ship rolled, and sometimes took in so much water on the deck as to wash people off their legs. Several sailors were washed along the deck this way, and came near getting washed overboard. And this reminds me of a very sad thing that happened on the very morning we were off the Cape—I mean the very *pitch* of the Cape. —It was just about day-light; it was blowing a gale of wind, and Uncle Tom ordered the topsails (big sails) to be furled. Whilst the sailors were aloft on one of the yards, the ship rolled and plunged terribly; and it blew with sleet and hail, and was very cold & biting. Well, all at once, Uncle Tom saw something falling through the air, and then heard a thump, and then,—looking before him, saw a poor sailor lying dead on the deck. He had fallen from the yard, and was killed instantly.—His shipmates picked him up, and carried him under cover. By and by, when time could be spared, the sailmaker sewed up the body in a piece of sail-cloth, putting some iron balls—cannon balls—at the foot of it. And, when all was ready, the body was put on a plank and carried to the ship's side in the prescence of all hands. Then Uncle Tom, as Captain, read a prayer out of the prayer-book, and at a given word, the sailors who held the plank tipped it up, and immediately the body slipped into the stormy ocean, and we saw it no more.—Such is the way a poor sailor is buried at sea. This sailor's name was Ray. He had a friend among the crew; and they were both going to California, and thought of living there; but you see what happened.

We were in this stormy weather about forty or fifty days, dating from the beginning. But now at last we are in fine weather again, and the sun shines warm.

When he reached San Francisco, Melville discovered that his poems had been rejected for publication. Disappointed, he abandoned the voyage with Thomas and returned to his family in New York.

SAM HOUSTON TO SAM HOUSTON, JR.

"If Texas demands your services or your life, in her cause, stand by her."

Sam Houston never wanted his state to secede and in 1861, as the governor of Texas and a slaveholder, he stood alone as a Southern Unionist. Yet when the Texas legislature made it plain that secession was in fact the will of the people, Houston quietly relinquished the governor's office and told a supporter, "I have done all I could to keep her from seceding, and now if she won't go with me I'll have to turn and go with her." He had fought for the independence of Texas, led her as nation, maneuvered her into the Union, and served as her senator and governor: Sam Houston's loyalty to Texas never wavered.

Here he writes to the eldest of his eight children, Sam Houston, Jr., who at eighteen years old was eager to join the Confederate Army. Sam, Jr., did enlist the following year, was wounded at Shiloh, taken as prisoner by northern forces, and returned to Texas before the war's end and before his father's death. Sam Houston died with his family at his side at home in Huntsville in 1863. He was never to know the outcome of the war nor the fate of his beloved Texas.

Cedar Point, 23rd July, 1861

My Dear Son:

Supposing that on last night you had a fine wet time of it, and the benefit of a pleasant today for drill, I write to you as I can send it by Mr. Armstrong, who wishes to take Tom some shoes.

I am happy to tell you that we are all well, except Willie, who has a chill, but I hope that it will be the last; and Sally has been ill of fever, but today she is much better. Will be well I hope soon. Had my friend Dr. Smith been at home, I would have sent for him. Now a days Esculapius is transformed to Mars.

I had hoped, my dear son, that in retirement my mind would be engrossed, so far as I am concerned with the affairs of the times, in the cares of my Domestic circle and matters concerning my family alone, and that I could live in peace. In the train of events now transpiring, I think I perceive disasters to Texas. The men and arms are all leaving this quarter of the theatre in the great Drama, which is playing, and is to be played. I know not how much statesmanship Lincoln may have, or Generalship at his command, and therefore I would not be wise to Prophesy. But looking at matters as they seem to me, his wise course, I would say is, that Texas is his great point in which to make a lodgment and thereby make a diversion from the seat of war. Texas in his possession, and the Gulf is his with Fort Pickens as a convenient Point. The assault upon Texas will require two armies & weaken the army of Eastern operations. If Texas is attacked she must be in her present isolated condition. She can look for no aid from the Confederacy, and must either succumb or defend herself. Are our means sufficient to do this? What is her situation as has been represented by the newspapers? Has she arms, men, ammunition, in an emergency to defend herself? Arkansas is crying for help. Our frontier is again assailed by the Indians, and she will be left alone in her straits without means. Missouri must yield to the pressure by which she is surrounded. The States of Illinois, Iowa, Indiana, Minnesota, Nebraska, and Kansas must soon silence her, and then Arkansas without means, as she says, must be overrun, and then Texas must be the Ultimate Point in the campaign of subjugation and spoil. Under these circumstances, it is wise for her to send, unasked and at the instigation of "Major Marshall," her men and arms? That wretch has been a blotch on humanity and will be a scab on Texas. I am ready, as I have ever been, to die for my country, but to die without a hope of benefit by my death is not my wish. The well-being of my country is the salvation of my family; But to see it surrendered to Lincoln, as sheep in the shambles, is terrible to me.

I fear that within twenty days, or less, an assault will be made upon some part of our coast, and how are we prepared to repel it? Have we men? Will we have means? Our troops with leaders, have never been beaten, and with good ones, they will always be invincible. Will Major Marshall, McLeod, Sherman, or the gallant men made by the Convention, or the Committees of vigilance, save us in an hour of peril? Does anyone suppose that proclamations by a Clark will save the Country in the hour of her peril; yet no one else has power but those to whom I have referred! The fact that a park of flying artillery is on the vessel now in our harbor is proof that a landing is designed somewhere on the coast. The question arises: is it wise to send our men and arms at the instance of Major Marshall!

These matters, my son, I have written to you, and have to say in conclusion, if Texas did not require your services, and you wished to go elsewhere, why then all would be well, but as she will need your aid, your first allegiance is due to her and let nothing cause you in a moment of ardor to assume any obligation to any other power whatever, without my consent. If Texas demands your services or your life, in her cause, stand by her.

Houston is not, nor will be a favorite name in the Confederacy! Thus, you had best keep your duty and your hopes together, and when the Drill is over, come home. Your Dear Ma and all of us send best love to you and Martin. Give my regards to General Rogers, Colonel Daly, & Dr. Smith. When will you be home my son! Thy Devoted Father,

Sam Houston

RICHARD E. BYRD TO RICHARD E. BYRD

"I have named a big new land after mommie . . ."

In September 1928, Richard E. Byrd was preparing to depart on his immense exploratory expedition to Antarctica. He spent his last days at home in Boston filling his mind with impressions of his wife and four children, "snatching them like a glutton," he wrote. As he began his journey, filled with "heart-sinking doubt," he asked himself, "Why are you doing this?" His answer was found in a quota-

tion from the Norwegian explorer Fridtjof Nansen, "Man wants to know and when he does not want to know he ceases to be a man."

Plans for the expedition had been in the works for years. It was an enormous undertaking, privately funded with more than $500,000, and included four ships, sixty-five men, four airplanes, and 178 dogs. In the end, after nearly two years in the polar freeze, the expedition had made the first flight over the South Pole, photographed some 150,000 square miles of Antarctica, discovered two mountain ranges and a ten-thousand-foot peak, and claimed for the United States a vast new area that had never been seen before, Marie Byrd Land, named for the admiral's wife.

Here forty-year-old Byrd writes from Antarctica to eight-year-old "Dickie."

[February 22, 1929]

Dear Dickie—

I have named a big new land after mommie because mommie is the sweetest finest and nicest and best person in the world. Take good care of her and be awfully sweet to her while I'm away.

I love you my dear boy.

Daddy

Little America
Antarctica

LINCOLN STEFFENS TO PETE STEFFENS

". . . horses, pigs and sheep were frightened by us . . . while farmers looked up at us and automobiles halted to watch us as we zoomed along."

In 1931, journalist and reformer Lincoln Steffens was enjoying a renewed success at age sixty-five. He published his autobiography that year—during the hard times of the Great Depression—and it had become a major best seller. Delighted, Steffens wrote to his sister, "My humble lecture tour is developing into a triumph. Everybody seems to have read (and bought) my book and . . . most of them have an emotional sense of it."

Here, on tour for The Autobiography of Lincoln Steffens, *during the very early years of commercial aviation, the author writes with exhilaration and wonder to seven-year-old Pete, at home in Carmel, California.*

Plaza Hotel
San Antonio, Texas,
Dec. 9, 1931

Dear Pete,

I flew yesterday in one of those big passenger planes from Louisville to Memphis and I meant to fly farther to near here, but the rain and fog stopped all flights that day, so I came on by train. I'll tell you about it.

The plane I was to take was coming from Cincinnati, so I took a taxi and went to the airport in Louisville to meet it. There were some clouds out there but the weather man said we could fly, and when the big plane came swooping in and the other passengers got out, we were told to "all aboard." I ducked low to get in and took a seat on the right side, buckled the strap around me and settled down comfortably. My bag had been checked like on a train. I had a window to myself and there were eight other passengers. The pilots were two young men, about 20–24, who looked strong, confident, very competent. Both went up to their station, which is closed off, apart; they had the motors going already. With one glance around at us, one of them started us across the field; he paused, started the motors flying so fast you could not see them and we raced around the field, took off,—we were flying. The ground sank away as we lifted and turned to take our direction, and what surprised me was they did not seem to go fast. You could see by the way we passed trains and autos that we were going at great speed, but it did not seem fast. That is because, up there, you can see so far ahead objects, like hills, rivers and towns, that you seem to approach them slowly. We sailed along making a great, regular noise (the motors) but we moved evenly, steadily, and swung around heights very smoothly, bending way over. We were going fast, to Memphis, I thought. There was nothing to do for a long while. Some passengers read papers. I watched the country,—all marked up in farms,—blow by under us for perhaps two hours.

Then the motors slowed and we began to swoop down around in a circle. I saw a big town nearby and somebody said it was Nashville, Tenn., but I was surprised; and I was glad, too, when we came down on the landing field of an airport, a muddy field which we tore up badly. And I learned that it was a regular stop-off station. I darted into the rest-room, got a sandwich and a Coca-cola while some passengers got out and others were buying tickets. We did not stop long. Climbing in again, we raced through the mud, paused, set the motors going full power and so again up, but not so high this time. It was raining, the clouds hung low,—what they called a low ceiling,—and the pilot to see and keep his course had to stay near the ground.

Then we came to high hills,—almost mountains, and we ran into big pieces of fog. That drove the pilot down lower, and from then on we always followed a river or railroad that was going our way. Cars and horses, pigs and sheep were frightened by us,—so close,—and ran and kicked up, while farmers looked up at us and automobiles halted to watch us as we zoomed along. For now we seemed to be going fast, very fast. The boy pilots took turns and sometimes they were both out there together. A passenger I met afterward, one who had flown a lot, told me he was scared; and that the pilots were, of the fog. Anyway, it was 1 hour 50 minutes, this time, when we settled again to Memphis; as I was going out, I asked the pilot how long before we would go on. He shook his head and said: "Not today: we'll cancel this afternoon's flight." And they did. My ticket was to Dallas, Texas, where we were to arrive at 5:30 P.M. The agent bought me a railroad ticket and berth on the Pacific Missouri Railroad to here instead of to Dallas. And to make up, the agent took us to a hotel, gave us luncheon and a room to wait in till 7:15 that (yesterday) evening. I had a bath, a nap and came on last night this long, long journey down to San Antonio, which is in Texas near the Mexican border.

It is sunny here. I have to stay here and try to get over my bronchitis in time to speak here on Monday (today is Wednesday): to Houston on Tuesday: and then next Wednesday, I have to fly again from Houston to Amarillo so as to speak at Canon, Texas, at a college. But flying is good here: it is almost always clear, and usually sunny. After that, Pete, I'll be going home, stopping only for a day at Los Angeles. I can't name my date yet: I'll wire that to Anna later, but I think it will be about December 21 or 22: Carmel, and I'll be so glad.

Love to all: Betty Ann, Leslie, Pete, your teacher and the whole town.

Dad

Harry S. Truman to Margaret Truman

"Stalin and Churchill paid your pop a most high compliment by saying that my presiding had been the ablest they'd ever seen."

In July 1945 Harry Truman met with Winston Churchill and Joseph Stalin ("Uncle Joe") at the Potsdam Conference to discuss the future of postwar Europe and how best to bring an end to the continuing war with Japan. Before this trip to Germany, Truman had traveled to Europe just one other time—as a reserve officer in World War I. He had never been to college and he had been president of the United States for only three and a half months.

Here the sixty-one-year-old Harry Truman writes to his only child, twenty-one-year-old Margaret. The day before he wrote the letter, on the twenty-fourth of July, it had apparently been decided that, if everything went as expected, within weeks a new weapon, the atomic bomb, would be used against Japan.

Berlin, July 25, 1945

Dear Margie:

—We went to the British dinner night before last—and was *it* a show piece too! Mr. Byrnes and I walked from the Berlin White House (it's still yellow trimmed in a dirty red—dirty yellow too) to Mr. Churchill's place about three blocks down the street or up (it's level so either one is all right). Churchill had phoned Gen. Vaughan, my *chief* of protocol, that he would greatly, very greatly appreciate it if I would arrive a few minutes late as I happened to be the senior guest and Uncle Joe should realize it. Well we arrived as directed and were received by the P.M and his nice daughter, Mary. I had to shake hands with Marshall, now Generallisimo Stalin, General of the Army Antonov, Marshall Zhukov, Field Marshall Montgomery, Lord this & that and a lot more Ruskies and Limies, we went out to dinner. It was a very colorful affair, as you can see. I am enclosing you the menu and the list of guests. The menu is signed to you by J. Stalin & Winston Churchill and the guest list is signed by all the guests. Stalin and Churchill paid your pop a most high compliment by saying that my presiding had been the ablest they'd ever seen. That's what Adm. Leahy and all the rest say but it is hard to believe because I've had plenty of trouble.

Churchill said his crowd went home today to see how the vote in England came out. I am going to Frankfurt tomorrow and inspect some American divisions.

Friday we resume sessions and I believe we shall wind up Sunday so I should be out to sea on Tuesday and home by Sunday August 4th.

Had a telegram today saying Harry had safely landed at Washington Air Port. He should be home by the time this letter gets to you. I hope you and your mamma will be at the White House when I get back to Washington. That old barn is terribly lonely for me alone. Especially since I'm so hemmed in.

Kiss Mamma & lots for you

XXXXXXXXXXXX Dad

Rosetta Douglass

Woodrow Wilson (center) and family (Jessie second from left)

Loss

JOHN QUINCY ADAMS TO JOHN ADAMS

*"May it be your lot in life to enjoy the society even
of a few spirits, so nearly approaching
to perfection as hers . . ."*

Upon reading heartbreaking news in a letter from his fifteen-year-old son, Secretary of State Adams immediately left his Washington office and went home. He
had just learned that his mother, Abigail Adams, at seventy-four years old had died
in her bedroom in Quincy, Massachusetts, on October 28 of typhoid fever. John
Quincy Adams adored and revered his mother, and he appreciated, too, that without her steadfast, intelligent, and "affectionate participation and cheering encouragement," his father, John Adams, could not have endured and accomplished all he
had. "There is not a virtue that can abide in the female heart but it was the orna-
ment of hers," John Quincy wrote in his diary.

To his second son, John, who was in school in Massachusetts, he wrote the following letter. The loss was particularly profound for young John and his brother
George, as the elder Adamses, Abigail and John, had cared for the boys entirely for
nearly six years, from 1809 to 1815, while their parents, John Quincy and Louisa
Catherine, were serving the United States government in Russia.

Washington 2 November 1818

My dear Son:

Your letter of the 28th of last month, has this day brought me the most distressing intelligence that I ever received, yet my dear John, if there was any thing that could soften its bitterness, it was that it should first come from a beloved and affectionate hand. Such it was coming from yours, and I thank you, for the kind and filial attention with which you immediately communicated the event, by which it has pleased God to remove my ever blessed Mother to a better world. I thank you too for the same attention, with which you repeatedly wrote to your mother, during the illness of mine, and which apprised us of her real situation, when we were too ready to trust in the hopes, which other friends fondly cherished by listening to their ardent wishes. I pray you to return your mothers and my most affectionate and grateful thanks to Miss Harriet Welsh both for her kind and unwearied attendance on my mother in her illness, and for the assiduous and active friendship with which she wrote from time to time, while a lingering hope was left, to keep it alive in our breasts.

You have lost, my dear son, one of the kindest, and most precious of parents, for such she truly was to you, and to all my children. If you live, as I hope and pray you may, to an age as advanced as hers, you will never meet on earth one, to whom you will owe deeper obligations, or who will be to you a more faithful and affectionate friend. May it be your lot in life to enjoy the society even of a few spirits, so nearly approaching to perfection as hers, and above all, my son, may he who is the supreme God, inspire and guide your conduct through your earthly career, so that at the final scene, you may surrender your spirit to its creator as unsullied as was hers. I have no greater blessing to bestow. Be it yours, and be it that of your brothers!

From your affectionate father

John Quincy Adams

Daniel Webster to Charles Webster

"But ah! thy little day is done,—"

Just before his third birthday, Charles Webster died at home after a two-week battle with "lung fever." At the time of the little boy's death, his father, Congressman Daniel Webster, was departing from Monticello after a meeting with eighty-one-year-old Thomas Jefferson. Upon hearing the news, Webster, having already endured the loss of a daughter to tuberculosis, now lamented being absent at the time of his son's death. He wrote this short poem to his dead son in an effort to console his grief-stricken wife.

[c. January 1, 1825]

My son, thou wast my hearts delight
Thy morn of life was gay & cheery:
That morn has rushed to sudden night.
Thy fathers house is sad & dreary

I held thee on my knee, my son!
And kissed thee laughing, kissed thee weeping:
But ah! thy little day is done,—
Thou'rt with thy angel sister sleeping.

The staff, on which my years should lean,
Is broken, 'ere those years come over me,
My funeral rites thou should'st have seen,
But thou art in the tomb before me

Thou rear'st to me, no filial stone.
No parents grave, with tears, beholdest;
Thou are my ancestor, my son!
And stand'st in Heaven's account, the oldest.

On earth my lot was soonest cast,
Thy generation after mine;
Thou has thy predecessor past.
Earlier Eternity is thine.

I should have set before thine eyes
The road to Heaven, & showed it clear;
But thou, untaught springest to the skies teacher
And leavest the father lingering here

Sweet Seraph, I would learn of thee
And hasten to partake thy bliss!
And oh! to thy world welcome me,
As erst I welcomed thee to this.

Dear Angel, thou art safe in Heaven:
No prayers for thee need more be made
Oh! let thy prayer for thee be given,
Who oft have blessed thine infant head.

My Father, I beheld thee born,
and led thy tottering steps with care;
Before me risen to Heaven's bright morn
My Son! My Father! Guide me there—

FREDERICK DOUGLASS TO ROSETTA DOUGLASS SPRAGUE

"The peace of death is with the living not with the dead."

In a baritone voice that was thunderous and clear, Frederick Douglass exposed nineteenth-century Americans of the North to the evils of slavery in a way no one ever had before. With broad shoulders and a deep chest, he stood over six feet tall and he knew his subject well as he himself was an escaped slave. He moved and stirred the nation with his speeches and best-selling autobiographies. When the Civil War was over, Douglass at first felt all he had worked for had been accomplished. Yet the struggle "for the ultimate peace and freedom of [his] race" continued throughout his life and he consistently protested publicly against racial discrimination of any kind.

He was the father of five children, one of whom, Annie, died when she was just eleven years old. His concern for his children never dwindled, even when they reached adulthood. He worked to help find them careers and to set them on solid paths toward their futures, but they were always a financial drain and concern to him. Of particular worry was his eldest child, Rosetta, who married Nathan Sprague, a man who seemed to fail and disappoint at every opportunity. It was Rosetta who stood as the main support for her seven children.

In 1875, from his new home in Washington, D.C., Douglass wrote to his daughter in Rochester, New York. Exactly three years earlier the Douglass house in Rochester was burned to the ground by an arsonist. The circumstances of the illness and death of Rosetta's daughter, Alice, described in the following letter are unclear. Likely Douglass wrote to Rosetta for himself and for her mother, Anna Murray Douglass, his wife of thirty-seven years, who remained illiterate until her death.

Washington, D.C. June 3, 1875

My dear Rosa:

Nearly six weeks ago, I received a telegram from dear Nathan, almost in the precise words of the one which came yesterday, and since that time I have been waiting daily expecting to learn that the dear suffering child had passed beyond the reach of care, trouble, sickness and pain. Since it now seems that the dear child cannot live and that she could never be strong and healthy if she did live, her passing away will be a happy release from a life of misery. With her high spirit, a life of weakness and dependence would be intolerable.

I hope dear Rosa, that you are thoroughly nerved for the event, that you are wholly emancipated from the superstitious terrors with which priest craft has surrounded the great and universal fact of death and that you will be able to look with calmness upon the peaceful features of the dear child whose sufferings are ended. Death is the common lot of all and the strongest of us will soon be called away. It is well! Death is a friend not an enemy. It comes at the right time when it comes naturally, and not by violence. It takes the feeble infant from prospective misery and releases the aged from continued aches and pains. The peace of death is with the living not with the dead. We shall all miss our dear little Alice. She was the remarkable child of your flock, a real character. The memory of her words and ways will live with us all. I do not dogmatize as to the life of the future. I know not and no man can know what is beyond or what is the condition of existence, whether conscious or unconscious, beyond this life, but whatever else it may be, it is nothing that our taking thought about can alter or improve. The best any of us can do is to trust in the eternal powers which brought us into existence and this I do for myself and for all.

I do not think our house should be left alone or entirely in the hands of strangers. We have been burnt out once and may be burnt out again, and if burnt out a second time I have no more strength to start life anew again and build up another house.

We are not among friends here any more than in Rochester. It is our misfortune to create envy wherever we go. The white people don't like us and the colored people envy us. I do not wish to burden Amelia with the responsibility of taking care of all here and she told mother before she went away that she did not want to take the responsibility.

Your father,
Fred K Douglass

HARRIET BEECHER STOWE TO GEORGIANA STOWE

". . . mamma is sitting weary by the wayside, feeling weak and worn, but in no sense discouraged."

Author of Uncle Tom's Cabin, *Harriet Beecher Stowe was America's first great female novelist. She was a member of the socially reforming and outspoken Beecher family and the mother of seven children. By 1858 Stowe had already lost two sons; eighteen-month-old Charley died during a cholera epidemic, and nineteen-year-old Henry, a sophomore at Dartmouth College, drowned in the currents of the Connecticut River. Here, at forty-seven years old, she writes to her fourteen-year-old daughter, Georgiana, nearly two years after Henry's death.*

February 12 [1858]

My dear Georgie,

Why have n't I written? Because, dear Georgie, I am like the dry, dead leafless tree, and have only cold, dead, slumbering buds of hope on the end of stiff, hard, frozen twigs of thought, but no leaves, no blossoms; nothing to send to a little girl who does n't know what to do with herself any more than a kitten. I am cold, weary, dead; everything is a burden to me.

I let my plants die by inches before my eyes, and do not water them, and I dread everything I do, and wish it was not to be done, and so when I get a letter from my little girl I smile and say, "Dear little puss, I will answer it"; and I sit hour after hour with folded hands, looking at the inkstand and dreading to begin. The fact is, pussy, mamma is tired. Life to you is gay and joyous, but to mamma it has been a battle in which the spirit is willing but the flesh is weak; and she would be glad, like the woman in the St. Bernard, to lie down with her arms around the wayside cross, and sleep away into a brighter scene. Henry's fair, sweet face looks down upon me now and then from out a cloud, and I feel again all the bitterness of the eternal "No" which says I must never, never, in this life, see that face, lean on that arm, hear that voice. Not that my faith in God in the least fails, and that I do not believe that all this is for good. I do, and though not happy, I am blessed. Weak, weary as I am, I rest on Jesus in the innermost depth of my soul, and am quite sure that there is coming and inconceivable hour of beauty and glory when I shall regain Jesus, and He will give me back my beloved one, whom He is educating in a far higher sphere than I proposed. So do not mistake me,—only know that mamma is sitting weary by the wayside, feeling weak and worn, but in no sense discouraged.

Your affectionate mother,
H. B. S.

ROBERT E. LEE TO
CHARLOTTE WICKHAM LEE

"My horse is waiting at my tent door . . ."

In the months before December 1862 General Robert E. Lee had led Confederate troops in the battles of Second Manassas and Antietam; he had broken bones in one hand and sprained his other wrist in a riding accident; and he had suffered the loss of his beloved twenty-three-year-old daughter to typhoid fever. Lee wrote the following letter to his daughter-in-law upon learning of the death of his only living grandchild, a baby girl. Outside his tent door Lee's troops awaited a Union attack. Three days later, on December 13, at the Battle of Fredericksburg, the Confederacy suffered more than four thousand casualties and the Union more than twelve thousand.

Camp Fredericksburg
December 10, 1862

I heard yesterday, my dear daughter, with the deepest sorrow, of the death of your infant. I was so grateful at her birth. I felt that she would be such a comfort to you, such a pleasure to my dear Fitzhugh, and would fill so full the void still aching in your hearts. But you have now two sweet angels in heaven. What joy there is in the thought! I can say nothing to soften the anguish you must feel, and I know you are assured of my deep and affectionate sympathy. May God give you strength to bear the affliction He has imposed, and produce future joy out of your present misery, is my earnest prayer.

I saw Fitzhugh yesterday. He is well, and wants much to see you. When you are strong enough, cannot you come up to Hickory Hill, or your grandpa's, on a little visit, when he can come down and see you? My horse is waiting at my tent door, but I could not refrain from sending these few lines to recall to you the thought and love of

Your devoted father
R. E. Lee

MARK TWAIN (SAMUEL CLEMENS) TO CLARA CLEMENS GABRILOWITSCH

"I shall never be melancholy again, I think."

He was feeling chest pains with increasing frequency and severity, and Samuel Clemens suspected he might not have long to live. The celebrated writer and lecturer had already lost his wife, a son, and a daughter; a second daughter, Clara, had recently married and moved to Europe with her husband, Ossip Gabrilowitsch. Clemens lived in Connecticut with his remaining daughter, Jean, who was an epileptic, and he worried about what would become of her if he should die. On the morning of December 24, he received the news from the family maid that Jean, twenty-nine years old, had suffered a fatal seizure and was dead in the bathtub upstairs. "Possibly I know now what the soldier feels when a bullet crashes through his heart," he wrote.

Here, seventy-four-year-old Samuel Clemens writes to his remaining child, Clara, five days after Jean's death. Just four months later, Twain himself was in his grave.

Redding, Conn.,
Dec. 29, '09.

O, Clara, Clara dear, I am so glad she is out of it and safe—safe! I am not melancholy; I shall never be melancholy again, I think. You see I was in such distress when I came to realize that you were gone far away and no one stood between her and danger but me—and I could die at any moment, and *then*—oh then what would become of her! For she was wil-full, you know, and would not have been governable.

You can't imagine what a darling she was, that last two or three days; and how *fine*, and good, and sweet, and noble—and *joyful*, thank Heaven!—and how intellectually brilliant. I had never been acquainted with Jean before. I recognized that.

But I mustn't try to write about her—I *can't*. I have already poured my heart out with the pen, recording that last day or two. I will send you that—and you must let no one but Ossip read it.

Good-bye. I love you so! And Ossip.

Father

WOODROW WILSON TO
JESSIE WILSON SAYRE

"I find that the only way to sustain a broken heart is to try to do what she would have done."

On August 6, 1914, just five days after World War I erupted in Europe, Woodrow Wilson's wife, Ellen Axson Wilson, died in her sickroom at the White House. Months before she had been diagnosed with Bright's disease, a disease of the kidneys. Her death that summer afternoon "nearly paralyzed" her husband of twenty-nine years and shocked their three daughters, Margaret, Jessie, and Eleanor. The last words Mrs. Wilson spoke were to the White House physician, Dr. Grayson—"Doctor, if I go away, promise me that you will take good care of my husband."

Two months after Mrs. Wilson passed away, a devastated president wrote the following letter to his second daughter, twenty-seven-year-old Jessie Sayre of Williamstown, Massachusetts. Mrs. Sayre joined her father in the White House for the holidays and then remained in Washington, D.C., for the birth of her first child. To the president's and the country's delight, the baby, a seven-and-a-half-pound boy, Francis Sayre, was delivered in the White House by Dr. Grayson on January 17, 1915. He was Wilson's first grandchild, the eleventh and, to date, last baby to claim the executive mansion as his birthplace.

The White House 15 October, 1914

My precious Daughter,

My heart has long ago answered your sweet letter, though without words. I *long* to see you and Frank in your own home! I would give my head to turn away from things here and run up for a little visit. But, alas! I must not. Every day it is plain that I would simply be neglecting my duty if I were to go away. Much as it hurts, I must deny myself and stick at the endless job.

My heart carries thoughts of you all day long. I think your mother's feelings have been left with me, in addition to my own. The doctor and I have worked out a lovely plan for Christmas and the two months following. I shall have the chance to look after you for a little while, at least, and do very poorly what she would have done so wonderfully. I find that the only way to sustain a broken heart is to try to do what she would have done. So long as I act in her spirit and, as nearly as I can, as she would have acted I experience a sort of sweet relief and happiness that helps to carry me through the day.

Helen seems quite herself again (though I fear she must be rather lonely, poor little girl) and I am perfectly well. The days are, fortunately too full of pressing tasks to give me time for weakness and thoughts of myself.

It will not be very long before the Christmas holidays, and then we shall all be together again! How fine! God bless you, my darling! It is so fine to hear how well you are! Dear love to Frank.

Your devoted Father

Biltmore N.C.
10th May, 1895.

Dear John; It has today,
for the first time, become evident to me that my memory
as to recent occurrences is no
longer to be trusted. If Rick
had not been with me and
had not privately set me
right I should have left an
untrue fact in a flagrant way
to Mr Vanderbilt. I think it
my duty to tell you this at
once in order that you may
take measures to guard the
business from possible consequences. I try to look at the
situation from an outside
and impersonal point of view

Frederick Law Olmsted (above) and
first page of his letter to his son John

Aging

William Lloyd Garrison to
Wendell Phillips Garrison

*"The matter of death, regarding it as I do as simply
an exchange of spheres for the better, grows more
and more insignificant as I advance."*

*In December 1878, William Lloyd Garrison was entering the final months of
his life. With the end of slavery accomplished, thirteen years had passed since the
publication of the last issue of Garrison's stalwart and influential abolitionist newspaper,* The Liberator. *He had become a private person during these last years, but
he remained until the end reform-minded and committed to improving the lives and
education of freed slaves.*

*Here a contented seventy-three-year-old Garrison responds to birthday wishes
from his son.*

Roxbury, Dec. 12, 1878

My dear Wendell:

Thanks for your congratulatory letter, with its filial remembrance of the day, which certainly completes at least seventy-three years of my earthly pilgrimage. Notwithstanding this advanced period of life, to which so few comparatively attain, you propose for me additional "length of days," even to a centennial climax! However that may be, while it will be hard for me at any stage to part with my beloved children and grandchildren, I trust to be ready for the summons to "go hence," come when they may. The matter of death, regarding it as I do as simply an exchange of spheres for the better, grows more and more insignificant as I advance; and what may be a painful separation from loved ones here will, I doubt not, prove a joyful reunion with loved ones gone before. I shall not object to being permitted to see myself enrolled on the list of great-grandfathers; but I could hope that I might pass on before my faculties are essentially impaired, or the body bowed down with hopeless infirmities. The first two I desire to meet on "the other side of Jordan" are your fond mother and my own. It is something curious that, while my mother was only forty-seven years old when she died, and I am now seventy-three, I feel my filial impulses bounding within me as though I were again a child, whenever I think of the possibility of coming into her presence; and though our ages are reversed, according to earthly dates, there still seems to be the same relative distance between us, as to the point of time, that existed when she was here in the body.

I am often congratulated on being blessed with such good children—by those who mean no flattery, but who know from personal knowledge whereof they affirm. I have every reason to be devoutly thankful that you have all grown up to adult life with no stain upon your character, no youthful excesses to deplore, no vicious or unseemly habits to overcome; that your affection for me, and concern for my welfare and happiness, have been without measure; and that you have always shown a mutually disinterested regard for each other, without the slightest alloy. In all these respects my cup of bliss has been full to overflowing. I feel that I can safely trust all of you to maintain an upright character to the end, no matter by what temptations you may at any time be surrounded.

With your letter one of a similar nature comes from my darling daughter, and a brief one from dear little Helen.

The violent rain-storm which you report as so damaging at the Park was felt in all this region. Indeed, it covered all New England, besides New York and Pennsylvania; and the pecuniary loss sustained by it is to be counted by millions of dollars in the aggregate. I doubt if it has ever been equalled since I came upon the stage of action. Happily, as you know, my house is founded upon a rock; and though the rains descended, and the winds blew, and beat upon it, it did not fall as it might have done if it had been built upon a sandy foundation.

On the coming Sunday old lady May will complete her ninety-first year. On Monday Fanny will have achieved her thirty-fourth year. So we ripen.

Receive my benediction. Affectionate remembrances to dear Mrs. McKim, Lloyd, Phil, and queen Katharine.

Your loving Father.

No doubt John Ritchie and his lovable wife must have greatly enjoyed their visit to the Park. They were in luck as to the storm. I have not yet seen them.

HARRIET BEECHER STOWE TO CHARLES STOWE

"It gives me a sort of dizzy feeling of the shortness of life and nearness of eternity . . ."

Residing with her husband and twin spinster daughters, Hattie and Eliza, Harriet Beecher Stowe busied herself during 1882 by putting her papers in order. She made her last public appearance that year and wasn't writing much anymore, aside from letters and notes. Life for Stowe had been filled with family, faith, and unprecedented accomplishment, yet she had also suffered nearly unimaginable sorrow—of her seven children, only three would survive her. In the following letter she mentions the loss of two sons, but of a third son, Frederick, she says nothing. A troubled alcoholic, thirty-one-year-old Frederick sailed around Cape Horn in 1871, landed in San Francisco, and was never heard from again.

Here, in the midst of arranging a lifetime of papers, at seventy-one years old, Stowe writes to her only remaining son, Charles, a minister, husband, father, and a bright spot in his mother's life.

My Dear Charley,

My mind has been with you a great deal lately. I have been looking over and arranging my papers with a view to sifting out those that are not worth keeping, and so filing and arranging those that are to be kept that my heirs and assigns may with the less trouble know where and what they are. I cannot describe (to you) the peculiar feelings which this review occasions. Reading old letters, when so many of the writers are gone from the earth, seems to me like going into the world of spirits,—letters full of warm, eager, anxious, busy life, that is *forever* past. My own letters, too, full of bygone scenes in my early life and the childish days of my children. It is affecting to me to recall things that strongly moved me years ago, that filled my thoughts and made me anxious, when the occasion and emotion have wholly vanished from my mind. But I thank God there is *one* thing running through all of them from the time I was thirteen years old, and that is the intense unwavering sense of Christ's educating, guiding presence and care. It is *all* that remains now. The romance of my youth is faded; it looks to me now, from my years, so *very* young—those days when my mind only lived in *emotion*, and when my letters never were dated, because they were only histories of the *internal*, but now that I am no more and never can be young in this world, now that the friends of those days are almost all in eternity, what remains?

I was passionate in my attachments in those far back years, and as I have looked over the files of old letters, they are all gone (except one, C. Van Rensselaer), Georgiana May, Delia Bacon, Clarissa Treat, Elizabeth Lyman, Sarah Colt, Elisabeth Phenix, Frances Strong, Elisabeth Foster. I have letters from them all, but they have been long in spirit land, and know more about how it is there than I do. It gives me a sort of dizzy feeling of the shortness of life and nearness of eternity when I see how many that I have traveled with are gone within the veil. Then there are all my own letters, written in the first two years of marriage, when Mr. Stowe was in Europe and I was looking forward to motherhood and preparing for it— my letters when my whole life was within the four walls of my nursery, my thoughts absorbed by the developing character of children who have now lived their earthly life and gone to the eternal one,—my two little boys, each in his way good and lovely, whom Christ has taken in youth, and my little one, my first Charley, whom He took away before he knew sin or sorrow,—then my brother George and sister Catherine, the one a companion of my youth, the other the mother who assumed the care of me after I left home in my twelfth year—and they are gone. Then my blessed father, for many years so true an image of the Heavenly Father,— in all my afflictions he was afflicted, in all my perplexities he was a sure and safe counselor, and he too is gone upward to join the angelic mother whom I scarcely knew in this world, who has been to me only a spiritual presence through life.

Harriet Beecher Stowe lived for another fourteen years.

FREDERICK LAW OLMSTED TO JOHN CHARLES OLMSTED*

"It has today for the first time become evident to me that my memory as to recent occurrences is no longer to be trusted."

In the spring of 1895, at the age of seventy-three, Frederick Law Olmsted knew his mind was slipping. He had been pushing himself especially hard for the past few years, working at full steam on major projects in Chicago, Milwaukee, Boston, Louisville, Atlanta, and Washington, D.C. Details and names were beginning to escape him, and his sons John and Rick, both members of his landscape architecture firm, noticed the deterioration. They began briefing their father before client meetings and sometimes even made decisions in his name.

By 1895, the firm had been working for seven years to develop the grounds and an arboretum at the Biltmore, George W. Vanderbilt's magnificent two-thousand-acre Asheville, North Carolina, estate. Here, after a meeting with Mr. Vanderbilt, Olmsted writes to forty-four-year-old John at home in the Massachusetts office of Olmsted, Olmsted and Eliot.

Biltmore, North Carolina
10th May, 1895

Dear John:

It has today for the first time become evident to me that my memory as to recent occurrences is no longer to be trusted. If Rick had not been with me and had not privately set me right I should have shown that fact in a flagrant way to Mr. Vanderbilt. I think it my duty to tell you this at once in order that you may take measures to guard the business from possible consequences. I try to look at the situation from an outside and impersonal point of view and so looking at it I see that I ought no longer to be trusted to carry on important business for the firm alone. This simply because I am liable to such lapses of memory as to recent experiences, as, for example, as to instructions issued verbally, that I cannot be depended on to properly represent the firm. I think that I have no right to conceal this, or to delay telling you of it. I have no reason to think I have lost capacity in respect to invention, design or reasoning powers in any respect, only that my memory (or presence of mind) in regard to recent occurrences is less trustworthy than it has been. It follows, simply, for the present, that it will be prudent for you and Eliot to trust a little less to my presence of mind in interviews with clients than you prudently might hitherto; to recognize that I am instinctively less ready to take risks and more distrustful of myself than I have been and that I have a *slower-working* memory of recent occurrences.

I do not quite like to undertake alone such business as ought to come in Washington and Philadelphia next week. Perhaps this is in a considerable degree because I do not think that I am as well versed in the facts of the present situation of affairs in these places as I should be, but it is also in part because of a growing distrust of my presence of mind in matters the consideration of which involves action of memory of comparatively recent occurrences. Precisely this condition, I suppose, which lends to the rule that military and naval officers shall be retired at seventy.

I suppose that I am a little afflicted physically, as I always have been in previous visits, by the elevation of this place, but I do not think that I can rightly conceal from you the fact that I am more distrustful of myself than I have ever before been and am less willing to operate alone in matters of considerable importance, like this of the Biltmore arboretum, for example.

As to [?] at Washington, Brooklyn &c, we will do the best we can by telegraphic correspondence. I simply now do not want to deal with these matters alone.

Yours affectionately,
Frederick Law Olmsted

* *John Charles Olmsted was actually Frederick Law Olmsted's nephew and adopted son. In 1859, Olmsted married his brother's widow, Mary, and adopted their three children, John, Charlotte, and Owen. Then, together Olmsted and Mary had four children, two of whom, Marion and Frederick, Jr., survived beyond infancy.*

FREDERICK LAW OLMSTED TO
FREDERICK LAW OLMSTED, JR.

*"As long as I have interest in anything earthy
it will be in what interests you."*

Throughout 1895, Olmsted's condition worsened. He was becoming more and more forgetful, so much so that one day he wrote the same letter to Mr. Vanderbilt three times without realizing what he had done. He had "rarely felt so little master of [him]self," yet he continued to be keenly interested in the work of the firm, and especially in twenty-five-year-old Rick's development as a landscape architect. Sensing that time was short, he wrote page after page of advice to the young man and pleaded with him to be kept apprised of the continuing work at the Biltmore. News from Rick lifted Olmsted out of his feeling of desolation and gave him, he wrote, "the assurance that you are taking up what I am dropping."

By October, when he sent the following letter to his youngest son, Olmsted knew a shade in his mind was about to be drawn. He spent the last five years of his life in a cottage at the McLean Asylum in Waverly, Massachusetts, where he was surrounded by a landscape he himself had created.

Brookline, 15th October, 1895

Dear Rick:

I write only in yielding to a constant impulse, vain tho' I feel it to be, to be doing something for you. My time for that has past. I can only pray, and I am a poor hand for that. I try in vain to think of something that I can yet do. I am sure that you do not need advice. You can give yourself better advice than I can offer you. It all comes back again to Sir Walter's "Be good."

You can still write me for some time I hope. As long as I have interest in anything earthy it will be in what interests you.

Your affectionate father

WILLIAM DEAN HOWELLS TO
WILLIAM W. HOWELLS

"Hold fast to my hand, dear little boy,
and keep me with you . . ."

William Dean Howells was one of the most important American writers of the late nineteenth century. The author of travel books, fiction, campaign brochures, autobiography, and hundreds of essays, he had a sharp eye for talent and was the editor of the influential Atlantic Monthly *magazine. Howells was considered a pillar of cultural life in America, so when he reached his seventy-fifth birthday, it was an occasion for a national celebration. He was a man who throughout his life made hard work a habit, finding comfort and refuge in it; he distrusted anything that came easily.*

By 1909, he was still writing, but most of his best work was behind him. Younger writers, feeling Howells's form of realism was outdated, were beginning to call his work vapid and timid. He sensed the era to which he and his work belonged had already passed. For his seventy-second birthday he was sent a card by his grandson, Billy. The card was sent in the boy's name, as Billy was just three months old at the time. Here grandfather William Dean Howells responds.

130 West 57th st.,
March 1, 1909.

Dear Billy:

It is very sweet of you to send that birthday card, where we are walking toward the sunset together. It is a lovely sunset, but sad, and the night is beyond it. Hold fast to my hand, dear little boy, and keep me with you as long as you can. Some day, I hope not too late, you will know how I love you.

Your aff'te grandfather,
W. D. Howells.

N. C. WYETH TO PETER AND
HENRIETTE WYETH HURD

*"This watching of the unfolding of all the younger
members of the family is a glorious episode in my
life . . . But . . . I am still in the battle myself, in spirit
at least, and I still have a fairly clear vision of what
lies ahead to be done before a real mark is achieved."*

*N. C. Wyeth, the greatest American illustrator of his day, felt illustration was
but a lowly craft, yet to be a "painter" was noble. It was as a painter, not an illustrator, that he wanted to make "a real mark." Though he painted landscapes,
still lifes, portraits, and enormous murals, it was for his powerful illustrations that
he was known and celebrated. As the father of five remarkably creative and successful adult children, he was both exhilarated by their achievements and depressed
by his own struggle. Upon seeing his son Andrew's paintings he wrote, "I am at
once stimulated beyond words to new, purer effort, and plunged into black despair."*

*In 1939, at fifty-six years old, N. C. Wyeth had been painting for thirty-seven
years. He and his wife, Carol, were at their house in Maine where the family gath-
ered in the summer. Here he writes to his eldest daughter, Henriette, and son-in-
law, Peter Hurd, both accomplished painters, who lived and worked, far beyond the
Wyeth family fold, in remote New Mexico.*

Port Clyde, Maine
August 27, 1939

Dear Henriette and Pete:

Ironically enough, this day has blazed forth into brilliant sun, jewel-
blue sky and water, with a "westerly" pouring over us from Caldwell's Island like some crystal liquid. I say ironically, because Nat and Caroline
vanished from our doorway yesterday in a thick murk of fog, a condition
which dominated their two weeks with us. However, we all had an unusually splendid time, and every hour of clearing weather was used for ex-
citing explorations of islands, events usually garnished with clam bakes or
lobster boils—and in one case the return to "Eight Bells" in an impene-
trable fog cleverly mastered by Nat with chart and compass so that we
landed within thirty yards of our wharf.

Four days after Nat's arrival, I completed the last vestige of work for

The Yearling. This included two extra drawings for the special edition, besides the thirteen panels in color. Three others, of course, were done at home, as you know.

It's a long, long time since I've written a letter and I seem to have lost what little I had of spontaneity and free flow of expression. Your own letters are full to bursting of truly "winged words," and they have given joy to all who have read them—and many have! You will never realize what pleasure they've given.

When I think of the gamut of experiences that Pete has gone through since he left Chadds Ford, I feel hopeless to express my own reaction to it all, except to say that I have followed it all like a small boat tossing in the wake of a ship, rising, falling and rising, but exhilarated in the end over an experience based upon life, energy and enthusiasm.

This watching of the unfolding of all the younger members of the family is a glorious episode in my life. As you both know I am asked interminably, "Aren't you proud of it all?" Of course I am, beyond the expression of any words. But my answer is always restrained because I am still in the battle myself, in spirit at least, and I still have a fairly clear vision of what lies ahead to be done before a real mark is achieved. I believe, as I never believed before, that we, as a group, *have got something* and that there is a real promise of sound achievement—of *major* achievement in the offing. Based upon the sound and constant seeking for the truth, and out of all this the gradual unfolding of personal spirit and mood, and all based upon intensive and simple living, the possibilities are limitless.

You will like to know that John has made *extraordinary* progress in his watercolors, and under the stimulation of very busy people around him, has done a quantity of work.

Andy's results are to me astounding. Just at the conclusion of his summer's work he went starry-eyed over a very attractive young lady. She's really a splendid person, very handsome and very sound. Betsy James is her name. She hails from northern New York. Her family are, or at least seem to be, solid, sensible people. As long as such an event must happen, it is deeply gratifying not to have to worry about *what is a girl's background.*

Earlier in the season there were some very lurid distractions here in P.C. which can be told you better by word of mouth. That's all over now, thank heavens.

I start tomorrow on my first tempera panel for myself. I shall have a full month to do what I want. I hope it goes well.

The European situation is the only headache. I believe the present crisis a colossal bluff, one which conceals a very ominous one of the economic tie-up between Germany and Russia which, if allowed to progress through the years, will enslave the world in a terrible manner.

We may stay on here into October if my painting goes well. My first spell of freedom from commissions in a long time.

OSCAR HAMMERSTEIN TO
BILL HAMMERSTEIN

"What a good boy am I!"

Lyricist, playwright, director, and producer, Oscar Hammerstein 2nd made an unprecedented and enduring mark on the landscape of American theater. In collaboration with Jerome Kern and later with Richard Rodgers, Hammerstein's musicals brought a new form of theater into existence in which story lines, dialogue, songs, and dances were fully integrated to create the vibrant and cohesive new American musical.

In 1953 Oscar Hammerstein 2nd was fifty-seven years old. He had had brilliant success with Show Boat, Oklahoma!, Carousel, South Pacific, *and* The King and I. The Sound of Music *was still years ahead. He had experienced smash hits as well as disappointments, but many of his songs—like "Ol' Man River," "All the Things You Are," and "Some Enchanted Evening" had taken on lives of their own. Through life's ups and downs, he remained steadily and optimistically committed to the work at hand.*

With dark lashes and a heavy brow, he was a large, gentle, and soft-spoken man. As the father of three and stepfather of two, he felt that "to be a good man" was the best any father could be for his children.

His eldest son, Bill, asked his father to write letters to him about the early years in the hopes of helping his father assemble an autobiography. The project was never completed, but this letter remains a fascinating example of Hammerstein's personal philosophies about life, philosophies that permeated his works.

January 18, 1953

Dear Bill:

I have just started to read Carl Sandburg's autobiography of the first twenty one years of his life, "Always The Young Strangers." I cannot help contrasting it with these haphazard memories I am giving you. His life starts a little earlier than mine in a small town, Galesburg, Illinois, and how simple and pure and orderly it seems compared to mine. He was the son of a poor but industrious Swedish carpenter. It was a good clean orderly family life they all led, he and his mother and father and eight other children. They seemed never to have wanted for meals or shelter, but they all had to work pretty hard at one chore or another. A political parade was a big event to be seen and cherished. Carl Sandburg built his experiences slowly but solidly into a philosophy, and a talent for expressing his philosophy. Whatever order or form I have got out of life has been extracted from chaos. This was true when I was a child, and it is true now. The farm and my determination to be down here as often and for as long a time as possible expresses my eagerness for peace and systematic living. As far back as I can remember I always wanted to live in the country. Even in the city, if I saw an empty lot with a few weeds and a tree in it I was attracted by it. In your first year we took a small cottage in Far Rockaway in a street jammed with cottages, but just across the street was a tall tree, and I used to sit on the small porch and look across at the tree against the sky as the light was fading in the evening, and it gave me a great feeling of peace and even happiness, and it made me thoughtful about life in the abstract, as I sometimes get thoughtful listening to a symphony without actually "hearing it." I remember telling Walter Redell about this feeling, and he used to kid me about the tree for a long time. It became a symbol to him of my naive idealism.

A psychologist would be skeptical of my professed groping for peace. He would say: "Why don't you take it? You have enough copyrights to live on. Why don't you stop working? Why don't you leave the hectic life of New York and the theatre, live in Doylestown, take care of your cows, and have the peace you've always been after?" These would be hard questions to answer. I often think of doing this "some day." Then I ask myself: "What would you do when the Kiwanis asked you to come down and speak to them? If you read an editorial in the *Intelligencer* which made you angry, would you not use your new leisure to sit down and write them a hot letter of protest? Would you not in a few years become as involved with as many friends and as many projects in and around Bucks county as you are now in New York? And would you have any more freedom as a big fish in a small pond than you have as a medium sized fish in a metropolitan pond?" I suppose I would not have more freedom—not at my present age anyway. I suppose you get free of these things when you get so old and feeble that they say: "Don't ask him to do that. He's an old man, and he hasn't been very well." Sometimes I see myself as a lean and slippered pantaloon with white hair, wearing tweeds whose cut has become out of date, sitting on the porch watching the younger people playing tennis and receiving my sons and daughters when they come to visit me, and listening to them tell me of their doings in the great world outside. If this is the stage I must get to before I find peace and the orderly and systematic life, then the whole idea is very discouraging.

Using the word peace makes me rush to confess that if peace means peace of mind, I have this to an amazing degree compared to all the other people I know. I have always had this somehow. I have never been harried or extremely worried except for temporary specific causes. In a confused world I am confused, but I am not thrown into a panic by confusion. I am not unduly distressed by it. I can take confusion and imperfection in my stride.

All this brings me back to where we left off—my childhood. It is possible that there were many lucky accidents in my upbringing that were good for me. My strange disorderly unsystematic family may have developed in me a tolerance for disorder which makes it possible for me to live in a disorderly world, even though I crave another kind. But there is no other kind. The world is very much like my family, filled with people of unharnessed passions, illogical impulses, inconsistent religions and clashing philosophies. All these whirling atoms are held together loosely and kept going slowly in the same general direction by one element—love. You may substitute another word for this if you please. You may call it God or you may call it goodness. You may call it Seventh Day Adventism or Free Masonry or Democracy or Communism or the American Legion or the Doylestown sewing circle or Local 802—but it is the desire to be with a group of other people, all working with one another in an effort to do something which all consider a good thing to do. What one group considers a good thing to do may be thought the worst thing in the world by another group, but if you don't belong to a group that is doing something or thinks it is doing something, you haven't a chance. Within that group is the justification of that small atom that is you, and some day you hope to do something very fine which will make the group applaud you. The biggest and truest and most significant line in all nursery rhymes is a line in Little Jack Horner—"What a good boy am I!" That is what everybody wants to say to himself, but he can have little assurance of his belief unless it is endorsed by other members of his group. Everyone has this desire for approval. The trouble is that many people do not work hard enough to get it. Then they become unhappy paranoiacs, clinging for the life of their egos to their own self-approval, and blaming the rest of the world for not endorsing it.

This whole essay springs from what I have been telling you about my family and what I am going to tell you about them. In the light of the earnest and scientific approach that all the young people of your generation bring to the task of bearing and breeding and educating your young, my family and many families of that day, and indeed many families of today, seem like irresponsible maniacs, but all the science in the world is no good without this thing I have quickly and carelessly called love. There must be love, unselfconscious, spontaneous and unscientific, shining out of all the dusty corners of the disorderly household. And specifically, the little atom whirling around among millions of other atoms very like himself must be given the illusion that they are not so like himself, that he is something very special, worth promoting, worth perfecting, worth building up to that position of prominence and achievement where he can lie in his bed or stand on a hill or walk down the street and say to himself with conviction: "What a good boy am I."

M. F. K. FISHER TO NORAH KENNEDY BARR, ANNA PARRISH, AND MARY KENNEDY WRIGHT

"I wish and want and hope to die in my own home."

As a food aficionado and writer, in her more than twenty books and scores of articles, Mary Frances Kennedy Fisher essentially told her readers, "Look, if you have to eat to live you may as well enjoy it." She created a new genre for the written word and her work elevated the preparation and consumption of food from mere necessity to important and gratifying social occasion and opportunity for self-expression. She was tough and funny, tall and sometimes beautiful, and as the daughter of Rex Kennedy, a lifelong and fifth-generation newspaperman, from childhood she knew she would write. And write she did, but her adult life was more complicated than she ever expected—divorced, widowed, and divorced again—she

evolved into a courageous mother who achieved nuch professionally and, by herself,
raised two daughters.

As Fisher grew older she trained herself to remain detached from, yet keenly
aware of, her own progressive aging. She "meant to work longer, and say more,"
but by the 1980s her eyesight was failing and she was increasingly debilitated by
arthritis and Parkinson's disease. At seventy-six years old, she wrote the following
letter to her two daughters and her younger sister, Norah. She lived for another
eight years, all the while working and writing as best she could.

[Last House, Glen Ellen, California]
February 9, 1984

To: Norah Kennedy Barr, Anna Parrish, and Mary Kennedy Wright . . .

I want to tell you what some of you may have to think about, since
chronologically I'll not outlive any of you . . .

I wish and want and hope to die in my own home. Some of you may
want to help me do this.

Rex Kennedy told us that he wanted to die in his own house, "at
home." It was difficult at times, and even painful and unpleasant, but we
brought it off. And I must tell you that I myself feel that it was worth any
physical and perhaps spiritual inconveniences I had to put up with for a
time . . . quarrelling nurses, sad and sometimes scary character-changes in
my father. A few hours before Rex died, in a cosmic rage at finding himself only mortal . . . and I know he was frightened too . . . Dr. Bruff said,
"You must keep in your mind that this is not your father, the man you
have known." This helped me accept the raging roaring old lion in his
next-to-last hours, and the suspicious wily fox of perhaps five days before
that. It was *not* Rex, really, or at least it was not the man I knew as my father and friend.

And this may happen with me, although I, and all of you, devoutly
hope it will not, and that I can leave the scene easily.

BUT . . .

I want to leave it either by myself or with a few friends, HERE, or with
you.

I know that nurses, either RN or "practical," are hard to find and hard
to live with. But they exist. And the situation by the time they are needed
is a temporary one. As for the expense, they cost no more than the kind
of rest-home or nursing-home you might find, that you would want me

to end my life in. There are a few, perhaps, but we all know that most of them are simply living graveyards . . . and that living corpses are not often treated as decently as dead ones.

I hope to leave enough available cash to take care of such possible expenses. If there is not enough, you will simply have to borrow for more. It will be worth the doing, believe me, a few years along . . .

As for the personal physical side, I feel sad if you must try to carry out this wish of mine. I apologize to you now, for whatever trials it may put you through, and I thank you with all my heart. Between and among you, there will be enough energy and love to see the thing through. It may mean a temporary displacement, and it may even change the lives of your children or your friends, but I believe that it will not be bad, eventually. And meanwhile, I'll send this little manifesto to you, and then leave it lay where Jesus flang it.

What it comes down to is that I hope somebody will enable me to die in my own bed, if I do indeed need help then.

With love and thanks . . .

On June 22, 1992, Fisher died at home.

GEORGE HERBERT WALKER BUSH TO HIS CHILDREN

*"Well, I'll be there ready when you are,
for there's so much excitement ahead . . ."*

That George Bush, the forty-first president of the United States, has been a lifelong and prolific writer of emotive, warm, thoughtful, and humorous letters came as a surprise to many Americans. He was the president who led the country into war with Iraq and deftly presided over the end of the cold war, but while in office was often thought of as stiff and unfeeling. In hindsight George Bush himself realized there was a gulf between the public perception of him and the reality of his personality: "I'm convinced the American people didn't know my heartbeat," he said. "I can't blame anybody but myself for that."

He is a man who believes that the best way to lead, in any situation, is by example and he is a father who is always conscious of the example he sets for his family. In 1992, the day after he lost the presidential election, Bush directed himself in his diary, "Be strong, be kind, be generous of spirit, be understanding and let the people know how grateful you are."

Here the seventy-four-year-old former president writes to his five grown children about himself and his advancing age. In less than two months, on election night 1998, his two sons George and Jeb were elected to the governorships of two of the largest states in the nation.

September 23, 1998

Dear Kids,

This letter is about aging. Not about the President's Conference on Aging and how we should play lawn bowling, get discounts at the movies, turn into skin-conscious sunblockers, take Metamucil and grow old gracefully. No it's about me, about what happened between last year and this, between being 73 and 74. It's interesting—well, *fairly* interesting to you maybe, therapeutic to me for I know I am getting older now.

Last year I could drop the anchor on Fidelity and worry only a little bit about falling off the bow. This year if Bill Busch or Neil isn't up there on the bow of Fidelity II to drop the anchor I can still do it; but I figure it's about a 75% chance that a wave will hit Fidelity, my balance will go and I'll be in the drink.

Last year I could fly fish on the end rocks at the Point, and not be too concerned about losing my balance. Oh, if I'd been casting at one target for a while way back in the summer of '97, my spike clad feet firmly placed on two rocks, and then I turned fast I'd feel a little—what's the word here—not "wobbly" but "unbalanced"—that's the feeling.

This year if I turn fast, I wobble. I recover as I go from rock to rock, but I look like one of the Wallenza brothers going across Niagara Falls. Arms in the air are more important this year.

In August I was floating down the Bow River near Calgary in a 14' open fishing boat—the kind with the bow that goes up—not high up but up enough to keep the water out if you hit some rapids. Well we pulled in for a shore lunch, and I couldn't bend my legs enough to get them over the freeboard.

You may have noticed that in Greece I leaned on the guys holding the rubber launch when we pulled into a beach or when in a chop I climbed back onto Alexander's gangway.

When I climb in or out of the Navigator I have to swing one leg in then lift the other with my hands. Last year—no problem!

Then there's memory. I'm still pretty good at faking it. "Well, I'll be darn, how in the heck are you?" or "long time no see!" or "What you been up to?" or if I want to gamble "How's your better half?" Careful of this last one at both 73 and 74 though. The better half crop is getting a little thinner. Death has claimed some "better halfs" and over the years some have been dumped.

But no question my memory is getting worse. I was introduced up in Calgary by a guy named Sandy. I thanked him—then near the end of the speech I wanted to mention him again, ad lib him in, but I couldn't remember whether it was Sandy or Randy—so I go "And let me again thank all of you and especially our great host" at which point I gestured toward the spot in the totally darkened hall to which I thought Sandy had repaired after introducing me. When the lights came on, my speech finished, there was Sandy right near where I had pointed. What a country!

Memory? A definite problem now. The twins invited friends from Biddeford Pool over to Walker's Point this summer. Mystery guests in a way for they'd leave one day midst warm embraces and farewells only to mysteriously reappear the next.

Jenna introduced me to them on Day 1 and on Day 2—then gave up on me when failing to recall names I kept saying "Biddeford Girls—I am sure glad you came back. How long are you going to be with us?" They were very nice about it, and after a week of seeing them eating here they wedged into my heart—always room for more nice kids.

Near the end of their tenure when I needled them "Hey Biddeford girls, glad to see you could make it for ice cream" I almost wish I hadn't seen them exchange that 'who is this whacko?' look.

Sometimes humor works, it kind of obscures the memory thing. At a huge corporate gathering I had just met Kevin's wife. Kevin was my host and had been the question screener at a forum. When I went to bid farewell to Kevin and to his wife whose name suddenly escaped me I go "Kevin thanks a lot"—then patting his wife on the arm—a kind of farewell pat I go "You sure over married, Kevin old boy." She never knew.

One last point on memory. I can remember things very clearly that happened a long time ago. The longer ago, it seems, the clearer my recall.

Examples:

I can vividly remember the bottom of my mother's feet. Yes, she played a much younger woman named Peaches Peltz in tennis back in 1935 or so. Peaches was smooth. Mum was tenacious. Mother literally wore the skin off the bottom of her feet. But I can't remember whom I played tennis with last week.

I remember Uncle Johnny Walker back about 1945 telling me that Mr. Frank Parker, then a distinguished NYC lawyer of around 50, liked to stand in a cold shower and let ice cold water hit him in the crack of his buttocks. But I can't remember with any clarity what Gorbachev told me in 1991, or what Kohl said when the wall came down in '89. Incidentally I don't like what Mr. Parker liked. Warm water there—sure, but icy cold water no way.

I remember a lot of detail about all five of you when you were little—all happy memories I retain; but alas I am vague on recent details in your lives. I am passionately interested but factoids escape me.

This summer, one or two of you, I am sure in an effort to be helpful, said "get a hearing aid" or "try listening." I heard you. I also heard a family member (I won't say of which generation) go: "The old fogy is getting deaf." But I had clearly heard what had gone before and I heard that "old fogy" thing too. Come to think back on it I am not sure the word used was "fogy"—not sure, not sure at all.

But on the hearing thing, here's my side of it. Each year I have my hearing checked at the Mayo Clinic. They keep telling me "very slight hearing loss—no need for a hearing aid." So there!

What happens this year unlike last is I just tune out more: because I do not want to know when they are all thinking of going to the movies and I don't want to sign off on having someone take them all the way to Portland. So, on purpose, I either look confused or simply proceed on my way pretending to have heard nary a sound. It works.

Many times this summer I'd walk by that cluttered room off the kitchen—the TV, Nintendo, sloppy pillows on the floor lolling around the room. I'd hear a voice go "Gampster, can we"—and I'd walk on by heading for the living room. The kids thought I was deaf when I was just in quest of tranquility. I was tuning them out.

I sleep about the same as last year, but I find I am going to bed earlier but I wake up when the first sea gull, beak wide open, sends out his earliest screechiest call. Seagulls don't crow or scream, what is it they do? I forget.

This year I am more philosophical. I don't feel old at all, and I still love sports, but things are without a question different. I ache more after tennis—I mean I'm talking real hip and knee pain. Body parts hurt at night. Daytime is OK. . . . Golf's a problem—less distance this year. . . . Horseshoes, I can still hold my own. . . .

Desire—no aging in the desire department. I still want to compete. I still drive Fidelity II fast—very fast. My best so far—63 mph in a slight chop with one USSS agent on board.

I desire to play better golf, but I am allergic to practice, so I just tee it up and play fast. I can still volley but I can't cover behind me. I have the desire though. I love being out on the course or court with the greats of today or yesterday. It's more than name dropping. It's being close to excellence that I enjoy. No aging in the desire category.

If I try to read after dinner I fall asleep on the third page no matter how gripping the mystery. Read a briefing paper in bed? No way—Sominex time!

A very personal note. Three times this summer—once in June, twice in August someone has sidled up to me and whispered "Your zipper is down." Once I responded by quoting General Vernon Walters' memorable line: "An old bird does not fall out of the nest."

The other two times I just turned side ways, mumbled my thanks, and corrected the problem. But the difference is, 10 years ago I'd have been embarrassed. Now I couldn't care less. Tragic!

Actually I learned this zipper recovery technique from Italy's Prime Minister Andreotti. In the Oval Office one time George Shultz whispered to Andreotti that his zipper was down. Though speaking little English, Andreotti got the drift. Turning his back to all of us he stood up as if to examine the Gilbert Stuart picture of George Washington that was hanging behind President Reagan; and then with no visible concern zipped his pants up.

Last year there was only a tiny sense of time left—of sand running through the glass. This year, I must confess, I am more aware of that. No fear, no apprehension, just a feeling like "let's go—there's so much to do and there might not be a lot of time left." And except for an ache here a pain there I feel like the proverbial spring colt. There is so much left to do.

Your kids keep me young even if I don't bend as easily or run as fast or hear as well.

Maybe I am a little grumpier when there are a whole bunch of them together making funny sounds and having too many friends over who leave too many smelly sneakers around.

And, yes, I confess I am less tolerant about the 7-up can barely sipped—left to get stale and warm or about all the lights left on or about the VCR's whose empty cases are strewn around, the tapes themselves off in another house—stuck into yet another VCR machine.

Though I try not to show it, I also get irritated now when I go to watch a tape and instead of the Hitchcock movie or my Costner film in the proper cover I find a tape of Bambi or of that horrible Simpson family—always a tape that needs rewinding, too.

This summer when he came to the Point, Kevin Costner his ownself gave me tapes of 7 of his movies. I now have 2 tapes in proper covers, empty cardboard covers for two others, the rest of the covers and the other 5 tapes gone—vanished—MIA. Am I being unreasonable here?

I have given up trying to assign blame. I did that when you all were young but I never had my heart and soul in the blame game. Now I find I tune out when someone says "Ask Jeb, he knows!" or "Gampy, I wasn't even in the boat when they hit the rock." Or after all five gallons of French vanilla turned to mush, the freezer door having been left open all night, "I didn't do it, and I'm not saying who did, but Robert took out two Eskimo Pies after dinner—honest!" I wasn't trying to find the culprit. I was trying to safeguard our future.

I realize "Keep the freezer door closed from now on and I mean it" lacks the rhetorical depth of "This will not stand" or "Read my lips," but back in the White House days Ramsey or George worried about closing the freezer door while I worried about other problems. The lines were more clearly drawn back then.

No there is a difference now and maybe when we reconvene next year, you'll notice even more of a gentle slide. I hope not. I want to put this "aging" on hold for awhile now.

I don't expect to be on the A team anymore; but I want to play golf with you. And I want to fish or throw shoes. And I want to rejoice in your victories be they political, or business, or family happiness victories.

And I want to be there for you if you get a bad bounce in life, and no doubt you will for the seas do indeed get rough.

When I say "be there" I don't mean just showing up—I mean in the game, in the lineup, viscerally involved in your lives even though I might be miles away.

I don't want you to pull your punches. If I call Lauren "Barbara" go ahead and give me your best shot—I can take it. But try not to say "C'mon, Alph, get with it."

If I shed tears easier now try not to laugh at me, because I'll loose more saline and that makes me feel like a sissy, and it might make my mouth dry later on, and might be bad for digestion, too. And besides it's OK to cry if you are a man—a happy man (me) or a man faced with sadness or hurt (not me).

Hey, don't point the first finger at whom ever is shedding the tear because all Bushes cry easily when we're happy, or counting our blessings, or sad when one of us gets bruised or really hurt inside.

As the summer finishes out and the seas get a little higher, the winds a little colder, I'll be making some notes—writing it down lest I forget—so I can add to this report on getting older. Who knows maybe they'll come out with a new drug that makes legs bend easier—joints hurt less, drives go farther, memory come roaring back, and all fears about falling off fishing rocks go away.

Remember the old song "I'll be there ready when you are." Well, I'll be there ready when you are, for there's so much excitement ahead, so many grandkids to watch grow. If you need me, I'm here.

Devotedly,
Dad

For my deare sonne
Simon Bradstreet

Parents perpetuate their liues
in their posterity, and their
maners in their imitation
Children do naturally rather
follow the failings then the ver
tues of their predecessors, but I
am perswaded better things of
you once desired me to leaue some
thing for you in writing that
you might look vpon, when you
should see me no more, I could
think of nothing more fit for you
nor of more ease to my self then
these short meditations follow
ing, such as they are I bequeath
to you, small legacys are accepti
by true friends much more, by
duty full children, I haue avoyded
incroaching vpon others conceptions
because I would leaue you nothing

but myne owne, though in value
they fall short of all in this kinde
yet I presume they will be
better prisd by you, for the
Authors sake. the lord blesse
you with grace heer, and Crown
you with glory heerafter, that I
may meet you with reioyceing
at that great day of appear
ing, which is the Continuall pray
er, of

                    your affectionate
March 20   mother :A B
1664

Anne Bradstreet's 1664 letter to her son Simon

Rules to
Live By

ANNE BRADSTREET TO SIMON BRADSTREET

"Many can speak well, but few can do well."

Anne Bradstreet was not only America's first female poet, she was the first American ever to have a book of poetry published. She was a Puritan who, in 1630, made the journey to New England with John Winthrop and his party aboard the Arabella. As the mother of eight children, keeping house in the newly settled towns of Ipswich and North Andover, she wrote poems for herself and for her family. That her work was printed at all was the doing of her brother-in-law, John Woodbridge, who in 1650, without Bradstreet's consent, published a book of her poems in London.

The following letter and "Meditations" for her second son, Simon, were discovered in Bradstreet's Massachusetts house after her death in 1672. The "Meditations," upon which she was still working, number seventy-seven. Included here are the first four.

March 20, 1664.

For my deare Sonne Simon Bradstreet.

PARENTS perpetuate their lives in their posterity, and their maners in their imitation. Children do natureally rather follow the failings then the vertues of their predecessors, but I am perswaded better things of you. You once desired me to leave something for you in writeing that you might look upon when you should see me no more. I could think of nothing more fit for you, nor of more ease to my self, then these short meditations following. Such as they are I bequeath to you: small legacys are accepted by true friends, much more by duty full children. I have avoyded incroaching upon others conceptions, because I would leave you nothing but myne owne, though in value they fall short of all in this kinde, yet I persume they will be better prif'd by you for the Authors sake. The Lord bless you with grace heer, and crown you with glory heerafter, that I may meet you with rejoycing at that great day of appearing, which is the continuall prayer, of

your affectionate mother,
A. B.

Meditations Divine and Morall.

I.

THERE is no object that we see; no action that we doe; no good that we inioy; no evil that we feele, or fear, but we may make some spirituall advantage of all: and he that makes such improvment is wise, as well as pious.

II.

MANY can speak well, but few can do well. We are better scholars in the Theory then the practique part, but he is a true Christian that is a proficient in both.

III.

YOUTH is the time of getting, middle age of improving, and old age of spending; a negligent youth is usually attended by an ignorant middle age, and both by an empty old age. He that hath nothing to seed on but vanity and lyes must needs lye down in the Bed of sorrow.

IV.

A SHIP that beares much saile, and little or no ballast, is easily overset; and that man, whose head hath great abilities, and his heart little or no grace, is in danger of foundering.

BENJAMIN FRANKLIN TO WILLIAM FRANKLIN

"The resolution you have taken to use more exercise is extremely proper . . ."

By the 1770s Benjamin Franklin was the most famous American in the world. His extremely popular Poor Richard's Almanac *series and the invention of the lightning rod made his name known in households in America and abroad. From 1757 through 1775, returning to America from 1762 to 1764, Franklin served as the American agent to Great Britian and, as always, continued with his scientific pursuits and interests. Intrigued by the cause and spread of the common cold, he concluded—against the wisdom of the day: "People often catch cold from one another when shut up together in small close rooms." Fresh air, he was certain, particularly fresh air taken during outdoor exercise, was the best preventative measure. Here, with a thoroughly modern view of physical exertion, sixty-seven-year-old Franklin responds to forty-year-old William, who had written of a recent "indisposition."*

London Augt. 19: 1772

To Governor Franklin, New Jersey

In yours of May 14th, you acquaint me with your indisposition, which gave me great concern. The resolution you have taken to use more exercise is extremely proper, and I hope you will steadily perform it. It is of the greatest importance to prevent diseases; since the cure of them by physic is so very precarious. In considering the different kinds of exercise, I have thought that the *quantum* of each is to be judged of, not by time or by distance, but by the degree of warmth it produces in the body: Thus when I observe if I am cold when I get into a carriage in a morning, I may ride all day without being warmed by it, that if on horse back my feet are cold, I may ride some hours before they become warm; but if I am ever so cold on foot, I cannot walk an hour briskly, without glowing from head to foot by the quickened circulation; I have been ready to say, (using round numbers without regard to exactness, but merely to mark a great difference) that there is more exercise in *one* mile's riding on horseback, than in *five* in a coach; and more in *one* mile's walking on foot, than in *five* on horseback; to which I may add, that there is more in walking *one* mile up and down stairs, than in *five* on a level floor. The two latter exercises may be had within doors, when the weather discourages going abroad; and the last may be had when one is pinched for time, as containing a great quantity of exercise in a handful of minutes. The dumb bell is another exercise of the latter compendious kind; by the use of it I have in forty swings quickened my pulse from 60 to 100 beats in a minute, counted by a second watch: And I suppose the warmth generally increases with quickness of pulse.

BENJAMIN AND JULIA RUSH TO
JOHN RUSH

"Remember at all times that while you are seeing
the world, the world will see you."

Benjamin Rush was involved in almost everything. He was a signer of the Declaration of Independence and served in the Revolutionary War. He was a well-known and celebrated physician who treated all of his patients, rich and poor, with equal attention and care. He opposed slavery and capital punishment, and championed the free American public school. He was involved in the founding of five institutions of higher learning, worked for the humane treatment of the mentally ill, was the first American-born person to hold the title of professor of chemistry and for sixteen years served as the treasurer of the United States Mint. Because of his fearless, though controversial, treatment of the afflicted during Philadelphia's terrifying yellow fever epidemic of 1793, he was a popular hero.

The eldest of Benjamin and Julia Rush's thirteen children, John Rush became a surgeon. Apparently, throughout most of his adult life, John struggled with mental instability and his medical career was spotty at best. Tragically, three years before his father's death, John went insane following a duel in which he killed a friend. He was institutionalized at the Pennsylvania Hospital (Benjamin Rush's hospital) and remained there for twenty-seven years until his death in 1837.

In 1796, when Benjamin and Julia Rush wrote the following letter to their son, it seemed that John's mental troubles had not yet begun. He was twenty-one years old and, having finished a medical apprenticeship with his father, he was headed to India.

[May 18, 1796]

Directions and advice to Jno. Rush from his father and mother composed the evening before he sailed for Calcutta, May 18th, 1796.

We shall divide these directions into four heads, as they relate to *morals, knowledge, health,* and *business.*

I. Morals

1. Be punctual in committing your soul and body to the protection of your Creator every morning and evening. Implore at the same time his mercy in the name of his Son, our Lord and Saviour Jesus Christ.

2. Read in your Bible frequently, more especially on Sundays.

3. Avoid swearing and even an irreverent use of your Creator's name. *Flee* youthful lusts.

4. Be courteous and gentle in your behavior to your fellow passengers, and respectful and obedient to the captain of the vessel.

5. Attend public worship regularly every Sunday when you arrive at Calcutta.

II. Knowledge

1. Begin by studying Guthrie's *Geography.*

2. Read your other books *through* carefully, and converse daily upon the subjects of your reading.

3. Keep a diary of every day's studies, conversations, and transactions at

sea and on shore. Let it be composed in a fair, legible hand. Insert in it an account of the population, manners, climate, diseases, &c., of the places you visit.

4. Preserve an account of every person's name and disease whom you attend.

III. Health

1. Be temperate in eating, more especially of animal food. Never *taste* distilled spirits of any kind, and drink fermented liquors very sparingly.

2. Avoid the night air in sickly situations. Let your dress be rather warmer than the weather would seem to require. Carefully avoid fatigue from all causes both of body and mind.

IV. Business

1. Take no step in laying out your money without the advice and consent of the captain or supercargo. Let no solicitations prevail with you to leave the captain and supercargo during your residence in Calcutta.

2. Keep an exact account of all your expenditures. Preserve as vouchers of them all your bills.

3. Take care of all your instruments, books, clothes, &c.

Be sober and vigilant. Remember at all times that while you are seeing the world, the world will see you. Recollect further that you are always under the eye of the Supreme Being. One more consideration shall close this parting testimony of our affection. Whenever you are tempted to do an improper thing, fancy that you see your father and mother kneeling before you and imploring you with tears in their eyes to refrain from yielding to the temptation, and assuring you at the same time that your yielding to it will be the means of hurrying them to a premature grave.

Benjn Rush
Julia Rush

John D. Rockefeller, Jr., to John D. Rockefeller, III

"At the end of each week during which John has kept his accounts accurately and to Papa's satisfaction . . ."

Ever conscious of the responsibilities of his position, John D. Rockefeller, Jr., made certain his father's vast Standard Oil fortune was used for the betterment of mankind. The list of his philanthropic efforts is staggering and includes such contributions as financial support for the restoration of Versailles and the Rheims Cathedral, providing forty-six thousand acres to the United States government to establish Acadia National Park and Grand Teton National Park, preserving land along the Hudson River to forever protect the spectacular view from northern Manhattan, donating the land for the United Nations headquarters and spearheading the restoration and establishment of Colonial Williamsburg.

By 1920 the eldest John D. Rockefeller had shifted the balance of the fortune, money and burden, to his forty-six-year-old son and namesake. Here the second generation, John D. Rockefeller, Jr., lays out the financial expectations for the third generation, his son, fourteen-year-old John D. Rockefeller, III.

Memorandum between
PAPA and JOHN.
Regarding an Allowance.

1. Beginning with May 1st, John's allowance is to be at the rate of One dollar and fifty cents ($1.50) per week.

2. At the end of each week during which John has kept his accounts accurately and to Papa's satisfaction, the allowance for the succeeding week will be increased ten cents (10¢) over the week just ended, up to but not beyond a total per week of two dollars ($2.00).

3. At the end of each week during which John has not kept his accounts accurately and to Papa's satisfaction, the allowance for the succeeding week shall be reduced ten cents (10¢) from the week just ended.

4. During any week when there have been no receipts or expenditures to record the allowance shall continue at the same rate as in the preceding week.

5. During any week when the account has been correctly kept but the

writing and figuring are not satisfactory the allowance shall continue at the same rate as in the preceding week.

6. Papa shall be the sole judge as to whether an increase or a decrease is to be made.

7. It is understood that at least Twenty Per cent (20%) of the allowance shall be used for benevolences.

8. It is understood that at least Twenty Per cent (20%) of the allowance shall be saved.

9. It is understood that every purchase or expenditure made is to be put down definitely and clearly.

10. It is understood that John will make no purchases, charging the same to Mama or Papa, without the special consent of Mama, Papa or Miss Scales.

11. It is understood that when John desires to make any purchases which the allowance does not cover, he will first gain the consent of either Mama, Papa or Miss Scales, who will give him sufficient money with which to pay for the specific purchases, the change from which, together with a memorandum showing what items have been bought and at what cost and what amount is returned, is to be given to the person advancing the money, before night of the day on which the purchases are made.

12. It is understood that no governess, companion or other person in the household is to be asked by John to pay for any items for him, other than carfare.

13. To any savings from the date in this account which John may from time to time deposit in his bank account, in excess of the twenty per cent (20%) referred to in Item No. 8, Papa will add an equal sum for deposit.

14. The allowance above set forth and the agreement under which it shall be arrived at are to continue in force until changed by mutual consent.

> The above agreement approved and
> entered into by
> *John D. Rockefeller, Jr.*
> *John D. Rockefeller 3rd*

May 1, 1920.

F. Scott Fitzgerald to
Frances Scott "Scottie" Fitzgerald

"Things to worry about . . . Things not to worry about"

In the thirteen years following his smashing literary debut with This Side of Paradise, *F. Scott Fitzgerald's work was not very well received. His subsequent novels, including* The Beautiful and the Damned *and* The Great Gatsby, *were both critical and financial disappointments.*

During the summer of 1933, Fitzgerald was finishing Tender Is the Night *in a rented house near the Johns Hopkins hospital where his wife, Zelda, was receiving treatment for mental illness. He was drinking heavily and Zelda was at home in what turned out to be only a brief respite from a life in psychiatric institutions.*

Here Fitzgerald writes to his daughter and only child, twelve-year-old Scottie, away at summer camp.

La Paix, Rodgers' Forge,
Towson, Maryland,
August 8, 1933.

Dear Pie:

I feel very strongly about you doing duty. Would you give me a little more documentation about your reading in French? I am glad you are happy—but I never believe much in happiness. I never believe in misery either. Those are things you see on the stage or the screen or the printed page, they never really happen to you in life.

All I believe in in life is the rewards for virtue (according to your talents) and the *punishments* for not fulfilling your duties, which are doubly costly. If there is such a volume in the camp library, will you ask Mrs. Tyson to let you look up a sonnet of Shakespeare's in which the line occurs "*Lilies that fester smell far worse than weeds.*"

Have had no thoughts today, life seems composed of getting up a *Saturday Evening Post* story. I think of you, and always pleasantly; but if you call me "Pappy" again I am going to take the White Cat out and beat his bottom *hard, six times for every time you are impertinent.* Do you react to that?

I will arrange the camp bill.

Halfwit, I will conclude. Things to worry about:

Worry about courage
Worry about cleanliness
Worry about efficiency
Worry about horsemanship
Worry about . . .

Things not to worry about:

Don't worry about popular opinion
Don't worry about dolls
Don't worry about the past
Don't worry about the future
Don't worry about growing up
Don't worry about anybody getting ahead of you
Don't worry about triumph
Don't worry about failures unless it comes through your own fault
Don't worry about mosquitoes
Don't worry about flies
Don't worry about insects in general
Don't worry about parents
Don't worry about boys
Don't worry about disappointments
Don't worry about pleasures
Don't worry about satisfactions

Things to think about:

What am I really aiming at?
How good am I really in comparison to my contemporaries in
regard to:
    (a) Scholarship
    (b) Do I really understand about people and am I able to get along
    with them?
    (c) Am I trying to make my body a useful instrument or am I
    neglecting it?

With dearest love,

P.S. My come-back to your calling me Pappy is christening you by the word Egg, which implies that you belong to a very rudimentary state of life and that I could break you up and crack you open at my will and I think it would be a word that would hang on if I ever told it to your contemporaries. "Egg Fitzgerald." How would you like that to go through life with "Eggie Fitzgerald" or "Bad Egg Fitzgerald" or any form that might occur to fertile minds? Try it once more and I swear to God I will hang it on you and it will be up to you to shake it off. Why borrow trouble?

Love anyhow.

EDDIE RICKENBACKER TO
WILLIAM RICKENBACKER

"Never fail to live up to the rules of the game . . ."

Through determination and self-reliance, Eddie Rickenbacker reached acclaim in three distinct twentieth-century fields: In the early days of auto racing, Rickenbacker became a world-record-holding, Hall of Fame driver; then, under General Pershing in World War I, he was America's top fighter pilot, the "Ace of Aces," who destroyed twenty-six enemy aircraft and was awarded the Congressional Medal of Honor; later, as the president and chairman of the board of Eastern Airlines, he proved to the country that an airline company could in fact be profitable without government subsidies.

In 1941 on a government tour of World War II bases, the plane in which Rickenbacker was a passenger went down in the Pacific Ocean. He and seven of the eight others aboard survived twenty-two harrowing days adrift in a rubber raft.

Here, ten years after his crash into the Pacific and thirty-three years after Armistice Day, when he flew over the battlefield at Verdun, Capt. Eddie Rickenbacker sends his twenty-four-year-old adopted son, Bill, off to the United States Air Force.

January 11, 1951

My dear Son and Pal Bill:

With your departure to enter the military services of your country as a cadet in the Air Force of the United States of America, Mother and I hope that you will remember and follow a few of the simple rules of life which will be beneficial to you as time goes on:

Always remember that a million friends are worth more than a million dollars because if you have a million friends you will never need to worry about a million dollars.

Always be respectful to your superiors and elders as it is an acknowledgement of your capacity to appreciate the benefits acquired from experience.

This was evidenced by my answer to a query recently, "What advice can you give the younger generation, based on your greatest failure?" My answer was, "Failure to evaluate and understand the advice of my elders in my youth."

Naturally, modesty on the part of one who has been blessed with so many attributes as you in your limited years is a tribute to your good judgment.

Consideration of others at all times, be they right or wrong, is an acknowledgement of your own limitations.

Appreciation of acts of kindness and thoughtfulness will always make it possible for you to reciprocate in kind.

Never worry about protecting my name or my reputation. But always remember that it is your name you must protect and live with the balance of your life, which I am sure will be a constructive one as well as one of service to your fellow man.

Never fail to live up to the rules of the game, always play it in accordance with your knowledge and appreciation of the difference between right and wrong.

Always be a *good* soldier and not just a man in uniform.

Never try to impress other people with your superiority of knowledge, the latter of which you have been blessed with abundantly.

Never fail to remember that to have a strong and healthy mind you must first have a strong and healthy body.

Protect your body by limiting the abuses that go with every day life and you will automatically protect your mentality.

To become a good pilot and remain one never forget that an airplane is like a rattlesnake, you must keep your mind and eye on it constantly or it will bite you when you least expect it which could prove fatal.

Study the design, mechanics, and operation of your plane thoroughly and in detail.

Learn the detailed functioning and limitations of your plane, its accessories and its engines, and you will never abuse them to the degree that you will be the sufferer.

Learn to know and appreciate the mechanics who work on your plane and every unit of its operation because their appreciation of you at all times may mean the difference between a successful flight and one that is not.

Take advantage at all times, without interfering with your regular duties, to benefit through wholesome outdoor exercise such as golf at which you are very proficient.

For your peace of mind and emotional stability, play the piano when you feel the desire, when time permits, and when the opportunity is available.

Be certain to let your superior officer know the necessity to favor your left shoulder for some time to come in your daily exercises.

Make arrangements with the finance officer to have your checks sent to me in care of Eastern Air Lines, and I in turn will see that they are credited to your bank account, from which you may issue checks and will keep you advised of your balance.

Never hesitate to let me know if your requirements or needs exceed your earning power or bank balance.

By remaining strong physically and mentally remember you will be helping your country to develop the greatest and strongest air power in the world which is basically the salvation of this nation and the future of its people.

Always keep in mind the men at the head of the Kremlin only respect force and power.

Realize how blessed we of this land have been in our 160 odd years of existence. We have not suffered the penalties of starvation for generations at a time as other peoples of other lands have done. Neither have we suffered destruction of our homes, institutions of learning, commerce and finance.

There have been many times when I have felt that our standard of living had grown beyond reasonable proportions because we as a people have failed to appreciate the fruits and value thereof, and have become slaves to the philosophy of getting more for less or something for nothing.

There is no doubt that this country and our civilization are on trial and the problems of the future may be God's way of making us suffer for our lack of appreciation of our way of life and the blessings bestowed on us by the Supreme Power.

While it is an axiom in life, and has been since the beginning of the world, that suffering is the greatest developer for expanding mentality, it could become a great penalty imposed on us for our faithlessness.

You are certain as the years go on to have many heartaches, headaches, trials, and tribulations but when the hour looks the darkest never lose faith in that Power Above.

With faith in the Power Above you will have faith in yourself. And because of your faith your call to God in Heaven for help if needed will never go unheeded, and will bring you back to us, your family, and your fellow man for greater service when peace among men shall reign again.

Love as always,
Daddy

Barbara Bush to Her Children

"Keep trying."

Late one night, just after the death of her brother and the birth of a grandson, and soon after leaving the White House, Barbara Bush could not sleep. She rose from her bed to write her five living children about lessons learned during her sixty-seven years. The letter was never sent, but Mrs. Bush later published her words of advice to her children in her memoir, which she dedicated "To faith, family and friends; and to George Bush, who taught me that these are the most important things in life."

[c. May 1993]

. . . Faith, Family, and Friends.

Try—and oh boy, how hard it is—to find the good in people and not the bad. I remember many years ago that I wasted so much time worrying about my mother. I suffered so because she and I had a "chemical thing." I loved her very much, but was hurt by her. (I am sure that I hurt her a lot, too.) Grace Walker said to me once, "Think of all the lovely things about your mother . . . all the things you love and are proud of about her." There were so many that I couldn't count them all. I think that

I expected her to be perfect. Nobody is perfect. Certainly not me. So LOOK FOR THE GOOD IN OTHERS. Forget the other.

Clara Barton, the founder and president of the Red Cross, was once reminded of a wrong a friend had done to her years earlier. "Don't you remember?" the friend asked. "No," replied Clara firmly. "I distinctly remember forgetting that." Not bad advice. Take a lesson from your dad. He says that when I remind him that someone has been hateful, "Isn't it better to make a friend rather than an enemy?" He's right too.

Don't talk about money . . . either having it or not having it. It is embarrassing for others and quite frankly vulgar.

DO NOT BUY SOMETHING THAT YOU CANNOT AFFORD. YOU DO NOT NEED IT.

If you really need something and can't afford it . . . for heaven's sake call home. That's what family are all about.

Do not try to live up to your neighbors. They won't look down on you if you don't have two television sets. They will look down on you if you buy things that you cannot afford and they will know it! They are only interested in their possessions, not yours.

Be sure that you pay people back. If you have dinner at their house or they take you out, have them back, but remember you don't need the expensive thing. You can make the best spaghetti in the world. People love to come to your home. Plan ahead and it will be fun.

Value your friends. They are your most valuable asset.

Remember loyalty is a two-way street. It goes up and down. So be loyal to those people who are loyal to you. Your dad is the best example of two-way loyalty that I know.

Love your children. I don't have to tell any of you that. You are the best children any two people ever had. I know you will be as lucky. Your kids are great. Dad and I love them more than life itself. I think you know that about your dad. I do also.

Remember what Robert Fulghum says: "Don't worry that your children never listen to you; worry that they are always watching you."

For heaven's sake enjoy life. Don't cry over things that were or things that aren't. Enjoy what you have now to the fullest. In all honesty you really only have two choices; you can like what you do OR you can dislike it. I choose to like it and what fun I have had. The other choice is no fun and people do not want to be around a whiner. We can always find people who are worse off and we don't have to look far! Help them and forget self!

I would certainly say, above all, seek God. He will come to you if you look. There is absolutely *NO* down side. Please expose your children and set a good example for them by going to church. We, your dad and I, have tried to live as Christian a life as we can. We certainly have not been perfect. Maybe you can! Keep trying.

APPENDIX

Births, Deaths, Marriages, Children

Adams, Abigail (November 22, 1744—October 28, 1810)
    m. John Adams (married October 25, 1764; deceased 1826)
        Abigail (1765–1813)
        John Quincy (1767–1848)
        Susanna (1768–1770)
        Charles (1770–1800)
        Thomas (1772–1832)

Adams, Ansel (February 20, 1902—April 22, 1984)
    m. Virginia Best (married January 2, 1928; deceased 2000)
        Michael (1933–)
        Anne (1935–)

Adams, John (October 30, 1735—July 4, 1826)
    m. Abigail Smith (married October 25, 1764; deceased 1810)
        Abigail (1765–1813)
        John Quincy (1767–1848)
        Susanna (1768–1770)

Charles (1770–1800)

Thomas (1772–1832)

Adams, John Quincy (July 11, 1767—February 23, 1848)

    m. Louisa Catherine Johnson (married July 26, 1797; deceased May 14, 1852)

        George Washington (1801–1829)

        John (1803–1834)

        Charles Francis (1807–1886)

        Louisa Catherine (1811–1812)

Anderson, Sherwood (September 13, 1876—March 8, 1941)

    m. Cornelia Pratt Lane (married May 16, 1904; divorced July 27, 1916)

        Robert (1907–1951)

        John (1908–1995)

        Marion (1911–unknown)

    m. Tennessee Claflin Mitchell (married July 31, 1916; divorced April 1924)

    m. Elizabeth Prall (married April 5, 1924; divorced February, 1932)

    m. Eleanor Gladys Copenhaver (married July 6, 1933)

Audubon, John James (April 26, 1785—January 27, 1851)

    m. Lucy Bakewell (married 1808; deceased 1874)

        Victor (1809–1860)

        John (1812–1862)

        Lucy (1815–1817)

        Rose (1819–1820)

Bell, Alexander Graham (March 3, 1847—August 2, 1922)

    m. Mabel Hubbard (married July 11, 1877; deceased 1923)

        Elsie (1878–1964)

        Marian "Daisy" Hubbard (1880–1962)

        Edward (1881–1881)

        Robert (1883–1883)

Bradstreet, Anne (c. 1612—September 16, 1672)

    m. Simon Bradstreet (married c. 1628; deceased 1697)

        Dorothy (1633–1671/72)

        Samuel (c. 1632–1683)

        Sarah (c. 1636–1707)

        Simon (1640–1683/84)

        Hannah Ann (c. 1643–1707)

        Mercy (1647–1714)

Dudley (1648–1702)

John (1652–1717/18)

Elizabeth (1662/63–unknown)

Annie (1665–unknown)

Bush, Barbara (June 8, 1925–)

  m. George Herbert Walker Bush (married January 6, 1945)

    George (1946–)

    Robin (1949–1953)

    John Ellis "Jeb" (1953–)

    Neil (1955–)

    Marvin (1956–)

    Dorothy "Doro" (1959–)

Bush, George Herbert Walker (June 12, 1924–)

  m. Barbara Pierce (married January 6, 1945)

    George (1946–)

    Robin (1949–1953)

    John Ellis "Jeb" (1953–)

    Neil (1955–)

    Marvin (1956–)

    Dorothy "Doro" (1959–)

Byrd, Richard (October 25, 1888—March 11, 1957)

  m. Marie Ames (married 1915; deceased 1974)

    Richard Jr. (1920–1988)

    Bolling (1922–)

    Katherine (1924–)

    Helen (1926–1974)

Catlin, George (July 26, 1796—December 23, 1872)

  m. Clara B. Gregory (deceased 1845)

    [child died in 1836]

    Elizabeth Wing (1837–unknown)

    Clara Gregory (1839–unknown)

    Louise Victoria (1841–unknown)

    George, Jr. (1843–1846)

Chase, Salmon P. (January 13, 1808—May 7, 1873)

  m. Katherine Garniss (married March 4, 1834; deceased December 1835)

    Catherine Jane "Kate" (1835–1840)

m. Eliza Ann Smith (married September 1839; deceased September 29, 1845)
   Catherine Jane "Kate" (1840–1899)
   Elizabeth (1842–1842)
   Elizabeth (1843–1844)
m. Sarah Bella Dunlop Ludlow (married November 6, 1846; deceased January 13, 1852)
   Janet Ralston "Nettie" (1847–1925)
   Josephine Ludlow "Zoe" (1849–1850)

Cronyn, Hume (July 18, 1911—June 15, 2003)
   m. Emily Woodruff (married 1935; divorced 1942)
   m. Jessica Tandy (married September 27, 1942; deceased September 11, 1994)
   Susan Hawkins (Jessica Tandy's daughter from marriage to actor Jack Hawkins) (1934–)
   Christopher (1943–)
   Tandy (1945–)
   m. Susan Cooper (married 1996)
   (stepchildren Jonathan Grant and Kate Glennon)

Douglas, William O. (October 16, 1898—January 19, 1980)
   m. Mildred Riddle (married August 16, 1923; divorced 1954)
   Mildred (1929–)
   William (1932–)
   m. Mercedes Hester Davidson (married December 14, 1954; divorced 1963)
   m. Joan Martin (married August 1963; divorced 1966)
   m. Cathleen Heffernan (married July 1966)

Douglass, Frederick (ca. February 1817—February 20, 1895)
   m. Anna Murray (married September 15, 1838; deceased 1882)
   Rosetta (1839–1906)
   Lewis (1840–1908)
   Frederick (1842–1892)
   Charles (1844–1920)
   Annie (1849–1860)
   m. Helen Pitts (married January 24, 1884; deceased December 1, 1903)

Du Bois, W. E. B. (February 23, 1868—August 27, 1963)
   m. Nina Gomer (married May 12, 1896; deceased 1950)
   Yolande (1900–1960)
   Burghardt (1897–1899)
   m. Shirley Graham (married February 27, 1951; deceased April 4, 1977)

APPENDIX

Edison, Thomas Alva (February 11, 1847—October 18, 1931)
 m. Mary Stilwell (married December 25, 1871; deceased 1884)
  Estelle (1872–1965)
  Thomas Alva, Jr. (1876–1935)
  William (1878–1937)
 m. Mina Miller (married February 24, 1886; deceased August 24, 1947)
  Theodore (1898–1992)
  Madeleine (1888–1979)
  Charles (1890–1969)

Edwards, Jonathan (October 5, 1703—March 22, 1758)
 m. Sarah Pierpont (married July 1727; deceased 1758)
  Jerusha (1730–1748)
  Esther (1732–1758)
  Mary (1734–1807)
  Lucy (1736–1786)
  Timothy (1738–1813)
  Jonathan, Jr. (1745–1801)
  Pierpont (1750–1826)

Einstein, Albert (March 14, 1879—April 18, 1955)
 m. Mileva Maric (married January 6, 1903; divorced 1919)
  Lieserl (February 4, 1902–?)
  Hans Albert (1904–1973)
  Eduard (1910–1965)
 m. Elsa (married June 1919; deceased 1936)

Eliot, Charles W. (March 20, 1834—August 22, 1926)
 m. Ellen Peabody (married October 27, 1858; deceased March 13, 1869)
  Charles (1859–1897)
  Francis (1861–1861)
  Samuel (1862–1950)
  Robert (1866–1867)
 m. Grace Hopkinson (married October 30, 1877; deceased 1924)

Fisher, M. F. K. (July 3, 1908—June 22, 1992)
 m. Alfred Young Fisher (married 1929; divorced 1937)
 m. Dillwyn Parrish (married 1937; deceased 1941)
  Anna Kennedy (1943–)
 m. Donald Friede (married May 1945; divorced 1951)
  Mary Kennedy (March 1946–)

Fitzgerald, F. Scott (September 24, 1896—December 21, 1940)
    m. Zelda (married April 3, 1920; deceased March 10, 1948)
        Scottie (1921–1986)

Franklin, Benjamin (January 6, 1706—April 17, 1790)
    m. Deborah Read (married September 1, 1730; deceased December 19, 1774)
        William (1731–1813)
        Francis Folger (1732–1736)
        Sarah "Sally" (1743–1808)

Garrison, William Lloyd (December 10, 1805—May 24, 1879)
    m. Helen Benson (married September 4, 1834; deceased 1876)
        George Thompson (1836–1904)
        William Lloyd, Jr. (1838–1909)
        Wendell Phillips (1840–1907)
        Charles Follen (1842–1849)
        Helen Frances "Fanny" (1844–1928)
        Elizabeth Pease (1846–1848)
        Francis Jackson (1848–1916)

Gates, Henry Louis (September 16, 1950–)
    m. Sharon Lynn Adams (married September 1, 1979)
        Maude Augusta "Maggie" (1980–)
        Elizabeth Helen-Claire "Liza" (1982–)

Guthrie, Woody (July 14, 1912—October 3, 1967)
    m. Mary Jennings (married October 28, 1933; divorced 1945)
        Gwen (1935–1976)
        Sue (1937–1978)
        Will (1939–1962)
    m. Marjorie Greenblatt Mazia (married 1945; divorced 1953)
        Cathy Ann (1943–1947)
        Arlo (1947–)
        Joady (1948–)
        Nora (1950–)
    m. Anneke Van Kirk (married 1953; divorced 1956)
        Lorina Lynn (1954–1973)

Hammerstein, Oscar II (July 12, 1895—August 23, 1960)
    m. Myra Finn (married August 22, 1917; divorced 1928)

William (1918–2001)

Alice (1921–)

m. Dorothy Blanchard (married May 14, 1929; deceased 1987)

James (1931–1999)

Houston, Sam (March 2, 1793—July 26, 1863)

m. Eliza Allen (married January 22, 1829; divorced November 30, 1833)

m. Margaret Lea (married May 9, 1841; deceased December 3, 1867)

Sam (1843–1894)

Nancy (1846–1920)

Margaret (1848–1906)

Mary (1850–1931)

Antoinette (1852–1932)

Andrew Jackson (1854–1941)

William (1858–unknown)

Temple Lea (1860–1905)

Howard, Moses "Moe" (June 19, 1897—May 4, 1975)

m. Helen Schonberger (married 1925; deceased 1975)

Joan (1927–)

Paul (1935–)

Howells, William Dean (March 1, 1837—May 11, 1920)

m. Elinor Gertrude Mead (married December 24, 1862; deceased 1910)

Winifred (1863–1899)

John (1868–1959)

Mildred (1872–1966)

James, William (January 11, 1842—August 26, 1910)

m. Alice Howe Gibbens (married July 10, 1878; deceased 1922)

Henry III (1879–1947)

William (1882–1961)

Herman (1884–1885)

Mary Margaret "Peggy" (1887–1952)

Alexander "Tweedy" (1890–1946)

Jefferson, Thomas (April 13, 1743—July 4, 1826)

m. Martha Skelton (married January 1, 1772; deceased September 6, 1782)

Martha "Patsy" (1772–1836)

Jane (1774–1775)

unnamed son (1777–1777)
Maria "Polly" (1778–1804)
Lucy Elizabeth (1780–1781)
Lucy Elizabeth (1782–1785)

Lanier, Sidney (February 3, 1842—September 7, 1881)
    m. Mary Day (married December 21, 1867; deceased 1931)
        Charles (1868–1945)
        Sidney (1870–1918)
        Henry Wysham (1873–1958)
        Robert (1880–1912)

Lee, Robert E. (January 19, 1807–October 12, 1870)
    m. Mary Anne Custis (married June 30, 1831; deceased 1873)
        George Washington Custis (1832–1913)
        Mary Custis (1835–1918)
        William Henry Fitzhugh (1837–1891)
        Annie (1839–1862)
        Eleanor Agnes (1841–1873)
        Robert E., Jr. (1843–1914)
        Mildred Chase (1846–1905)

Lincoln, Mary Todd (December 13, 1818—July 15, 1882)
    m. Abraham Lincoln (married November 4, 1842; deceased April 15, 1865)
        Robert (1843–1926)
        Edward (1846–1850)
        William "Willie" (1850–1862)
        Thomas "Tad" (1853–1871)

London, Jack (January 12, 1867—November 22, 1916)
    m. Bess Maddern (married April 7, 1900; divorced, October 1905)
        Joan (1901–1971)
        Bess (1902–1992)
    m. Charmian Kittredge (married October 1905; deceased 1955)
        Joy (1910–1910)

Luce, Clare Boothe (April 10, 1903—October 9, 1987)
    m. George Tuttle Brokaw (married August 10, 1923; divorced 1929)
        Ann Clare (1924–1944)
    m. Henry Luce (married November 23, 1935; deceased February 28, 1967)

Mahan, Alfred Thayer (September 27, 1840—December 1, 1914)
    m. Ellen Lyle (married June 11, 1872; deceased 1927)
        Helen (1873–1963)
        Ellen Kuhn (1877–1947)
        Lyle Evans (1881–1966)

Marx, Groucho (Julius Henry) (October 2, 1890—August 19, 1977)
    m. Ruth Johnson (married February 4, 1920; divorced July 15, 1942)
        Arthur (1921–)
        Miriam (1927–)
    m. Catherine Gorcey (married July 21, 1945; divorced 1951)
        Melinda (1946–)
    m. Eden Hartford (married July 17, 1954; divorced 1969)

Melville, Herman (August 1, 1819–September 28, 1891)
    m. Elizabeth Shaw (married August 1847; deceased 1906)
        Malcolm (1849–1867)
        Stanwix (1851–1886)
        Elizabeth (1853–1908)
        Frances (1885–1938)

O'Hara, John (January 31, 1905–April 11, 1970)
    m. Helen Ritchie Petit (married February 28, 1931; divorced 1933)
    m. Belle Mulford Wylie (married December 3, 1937; deceased January 9, 1954)
        Wylie (1945–)
    m. Katharine "Sister" Barnes Bryan (married January 31, 1955; deceased 1974)

Olmsted, Frederick Law (April 26, 1822—August 28, 1903)
    m. Mary Perkins Olmsted (married June 13, 1859; deceased April 23, 1921)
        John Charles (1852–1920)
        Charlotte (1855–1908)
        Owen (1857–1881)
        John Theodore (1860–1860)
        Marion (1861–1948)
        unnamed boy (1866–1866)
        Henry (Frederick Law Olmsted, Jr.) (1870–1957)

O'Neill, Eugene (October 16, 1888–November 27, 1953)
    m. Kathleen Jenkins (married October 2, 1909; divorced July 1912)

Eugene, Jr. (1910—1950)
m. Agnes Boulton (married January 1918; divorced July 1929)
Shane (1919–1977)
Oona (1925–1991)
m. Carlotta Monterey (married July 1929; deceased November 18, 1970)

Patton, George (November 11, 1885—December 21, 1945)
m. Beatrice Ayer (married May 26, 1910; deceased 1953)
Beatrice (1911–1952)
Ruth Ellen (1915–1993)
George IV (December, 1923–)

Pershing, John J. (September 13, 1860—July 15, 1948)
m. Helen Frances Warren (married January 26, 1905; deceased August 27, 1915)
Helen (1906–1915)
Anne (1908–1915)
Francis Warren (1909–1980)
Mary Margaret (1912–1915)

Rickenbacker, Eddie (October 8, 1890—July 23, 1973)
m. Adelaide Frost (married 1922; deceased February 2, 1977)
David (1925–)
William (1928–)

Rockefeller, John D. (July 8, 1839—May 23, 1937)
m. Laura C. Spelman (married September 8, 1864; deceased March 12, 1915)
Elizabeth "Bessie" (1866–1906)
Alice (1869–1870)
Alta (1871–1962)
Edith (1872–1932)
John D., Jr. (1874–1960)

Rockefeller, John D., Jr. (January 29, 1874–May 11, 1960)
m. Abby Aldrich (married 1901; deceased April 5, 1948)
Abby (1903–1976)
John D. III (1906–1978)
Nelson (1908–1979)
Laurence (1910–)
Winthrop (1912–1973)

David (1915–)
m. Martha Baird Allen (married August 1951; deceased January 24, 1971)

Roebling, Washington (May 26, 1837—July 21, 1926)
    m. Emily Warren (married January 18, 1865; deceased February 28, 1903)
        John (1867–1952)
    m. Cornelia Witsell Farrow (married April 21, 1908; deceased 1942)

Roosevelt, Eleanor (October 11, 1884—November 7, 1962)
    m. Franklin Delano Roosevelt (married 1905; deceased April 12, 1945)
        Anna (1906–1975)
        James (1907–1991)
        Eliot (1910–1990)
        Franklin, Jr. (1909–1909)
        Franklin, Jr. (1914–1988)
        John (1916–1981)

Roosevelt, Theodore (October 27, 1858—January 6, 1919)
    m. Alice Lee (married October 27, 1880; deceased February 14, 1884)
        Alice (1884–1980)
    m. Edith Carow (married December 2, 1886; deceased September 30, 1948)
        Theodore (1887–1944)
        Kermit (1889–1943)
        Ethel (1891–1977)
        Archibald (1894–1979)
        Quentin (1897–1918)

Rush, Benjamin (January 4, 1746—April 19, 1813)
    m. Julia Stockton (married January 1, 1776; deceased 1848)
        John (1777–1837)
        Anne Emily (1779–1850)
        Richard (1780–1859)
        Susanna (1782–1782)
        Elizabeth Graeme (1783–1783)
        Mary Rush (1784–1849)
        James Rush (1786–1869)
        William (1787–1787)
        Benjamin (1789–1789)
        Benjamin (1791–1824)
        Julia (1792–1860)

Samuel (1795–1859)
William (1801–1864)

Sandburg, Carl (January 6, 1878—July 22, 1967)
    m. Lillian Steichen (married June 15, 1908; deceased February 18, 1977)
    Madeline (1913–1913)
    Margaret (1911–1977)
    Janet (1916–2001)
    Helga (1918–)

Seward, William (May 16, 1801—October 10, 1872)
    m. Frances Miller (married October 20, 1824; deceased June 21, 1865)
    Augustus Henry (1826–1876)
    Frederick William (1830–1915)
    Cornelia (1835–1836)
    William Henry, Jr. (1839–1920)
    Fanny (1844–1866)

Sexton, Anne (November 9, 1928—October 4, 1974)
    m. Alfred Muller "Kayo" Sexton (married August 15, 1948; divorced 1973)
    Linda (1953–)
    Joyce "Joy" (1955–)

Stanton, Elizabeth Cady (November 12, 1815—October 26, 1902)
    m. Henry Brewster Stanton (married 1840; deceased 1887)
    Daniel Cady (1842–1891)
    Henry B., Jr. (1844–1903)
    Gerrit Smith (1845–1927)
    Theodore Weld (1851–1925)
    Margaret Livingston (1852–1930)
    Harriet Eaton (1856–1940)
    Robert Livingston (1859–1920)

Steffens, Lincoln (April 6, 1866—August 9, 1936)
    m. Josephine Bontecou (married fall 1891; deceased 1911)
    m. Ella Winter (married August 1924)
    Pete (1924–unknown)

Steinbeck, John (February 27, 1902—December 20, 1968)
    m. Carol Henning (married 1930; divorced 1942)
    m. Gwyn Conger (married March 29, 1943; divorced 1948)
    Thomas (1944–)

John IV (1946–1991)
m. Elaine Scott (married December 26, 1950; deceased 2003)

Stowe, Harriet Beecher (June 14, 1811—July 1, 1896)
m. Calvin Stowe (married January 6, 1836; deceased 1886)
Harriet (1836–1907)
Eliza (1836–1912)
Henry Ellis (1838–1857)
Frederick (1840–1870?)
Georgiana (1843–1890)
Samuel Chase "Charley" (1848–1849)
Charles Edward "Charley" (1850–1934)

Truman, Harry S. (May 8, 1884—December 26, 1972)
m. Bess Wallace (married June 28, 1919; deceased October 18, 1982)
Margaret (1924–)

Twain, Mark (Samuel Clemens) (November 30, 1835—April 21, 1910)
m. Olivia Langdon (married 1870; deceased 1904)
Langdon (1870–1872)
Olivia Susan "Susie" (1872–1896)
Clara (1874–1962)
Jane "Jean" (1880–1909)

Washington, George (February 22, 1732—December 14, 1799)
m. Martha Dandridge Custis (married January 6, 1759; deceased May 22, 1802)
John Parke Custis (1754–1781)
Martha Parke "Patsy" Custis (1756–1773)

Webster, Daniel (January 18, 1782—October 24, 1852)
m. Grace Fletcher (married May 29, 1808; deceased January 21, 1828)
Grace (1810–1817)
Daniel "Fletcher" (1840–1865)
Julia (1818–1848)
Edward (1820–1848)
Charles (1821–1824)
m. Caroline Le Roy (married December 12, 1829; deceased 1882)

Wilder, Laura Ingalls (February 7, 1867—February 10, 1957)
m. Almanzo Wilder (married August 25, 1885; deceased 1949)

       Rose (1886–1968)

       unnamed son (1889–1889)

Williams, William Carlos (September 17, 1883—March 4, 1963)
    m. Florence Herman (married December 12, 1912; deceased 1976)
    William Eric (1914–1995)
    Paul (1916–)

Wilson, Woodrow (December 18, 1856—February 13, 1924)
    m. Ellen Louise Axson (married June 24, 1885; deceased August 6, 1914)
    Margaret (1886–1944)
    Jessie (1887–1933)
    Eleanor (1889–1967)
    m. Edith Bolling Galt (married December 18, 1915; deceased December 28, 1961)

Wyeth, N. C. (October 22, 1882—October 19, 1945)
    m. Carolyn Bockius (married April 16, 1906; deceased March 15, 1973)
    Carolyn (1906–1906)
    Henriette (1907–1997)
    Carolyn (1909–1994)
    Nathaniel (1911–1990)
    Ann (1915–)
    Andrew (1917–)

BIBLIOGRAPHY

Archives

The following archives, libraries, and institutions graciously made their collections available:

American Philosophical Society, Philadelphia, PA
Amherst College, Amherst, MA
Archive of American Art, Smithsonian Institution, Washington, DC
Archives of Labor and Urban Affairs, Walter Reuther Library, Wayne State
    University, Detroit, MI
Auburn University, Auburn, AL
Bancroft Library, University of California Berkeley, Berkeley, CA
California Institute of Technology, Pasadena, CA
Center for American Music, University of Pittsburgh, Pittsburgh, PA
Dartmouth College, Hanover, NH
Dwight Eisenhower Presidential Library, Abilene, KS
Franklin D. Roosevelt Presidential Library, Hyde Park, NY
Gerald Ford Presidential Library, Ann Arbor, MI
Harriet Beecher Stowe Center, Hartford, CT
Harry S Truman Presidential Library, Independence, MO

Haverford College, Haverford, PA
Herbert Hoover Presidential Library, West Branch, IA
Houghton Library, Harvard University, Cambridge, MA
James J. Hill Group, St. Paul, MN
Library of Congress, Washington, DC
Lyndon B. Johnson Library, Austin, TX
Maine Historical Society, Portland, ME
Massachusetts Historical Society, Boston, MA
Moorland-Spingarn Research Center, Howard University, Washington, DC
Morris Library, Southern Illinois University, Carbondale, IL
National John Steinbeck Center, Salinas, CA
Naval War College, Newport, RI
Newberry Library, Chicago, IL
Ohio State University, Columbus, OH
Olana State Historic Site, Saugerties, NY
Pierpont Morgan Library, New York, NY
Players Club, New York, NY
Princeton University, Princeton, NJ
Pusey Library, Harvard University, Cambridge, MA
Rockefeller Archive Center, Sleepy Hollow, NY
Rutgers University, New Brunswick, NJ
Schlesinger Library, Radcliffe College, Cambridge, MA
Schomburg Center for Research in Black Culture, New York Public Library,
    New York NY
Smithsonian Institution, Washington, DC
Stanford University, Stanford, CA
Studebaker National Museum, South Bend, IN
Texas State Library, Austin, TX
Theodore Roosevelt Association, Oyster Bay, NY
Thomas Edison Historic Site, West Orange, NJ
Union Theological Seminary, New York, NY
University of Chicago Library, Chicago, IL
University of Virginia, Charlottesville, VA
University of Wisconsin, Madison, WI
Woody Guthrie Archive, New York, NY
Yale University, New Haven, CT

Books and Periodicals

For individual introductions to the letters a number of reference materials were regularly consulted, including: *Dictionary of American Biography, Dictionary of Literary Biography, Current Biography*, and *Notable American Women*. Obituaries from *The New York Times*, when available, proved to be a consistently valuable resource as well.

Adams, Ansel. *Ansel Adams: An Autobiography*. Boston: Little, Brown & Company, 1986.

———. *Ansel Adams: Letters 1916–1984*. Edited by Mary Street Alinder and Andrea Gray Stillman. Boston: Little, Brown & Company, 2001.

Adams, John Quincy. *The Diary of John Quincy Adams: 1794–1845*. Edited by Allan Nevins. New York: Charles Scribner's Sons, 1951.

"Admiral Byrd Dies at 68; Made 5 Polar Expeditions." *New York Times*. March 12, 1957, 1.

Alter, Jonathan, and Howard Fineman, et al. "A Dynasty's Dilemma." *Newsweek*. July 29, 2002, 22.

Anderson, Sherwood. *Sherwood Anderson: Selected Letters*. Edited by Charles E. Modlin. Knoxville: University of Tennessee Press, 1984.

Andrist, Ralph, ed. *George Washington: A Biography in His Own Words*. New York: Newsweek Book Division, 1972.

Asbell, Bernard, ed. *Mother & Daughter: The Letters of Eleanor and Anna Roosevelt*. New York: Coward, McCann & Geoghegan, 1982.

Audubon, John James. *Audubon's Birds of America*. New York: Macmillan Publishing Company, 1950.

———. *Letters of John James Audubon 1826–1840: In Two Volumes: Volume Two*. Edited by Howard Corning. Boston: The Club of Odd Volumes, 1930.

———. *Writings and Drawings*. New York: Library of America, 1999.

"Baby Sayre Photographed." *New York Times*. January 31, 1915, 11.

Baldwin, Neil. *Edison: Inventing the Century*. Chicago: University of Chicago Press, 2001.

Barton, David. *Benjamin Rush: Signer of the Declaration of Independence*. Aledo, Tex.: WallBuilder Press, 1999.

Begley, Adam. "Henry Louis Gates Jr.: Black Studies' New Star." *New York Times Magazine*. April 1, 1990, 25–27, 48–50.

Bemis, Samuel Flagg. *John Quincy Adams and the Foundations of American Foreign Policy*. New York: Alfred A. Knopf, 1949.

Benson, Jackson J. *The True Adventures of John Steinbeck, Writer: A Biography*. New York: Viking Press, 1984. Reprint, New York: Penguin Books, 1990.

Beschloss, Michael, ed. *The American Heritage Illustrated History of the Presidents.* New York: Crown Publishers, 2000.

Betts, Edwin Morris, and James Adam Bear, Jr., eds. *The Family Letters of Thomas Jefferson.* Columbia: University of Missouri Press, 1966. Reprint, Charlottesville: University of Virginia Press, 1986.

Bird, William. "Byrd at Kings Bay, Landing His Planes." *New York Times.* May 1, 1926, 1.

———. "Byrd Expedition Will Reach Kings Bay Today; May Hop Off for the North Pole Within a Week." *New York Times.* April 29, 1926, 3.

———. "Byrd in Conference as He Nears Kings Bay." *New York Times.* April 28, 1926, 3.

———. "Byrd Tests Instruments and Fits Up Planes for Polar Dash as Chantier Nears Arctic Base." *New York Times.* April 27, 1926, 1.

Black, Stephen A. *Eugene O'Neill: Beyond Mourning and Tragedy.* New Haven: Yale University Press, 1999.

Blue, Frederick J. *Salmon P. Chase: A Life in Politics.* Kent, Ohio: Kent State University Press, 1987.

Blumenson, Martin. *The Patton Papers: 1940–1945.* Boston: Houghton-Mifflin Company, 1974. Reprint, Cambridge: Da Capo Press, 1996.

Bontemps, Arna. *Free at Last: The Life of Frederick Douglass.* New York: Dodd, Mead & Company, 1971.

Bowden, Henry Warner. *Dictionary of American Religious Biography: Second Edition, Revised and Enlarged.* Westport, Conn.: Greenwood Press, 1993.

Bradstreet, Anne. *The Works of Anne Bradstreet in Prose and Verse.* Edited by John Harvard Ellis. Gloucester, Mass.: Peter Smith Publisher, Inc., 1932.

Brands, H. W. *The First American: The Life and Times of Benjamin Franklin.* New York: Doubleday, 2000.

Brian, Denis. *Einstein: A Life.* New York: John Wiley & Sons, Inc., 1996.

Brinkley, Alan, and Davis Dyer, eds. *Reader's Companion to the American Presidency.* Boston: Houghton Mifflin, 2000.

Bruce, Robert V. *Bell: Alexander Graham Bell and the Conquest of Solitude.* Boston: Little, Brown, & Company, 1973.

Bush, Barbara. *Barbara Bush: A Memoir.* New York: St. Martin's Press, 1994.

Bush, George. *All the Best, George Bush: My Life in Letters and Other Writings.* New York: Touchstone, 2000.

Byrd, Richard E., "Byrd Extols Spirit of Volunteer Crew." *New York Times.* April 19, 1926, 3.

———. *Little America.* New York: Knickerbocker Press, 1930.

———. *Alone: The Classic Polar Adventure.* 1938. Reprint with an afterword by David G. Campbell, New York: Kodansha International, 1995.

Chase, Salmon P. *The Salmon P. Chase Papers: Volume 5: Correspondence, 1865–1873.* Edited by John Niven. Kent, Ohio: Kent State University Press, 1998.

Chernow, Ron. *Titan: The Life of John D. Rockefeller, Sr.* New York: Random House, 1998.

Clemens, Clara. *My Father Mark Twain.* New York: Harper & Brothers, 1931.

Clements, Kendrick A. *Woodrow Wilson: World Statesman.* Chicago: Ivan R. Dee, 1999.

Cronyn, Hume. *A Terrible Liar: A Memoir.* New York: William Morrow and Company, Inc., 1991.

Crowley, John W. *The Dean of American Letters: The Late Career of William Dean Howells.* Amherst: University of Massachusetts Press, 1999.

Davis, Burke. *Gray Fox: Robert E. Lee and the Civil War.* New York: Rinehart and Company, 1956.

Douglas, William O. *The Douglas Letters: Selections from the Private Papers of Justice William O. Douglas.* Edited by Melvin I. Urofsky with assistance of Philip E. Urofsky. Bethesda, Md.: Adler & Adler, 1987.

Du Bois, W. E. B. *The Correspondence of W. E. B. Du Bois: Volume I, Selections, 1877–1934.* Edited by Herbert Aptheker. Amherst, Mass.: University of Massachusetts Press, 1973.

———. *The Souls of Black Folk.* Introduction by Herb Boyd. New York: Modern Library, 1996.

Edwards, Jonathan. *Letters and Personal Writings.* Edited by George S. Claghorn. New Haven: Yale University Press, 1998.

Einstein, Albert. *The Collected Papers of Albert Einstein: Volume 8, The Berlin Correspondence, 1914–1918, Part A: 1914.* Edited by Robert Schulmann, A. J. Kox, Michel Janssen, and Jozsef Illy, et al. Princeton: Princeton University Press, 1998.

Eliade, Mircia, ed. *The Encyclopedia of Religion: Volume 5.* New York: Macmillan Publishing Company, 1987.

Ernst, Joseph W. *"Dear Father" / "Dear Son": Correspondence of John D. Rockefeller and John D. Rockefeller, Jr.* New York: Fordham University Press, in cooperation with Rockefeller Archive Center, 1994.

"First Great Goal Reached by Byrd." *New York Times.* December 27, 1928, 2.

Fisher, M. F. K. *M. F. K. Fisher, A Life in Letters: Correspondence 1929–1991.* Selected and compiled by Norah K. Barr, Marsha Moran, and Patrick Moran. Washington, D.C.: Counterpoint, 1998.

———. *A Welcoming Life: The M. F. K. Fisher Scrapbook.* Compiled and annotated by Dominique Gioia. Washington, D.C.: Counterpoint, 1998.

Fitzgerald, F. Scott. *A Life in Letters: F. Scott Fitzgerald.* Edited by Matthew J. Bruccoli with assistance of Judith S. Baughman. New York: Touchstone, 1995.

Flexner, James Thomas. *Washington: The Indispensable Man*. Boston: Little, Brown, & Company, 1974.

Foner, Philip S. *Frederick Douglass: A Biography*. New York: Citadel Press, 1964.

Fordin, Hugh. *Getting to Know Him: A Biography of Oscar Hammerstein II*. Introduction by Stephen Sondheim. New York: Unger Publishing Company, 1977. Reprint, New York: Da Capo Press, 1995.

Franklin, Benjamin. *The Papers of Benjamin Franklin: Volume 19, January 1 through December 31, 1772*. Edited by William B. Willcox. New Haven: Yale University Press, 1975.

Freeman, Douglas Southall. *Washington: An Abridgement in One Volume by Richard Harwell of the Seven-Volume George Washington by Douglas Southall Freeman*. New York: Collier Books, 1992.

Gardner, Joseph L. *Departing Glory: Theodore Roosevelt as ex-President*. New York: Charles Scribner's Sons, 1973.

Garrison, William Lloyd. *The Letters of William Lloyd Garrison, Volume IV: From Disunionism to the Brink of War, 1850–1860*. Edited by Louis Ruchames. Cambridge, Mass.: Belknap Press of Harvard University Press, 1975.

———. *The Letters of William Lloyd Garrison, Volume VI: To Rouse the Slumbering Land, 1868–1879*. Edited by Walter M. Merrill and Louis Ruchames. Cambridge, Mass.: Belknap Press of Harvard University Press, 1981.

Gates, Henry Louis Jr. *Colored People: A Memoir*. New York: Vintage Books, 1995.

Gelb, Arthur, and Barbara Gelb. *O'Neill*. New York: Harper and Row, 1973.

Griffith, Elisabeth. *In Her Own Right: The Life of Elizabeth Cady Stanton*. New York: Oxford University Press, 1984.

Griscom, Ludlow. Introduction to *Audubon's Birds of America*, by John James Audubon. New York: Macmillan Publishing Company, 1950.

Grizzard, Frank E. *George Washington: A Biographical Companion*. Santa Barbara, Calif.: ABC-CLIO, 2002.

Grosvenor, Edwin S., and Morgan Wesson. *Alexander Graham Bell: The Life and Times of the Man*. New York: Harry N. Abrams, Inc., 1997.

Haley, James L. *Sam Houston*. Norman: University of Oklahoma Press, 2002.

Harr, John Ensor, and Peter J. Johnson. *The Rockefeller Conscience: An American Family in Public and in Private*. New York: Charles Scribner's Sons, 1991.

Hatch, Alden. *Ambassador Extraordinary: Clare Boothe Luce*. New York: Henry Holt and Company, 1956.

Hedrick, Joan D. *Harriet Beecher Stowe: A Life*. New York: Oxford University Press, 1994.

Hirschfeld, Fritz. *George Washington and Slavery: A Documentary Portrayal*. Columbia: University of Missouri Press, 1997.

Hirshson, Stanley P. *General Patton: A Soldier's Life*. New York: HarperCollins, 2002.

Houston, Samuel. *The Writings of Sam Houston: 1813–1863: Volume IV: September 29, 1821—February 23, 1847*. Edited by Amelia W. Williams and Eugene C. Barker. Austin: Pemberton Press, 1970.

———. *The Writings of Sam Houston: 1813–1863: Volume VIII: April 1825–July*. Edited by Amelia W. Williams and Eugene C. Barker. Austin: Pemberton Press, 1970.

Howells, W. D. *W. D. Howells, Selected Letters, Volume 5: 1902–1911*. Edited by William C. Fischer with Christoph K. Lohmann. Boston: Twayne Publishers, 1983.

Israel, Paul. *Edison: A Life of Invention*. New York: John Wiley & Sons, Inc., 1998.

Jaggi, Maya. "Review: Profile: Henry the first." *The Guardian (London)*. July 6, 2002, 20.

James, Henry. *Charles W. Eliot: President of Harvard University 1869–1909 Volume I*. Boston: Houghton Mifflin Company, 1930. Reprint, New York: AMS Press, 1973.

———. *Charles W. Eliot: President of Harvard University 1869–1909 Volume II*. Boston: Houghton Mifflin Company, 1930. Reprint, New York: AMS Press, 1973.

James, William. *The Correspondence of William James, Volume 5, 1878–1884*. Edited by Ignas K. Skrupskelis and Elizabeth M. Berkeley with the assistance of Wilma Bradbeer. Charlottesville: University Press of Virginia, 1997.

Kanfer, Stefan. *Groucho: The Life and Times of Julius Henry Marx*. New York: Vintage Books, 2001.

Kaplan, Justin. *Lincoln Steffens: A Biography*. New York: Simon & Schuster, 1974.

———. *Mr. Clemens and Mark Twain: A Biography*. New York: Simon & Schuster, 1966.

Kershaw, Alex. *Jack London: A Life*. New York: St. Martin's Griffin, 1997.

Kleiman, Dena. "For Tandy and Cronyn, a New Play Echoes Years of Partnership." *New York Times*. April 20, 1986, sec. 2, p. 1.

Klein, Joe. *Woody Guthrie: A Life*. New York: Dell Publishing, 1980.

Kuhn, Ferdinand, Jr. "Mawson Declares Byrd Finds Vital." *New York Times*. February 23, 1929, 4.

Lanahan, Eleanor. *Scottie the Daughter of . . . : The Life of Frances Scott Fitzgerald Lanahan Smith*. New York: HarperPerennial, 1996.

Langhorne, Elizabeth. *Monticello: A Family Story*. Chapel Hill, N.C.: Algonquin Books of Chapel Hill, 1987.

Lash, Joseph P. *A World of Love: Eleanor Roosevelt and Her Friends 1943–1962*. New York: Doubleday, 1984.

———. *Eleanor: The Years Alone*. New York: W.W. Norton, 1972.

Lee, Robert E. *The Wartime Papers of Robert E. Lee*. Edited by Clifford Dowdy. Boston: Little, Brown & Company, 1961.

London, Jack. *The Letters of Jack London: Volume Three: 1913–1916*. Edited by Earle Labor, Robert C. Leitz III, and I. Milo Sheperd. Palo Alto: Stanford University Press, 1988.

Mariani, Paul. *William Carlos Williams: A New World Naked*. New York: McGraw-Hill, 1981.

Marx, Arthur. *The Groucho Letters*. New York: Simon & Schuster, 1967.

————. *Life with Groucho*. New York: Popular Library, 1960.

McCullough, David. *The Great Bridge*. New York: Simon & Schuster, 1972.

————. *John Adams*. New York: Simon & Schuster, 2001.

————. *Mornings on Horseback*. New York: Simon & Schuster, 1981.

————. *Truman*. New York: Simon & Schuster, 1992.

Meltzer, Milton. *Carl Sandburg: A Biography*. Brookfield, Conn.: Twenty-First Century Books, 1999.

Melville, Herman. *Correspondence: Herman Melville*. Edited by Lynn Horth. Evanston, Ill.: Northwestern University Press, 1993.

Meryman, Richard. *Andrew Wyeth: A Secret Life*. New York: HarperCollins, 1996.

Michaelis, David. *N. C. Wyeth: A Biography*. New York: Alfred A. Knopf, 1998.

Middlebrook, Diane Wood. *Anne Sexton: A Biography*. Boston: Houghton-Mifflin, 1991.

Morris, Sylvia Jukes. *Rage for Fame: The Ascent of Clare Boothe Luce*. New York: Random House, 1997.

"Mrs. Wilson Buried Beside Her Parents." *New York Times*. August 12, 1914, 9.

"Mrs. Wilson Dies in White House." *New York Times*. August 7, 1914, 1.

"Mrs. Woodrow Wilson." *New York Times*. August 7, 1914, 10.

Niven, John. *Salmon P. Chase: A Biography*. New York: Oxford University Press, 1995.

O'Hara, John. *Selected Letters of John O'Hara*. Edited by Matthew J. Bruccoli. New York: Random House, 1978.

O'Neill, Eugene. *The Selected Letters of Eugene O'Neill*. Edited by Travis Bogard and Jackson R. Bryer. New Haven: Yale University Press, 1988.

Owen, Russell. "Byrd Sees Vast New Antarctic Area from His Plane, Claims It for Nation; Names It for Wife, Marie Byrd Land." *New York Times*. February 21, 1929, 1.

Parini, Jay. *John Steinbeck: A Biography*. New York: Henry Holt and Company, 1995.

Parker, Hershel. *Herman Melville: A Biography, Volume 1, 1819–1851*. Baltimore: Johns Hopkins University Press, 1996.

————. *Herman Melville: A Biography, Volume 2, 1851–1891*. Baltimore: Johns Hopkins University Press, 2002.

Pershing, John J. *My Experiences in the World War, Volume II.* New York: Frederick A. Stokes Company, 1931.

Price, Bruce H., and E. P. Richardson, Jr. "The Neurologic Illness of Eugene O'Neill—A Clinicopathological Report." *The New England Journal of Medicine.* April 13, 2000, 1126–33.

Remini, Robert. *Daniel Webster: The Man and His Time.* New York: W.W. Norton & Company, 1997.

Rickenbacker, Edward. *From Father to Son: The Letters of Captain Eddie Rickenbacker to His Son William, from Boyhood to Manhood.* Edited with notes and introduction by William F. Rickenbacker. New York: Walker and Company, 1970.

Rockwell, Anne. *Paintbrush & Peacepipe: The Story of George Catlin.* New York: Atheneum, 1971.

Roosevelt, Theodore. *A Bully Father: Theodore Roosevelt's Letters to His Children.* Edited by Joan Paterson Kerr. New York: Random House, 1995.

————. *The Letters of Theodore Roosevelt.* Edited by Elting E. Morison. Cambridge, Mass.: Harvard University Press, 1954.

Roper, Laura Wood. *FLO: A Biography of Frederick Law Olmsted.* Baltimore: Johns Hopkins University Press, 1983.

Rush, Benjamin. *The Autobiography of Benjamin Rush: His "Travels Through Life" Together with His* Commonplace Book *for 1789–1813.* Edited with introduction and notes by George W. Corner. Princeton: Princeton University Press, 1948.

Rybczynski, Witold. *A Clearing in the Distance: Frederick Law Olmsted and America in the Nineteenth Century.* New York: Scribner, 1999.

Sandburg, Carl. *The Letters of Carl Sandburg.* Edited by Herbert Mitgang. New York: Harcourt, Brace & World, 1968.

Schuyler, Hamilton. *The Roeblings: A Century of Engineers, Bridge-builders and Industrialists; The Story of Three Generations of an Illustrious Family 1831–1931.* Princeton: Princeton University Press, 1931.

"Scientists Praise Byrd Achievement." *New York Times.* February 22, 1929, 1.

Seager, Robert II. *Alfred Thayer Mahan: The Man and His Letters.* Annapolis, Md.: Naval Institute Press, 1977.

Seale, William. *The President's House: A History.* Washington, D.C.: White House Historical Association with the cooperation of the National Geographic Society. New York: Harry N. Abrams, Inc., 1992.

Sexton, Anne. *A Self Portrait in Letters.* Edited by Linda Gray Sexton and Lois Ames. Boston: Houghton-Mifflin Company, 1977.

Simon, Linda. *Genuine Reality: A Life of William James.* New York: Harcourt Brace & Company, 1998.

Sklar, Dusty. "Radiant Fathers, Alienated Sons." *The Nation.* October 2, 1972, 279–81.

Smith, Gene. *Until the Last Trumpet Sounds: The Life of General of the Armies John J. Pershing.* New York: John Wiley and Sons, 1998.

Spaulding, Jonathan. *Ansel Adams and the American Landscape: A Biography.* Berkeley: University of California Press, 1998.

Steffens, Lincoln. "Becoming a Father at 60 Is a Liberal Education." *American Magazine.* August 1928, 48–49, 148–50.

———. *Lincoln Steffens Speaking.* New York: Harcourt, Brace & Company, 1936.

Steinbeck, John. *Steinbeck: A Life in Letters.* Edited by Elaine Steinbeck and Robert Wallsten. Viking Press, 1975. Reprint, New York: Penguin Books, 1989.

Stowe, Harriet Beecher. *Life and Letters of Harriet Beecher Stowe.* Edited by Annie Fields. Boston: Houghton-Mifflin and Company, 1898.

Sufrin, Mark. *George Catlin: Painter of the Indian West.* New York: Atheneum, 1991.

Sutton, William A. *The Road to Winesburg: A Mosaic of the Imaginative Life of Sherwood Anderson.* Metuchen, N.J.: Scarecrow Press, 1972.

Taylor, John M. *William Henry Seward: Lincoln's Right Hand.* New York: HarperCollins, 1991.

Townsend, Kim. *Sherwood Anderson.* Boston: Houghton-Mifflin Company, 1987.

Turner, Justin G., and Linda Levitt Turner. *Mary Todd Lincoln: Her Life and Letters.* New York: Alfred A. Knopf, 1972.

Twain, Mark. *Mark Twain's Letters: Volume II, 1884–1910.* Edited by Albert Bigelow Paine. New York: Harper and Brothers, 1917.

———. *Mark Twain's Letters: Volume VI, 1874–1875.* Edited by Michael B. Frank. Berkeley: University of California Press, 2002.

Vandiver, Frank E. *Black Jack: The Life and Times of John J. Pershing, Volume II.* College Station: Texas A&M University Press, 1977.

Ward, Geoffrey C. *Not for Ourselves Alone: The Story of Elizabeth Cady Stanton and Susan B. Anthony: An Illustrated History.* New York: Alfred A. Knopf, 1999.

Washington, George. *The Papers of George Washington: Revolutionary War Series: 1: June–September 1915.* Edited by W. W. Abbot. Charlottesville: University Press of Virginia, 1987.

Webster, Daniel. *The Papers of Daniel Webster: Correspondence, Volume 2, 1825–1829.* Edited by Charles M. Wiltse with Harold D. Moser. Hanover, N.H.: University Press of New England, 1976.

———. *The Papers of Daniel Webster: Correspondence, Volume 3, 1830–1834.* Edited by Charles M. Wiltse and David G. Allen. Hanover, N.H.: University Press of New England, 1977.

White, Timothy. "Theater's First Couple." *New York Times Magazine.* December 26, 1982, 20.

"White House Baby Francis." *New York Times.* January 21, 1915, 1.

Wilder, Laura Ingalls. *West from Home: Letters of Laura Ingalls Wilder, San Francisco, 1915.* Edited by Roger Lea MacBride, historical setting by Margot Patterson Doss. New York: Harper & Row, 1974.

Williams, William Carlos. *The Autobiography of William Carlos Williams.* New York: Random House, 1951.

———. *The Selected Letters of William Carlos Williams.* Edited with an introduction by John C. Thirwall. New York: McDowell Obolensky, 1957.

Wilson, Woodrow. *The Papers of Woodrow Wilson, Volume 38: August 7–November 19, 1916.* Edited by Arthur S. Link. Princeton, N.J.: Princeton University Press, 1982.

"Wilson Grandson Born in White House." *New York Times. January 18, 1915, 1.*

Wyeth, N. C. *The Wyeths: The Letters of N. C. Wyeth 1901–1945.* Edited by Betsy James Wyeth. Boston: Gambit, 1971.

Internet and Other Sources

Beatty, Mary Lou. "Biography." 2002 Jefferson Lecturer in the Humanities; Henry Louis Gates, Jr. http://www.neh.gov/whoeare/gates/biography.html. January 1, 2003.

Brokaw, Ann. Diary. Clare Boothe Luce Papers. Library of Congress.

Current and Upcoming Renwick Gallery Exhibitions. Fact Sheet; About George Catlin. "George Catlin and His Indian Gallery." http://americanart.si.edu/press/catlinbiofact.html. May 8, 2003.

"Former President George Bush Speaks at Rice Commencement," Rice University Weekly Online, Rice News Release. http://www.rice.edu/projects/reno/Newsrel/2000/20000513 bushspeech.shtml. January 29, 2003.

"Interview." 2002 Jefferson Lecturer in the Humanities: Henry Louis Gates, Jr. http://www.neh.gov/whoeare/gates/interview.html. January 13, 2003.

Mackintosh, Barry. "The National Park Service: A Brief History." http://www.cr.nps.gov/history/hisnps/MPSHistory/briefhistory.htm. May 8, 2003.

Wickett, Walton. Correspondence. Clare Boothe Luce Papers. Library of Congress.

"*The Wyeths: A Father and His Family.*" Interviews by David McCullough. Produced by David Grubin. Smithsonian World, videocassette.

SOURCES AND PERMISSIONS

Adams, Abigail, to John Quincy, January 19, 1780, and to Thomas, April 26, 1809; Collections of the Massachusetts Historical Society.

Adams, Ansel, to Michael, December 25, 1953: From Mary Street Adler and Andrea Gray Stillman, editors. *Ansel Adams: Letters 1916–1984* (Boston: Little, Brown and Company, 1988), 240–41. Published with permission from The Ansel Adams Publishing Rights Trust. All rights reserved.

Adams, John, to John Quincy, May 18, 1781; to John Quincy, May 26, 1794; to Abigail Adams Smith, February 21, 1797; Collections of the Massachusetts Historical Society.

Adams, John Quincy, to John, November 2, 1818; Collections of the Massachusetts Historical Society.

Anderson, Sherwood, to John, spring 1926, April 1927, and 1929: Manuscript Division, Newberry Library, Chicago. Published with permission from the estate of Sherwood Anderson: Charles Modlin, 1000 Chestnut, Christiansburg, VA 24073.

Audubon, John James, to Victor, January 14, 1834: Howard Corning, ed. *Letters of John James Audubon 1826–1840: In Two Volumes: Volume Two* (Boston: The Club of Odd Volumes, 1930), 3–7. Reprinted by permission of the American Philosophical Society.

Bell, Alexander Graham, to Elsie and Marian, November 13, 1887, and to Marian, May 4, 1901: Alexander Graham Bell Papers, Manuscript Division, Library of Congress.

Bradstreet, Anne, to Simon, March 20, 1664: John Harvard Ellis, ed., *The Works of Anne Bradstreet in Prose and Verse* (Gloucester, Mass.: Peter Smith Publisher, Inc., 1932), 45–48. Published by permission of Peter Smith Publisher, Inc.

Bush, Barbara, to children, May 1993: Barbara Bush, *Barbara Bush: A Memoir* (New York: St. Martin's Paperback, 1994), 552–53. Published by permission of Barbara Bush.

Bush, George Herbert Walker, to children, September 23, 1998: George Bush, *All the Best, George Bush: My Life in Letters and Other Writings* (New York: Touchstone, 1999), 621–26. Published by permission of George Bush.

Byrd, Richard, to Richard, April 28, 1926, and February 22, 1929: The Ohio State University Archives, Papers of Admiral Richard E. Byrd (RG56.1) 19961, Box 1, Folder 6. Published by permission of The Ohio State University Archives, Papers of Admiral Byrd.

Catlin, George, to Louise, April 22, 1861: George Catlin Papers 1821–1946, Archives of American Art, Smithsonian Institution, Washington, D.C.

Chase, Salmon P., to Kate, May 10, 1868: Salmon P. Chase Papers, Manuscript Division, Library of Congress.

Cronyn, Hume, to Tandy, May 26, 1961: Manuscript Division, Library of Congress. Published by permission of Hume Cronyn.

Douglas, William O., to Mildred, December 16, 1961: Papers of William O. Douglas, Manuscript Division, Library of Congress.

Douglass, Frederick, to Rosetta, June 3, 1875: The Frederick Douglass Papers, Manuscript Division, Library of Congress.

Du Bois, W. E. B., to Yolande, October 19, 1914: Herbert Aptheker, ed. *The Correspondence of W. E. B. Du Bois: Volume 1 Selections, 1877–1934* (Amherst: University of Massachusetts Press, 1973), 207–208. Published by permission of The University of Massachusetts Press.

Edison, Thomas, to Thomas, 1903: National Historical Site Archives. Box 1903, "Family."

Edwards, Jonathan, to Mary, July 26, 1749: George S. Claghorn, ed. *Jonathan Edwards: Letters and Personal Writings* (New Haven: Yale University Press, 1998), 288–90. Published by permission of Yale University Press.

Einstein, Albert, to Hans Albert, October 4, 1915: Robert Schulman, A. J. Kox, Michael Janssen, and Jozsef Illy, eds. *The Collected Papers of Albert Einstein. Volume 8, The Berlin Years Correspondence, 1914–1918* (Princeton: Princeton University Press, 1998), 189–90. Published by permission of Princeton University Press.

Eliot, Charles, to Charles Eliot, Jr., April 20, 1886: Courtesy of the Harvard University Archives.

Fisher, M. F. K., to Norah, Anne, and Mary, September 1984. *M. F. K. Fisher: A Life in Letters: Correspondence 1929–1991.* Selected and Compiled by Norah K. Barr, Marsha Moran, Patrick Moran (Washington, D.C.: Counterpoint, 1998), 455–56. Published by permission of Lescher & Lescher, Ltd.

Fitzgerald, F. Scott, to Scottie, August 8, 1933; October 20, 1936; and July 7, 1938: Matthew J. Buccoli, ed. *A Life in Letters: F. Scott Fitzgerald* (New York: Touchstone, 1994), 234–35, 313–14, 362–65. Reprinted with permission of Scribner, an imprint of Simon & Schuster Adult Publishing Group. Copyright © 1994 by the Trustees Under Agreement dated July 3, 1975, created by Frances Scott Fitzgerald Smith.

Franklin, Benjamin, to William, October 19, 1772: William B. Willcox, ed. *The Papers of Benjamin Franklin, Volume 19 January 1 through December 31, 1772.* To William, August 16, 1784: Department of Manuscripts, The British Library. Published by permission of The British Library.

Garrison, William Lloyd, to William, December 31, 1858: Garrison Family Papers, Sophia Smith Collection, Smith College, Northampton, Mass. To Wendell, December 12, 1878. bMS Am 1169 (101). Published by permission of the Houghton Library, Harvard University.

Gates, Henry Louis, to Maggie and Liza, July 8, 1993: Henry Louis Gates, Jr. *Colored People: A Memoir* (New York: Alfred A. Knopf, 1994), xi—xvi. Published by permission of Alfred A. Knopf, a division of Random House, Inc.

Guthrie, Woody, lines from "This Land Is Your Land" reprinted by permission of The Richmond Organization.

Guthrie, Woody, to Arlo, September 1956: Woody Guthrie Foundation Archives, Correspondence 1, Box 3, Folder 9. Published by permission of Woody Guthrie Publications, Inc.

Hammerstein, Oscar, to Bill, January 18, 1953: Papers of Oscar Hammerstein, Division of Performing Arts, Library of Congress. Unpublished letter reprinted by permission of The Rodgers and Hammerstein Organization. All rights reserved.

Houston, Sam, to Sam, June 15, 1846: Special Collections, The New York Public Library, Astor Lenox and Tilden Foundations. Published by permission of The New York Public Library. To Sam, July 23, 1861: Records of Governor Sam Houston, Texas State Library and Archives Commission. Published by permission of the Texas State Library and Archives Commission.

Howard, Moe, to Joan c. 1936: Private Collection of Joan Howard Maurer and Paul Howard. Published by permission of Joan Howard Maurer.

Howells, William Dean, to William, March 1, 1909: William C. Fischer with Christoph K. Lohmann, *W. D. Howells, Selected Letters, Volume 5: 1902–1911* (Boston: Twayne Publishers, 1983), 268. Published by permission of the Gale Group.

James, William, to Margaret, June 19, 1895: bMS Am 1092.9 (2980), Houghton Library, Harvard University. Published by permission of Houghton Library, Harvard University. To Margaret, May 26, 1900: bMS Am 1092.9 (3003) Houghton Library, Harvard University. Published by permission of Houghton Library, Harvard University.

Jefferson, Thomas, to Martha, March 28, 1717; April 7, 1787; June 14, 1787; and April 4, 1790: Thomas Jefferson Papers, Library of Congress.

Lanier, Sidney, to Charles, August 15, 1880, and July 20, 1881; Sidney Lanier Papers, Ms. 7, Special Collections and Archives, The Johns Hopkins University. Published by permission of Special Collections and Archives, The Johns Hopkins University.

Lee, Robert E., to Charlotte, December 10, 1862: Clifford Dowdy, ed. *The Wartime Papers of Robert E. Lee* (Boston: Little, Brown and Company, 1961), 357. Published by permission of Special Collections, Leyburn Library, Washington & Lee University.

Lincoln, Mary Todd, to Robert, June 19, 1876: Justin G. Turner and Linda Levitt Turner, *Mary Todd Lincoln: Her Life and Letters* (New York: Alfred A. Knopf, 1972), 615.

London, Jack, to Joan, August 17, 1913; August 24, 1913; September 5, 1913; October 11, 1913; and February 24, 1914; Earle Labor, Robert C. Leitz III, and I. Milo Sheperd, ed. *The Letters of Jack London: Volume Three: 1913–1916* (Palo Alto: Stanford University Press, 1988), 1215–16, 1218–19, 1225–26, 1257–60, 1298–1301. Published by permission of Stanford University Press.

Luce, Clare Boothe, to Ann, November 24, 1942, and February 4, 1942: Papers of Clare Booth Luce, Library of Congress.

Mahan, Alfred Thayer, to Helen, July 9, 1890: Naval Historical Collection, Naval War College. Published by permission of the Naval Historical Collection, Naval War College.

Marx, Groucho, to Arthur, 1940: Groucho Marx, *The Groucho Letters* (New York: Simon & Schuster, 1967), 43–45. Published by permission of Simon & Schuster Adult Publishing Group. To Arthur, February 16, 1945: Collections of the Manuscript Division, Library of Congress. Published by Permission of Groucho Marx Productions, Inc.

Melville, Herman, to Malcolm, September 1, 1860: bMS Am 188(176), Houghton Library, Harvard University. Published by permission of Houghton Library, Harvard University.

O'Hara, John, to Wylie, September 22, 1959, and September 29, 1959: Matthew J. Bruccoli, ed. *Selected Letters of John O'Hara* (New York: Random House,

1978), 300–304. Published by permission of United States Trust Company of New York.

Olmsted, Frederick Law, to Frederick, Jr., September 5, 1890; May 13, 1875; and October 15, 1895; to John, May 10, 1895: Papers of Frederick Law Olmsted, Library of Congress.

O'Neill, Eugene, to Eugene, Jr., February 20, 1930, and April 28, 1941; to Shane, October 1937, July 18, 1939, and April 18, 1941: The Yale Collection of American Literature, Beineke Rare Book and Manuscript Library, Yale University. Published by permission of Yale University.

Patton, George, to George, June 6, 1944: Papers of George Patton, Library of Congress.

Pershing, John J., to Warren, May 19, 1918, and February 28, 1925: Papers of John J. Pershing, Library of Congress.

Rickenbacker, Eddie, to William, January 1, 1951: Rickenbacker Papers, Special Collections & Archives, Auburn University. Published by permission of Special Collections & Archives, Auburn University.

Rockefeller, John D., to John, January 26, 1922, and June 13, 1929: Joseph W. Ernst, ed. *"Dear Father"/"Dear Son" Correspondence of John D. Rockefeller and John D. Rockefeller, Jr.* (New York: Fordham University Press, 1994), 133, 163. Published courtesy of the Rockefeller Archive Center.

Rockefeller, John D., Jr., to John, May 1, 1920: Rockefeller Archive Center. Collection: John Rockefeller III. Record Group: R65. Series: I, OMR. Box: 31. Folder: 2987. Item: Memo Between Papa & John. To Boys, December 21, 1943: Rockefeller Archive Center, collection: John Rockefeller III; Record Group: R65; Series: 1 OMR; Box: 31; Folder: 292; Item: John Jr–Boys December 21, 1943. Published courtesy of the Rockefeller Archive Center.

Roebling, Washington, to John, March 21, 1908: Special Collections and University Archives, Rutgers University Libraries. Published by permission.

Roosevelt, Eleanor, to James, September 22, 1949. Papers of Eleanor Roosevelt, Franklin D. Roosevelt Library. Published by permission of Nancy Roosevelt Ireland, Trustee, AER Estate.

Roosevelt, Theodore, to Alice, August 28, 1904. Published by permission of Joanna Sturm. To Kermit, March 5, 1904, and October 2, 1903: Manuscript Division, Library of Congress. To Theodore, Jr., April 9, 1904: Manuscript Division, Library of Congress. To Quentin, June 21, 1904: Manuscript Division, Library of Congress. To Quentin, December 24, 1917, and March 17, 1918: Houghton Library, Harvard University. Published by permission of the Theodore Roosevelt Association.

Rush, Benjamin, to John, May 18, 1796: Manuscripts Division, Department of Rare Books and Special Collections, Princeton University Library. Published by permission of Princeton University Library.

Sandburg, Carl, to Margaret, November 1921: Herbert Mitgang, ed. *The Letters of Carl Sandburg* (New York: Harcourt, Brace & World, Inc., 1968), 203. Published by permission of Harcourt, Inc.

Seward, William, to William, Jr., October 7, 1848: William Henry Seward Papers, Department of Rare Books and Special Collections, University of Rochester. Published by permission of University of Rochester.

Sexton, Ann, to Linda, April 1969: Linda Grey Sexton and Lois Ames, eds. *Anne Sexton: A Self Portrait in Letters* (Boston: Houghton-Mifflin Company, 1977), 424. Published by Permission of Linda Grey Sexton.

Stanton, Elizabeth Cady, to Margaret, December 1, 1872. Papers of Elizabeth Cady Stanton, Library of Congress.

Steffens, Lincoln, to Pete, June 23, 1926, and December 9, 1931; Lincoln Steffens Papers, Rare Book and Manuscript Library, Columbia University. Published by permission of Columbia University.

Steinbeck, John, to Thom, November 10, 1958, and to John, July 16, 1966: Elaine Steinbeck and Robert Wallsten, eds. *John Steinbeck: A Life in Letters* (New York: Penguin Books, 1989), 600–601, 835–36. Published by permission of Viking Penguin, a division of Penguin Group (USA) Inc.

Stowe, Harriet Beecher, to Georgiana, February 12, 1858, and to Charles, 1882: Anne Fields, ed. *Life and Letters of Harriet Beecher Stowe* (Detroit: Gale Research Company, 1898), 247–48, 382–83.

Truman, Harry, to Margaret, July 25, 1945: From the Collection of the Harry S Truman Library.

Twain, Mark, to Susie, December 25, 1875: Clara Clemens. *My Father, Mark Twain* (New York: Harper & Brothers, 1931), 36–39. Reprinted by permission of HarperCollins Publishers Inc. To Clara, December 29, 1909: Albert Bigelow Paine, ed. *Mark Twain's Letters, Volume II* (New York: Harper & Brothers Publishers, 1917), 835–36.

Washington, George, to John Parke Custis, June 19, 1775: George Bolling Lee Papers, Manuscripts and Archives, Virginia Historical Society. Published by permission of the Virginia Historical Society and the University of Virginia Press.

Webster, Daniel, to Charles, November 1825: Charles Wiltse, ed. *The Papers of Daniel Webster, Correspondence, Volume 2, 1825–1829* (Hanover, N.H.: University Press of New England, 1976), 3–4. Published by permission of University Press of New England. To Edward, June 23, 1834: Charles M. Wiltse, ed. *The Papers of Daniel Webster. Correspondence, Volume 3, 1830–1834* (Hanover, N.H.: University Press of New England, 1977), 351–52. Published by permission of University Press of New England.

Wilder, Laura Ingalls, to Rose, February 5, 1937: Collections of the Herbert Hoover Presidential Library. Published by permission of Little House Heritage Trust, its copyright owner.

Williams, William Carlos, to William, September 25, 1942: John C. Thirlwall, ed. *The Selected Letters of William Carlos Williams* (New York: McDowell, Obolensky, 1957), 201–203. Published by permission of New Directions Publishing Corp.

Wilson, Woodrow, to Jessie, October 15, 1914; Arthur S. Link, ed. *The Papers of Woodrow Wilson, Volume 38: August 7–November 19, 1916* (Princeton: Princeton University Press, 1982), 688–89. Published by permission of Princeton University Press.

Wyeth, N. C., to Ann and John, November 4, 1935; Peter and Henriette, August 27, 1939; Nat and Caroline, October 19, 1943; Andrew, February 16, 1944: Betsy James Wyeth, ed. *The Wyeths: The Letters of N. C. Wyeth 1901–1945* (Boston: Gambit, 1971), 750–51, 794–96, p. 828, 833–36. Published by permission of The Wyeth Foundation of American Art.

ACKNOWLEDGMENTS

My first gratitude is to those families, individuals, executors, archives, libraries, and publishing houses that granted me permission to publish these personal family correspondences. There would be no collection of this kind without their generosity.

The book could not have happened as it did without the imaginative and enthusiastic help of Mike Hill, who traveled the country, was driven after letters like a bloodhound in pursuit, provided valuable suggestions, made terrific finds, photocopied almost more than is humanly possible, and encouraged me all the while. He worked tirelessly on this project and always with genuine good cheer and sustaining humor.

For their assistance and suggestions I am particularly indebted to the following archivists, librarians, and specialists: Mary Wolfskill; Len Bruno; Alice Birney; Mark Horowitz; Bruce Kirby; Gerard Gawalt; David Wigdor; Barbara Bair; Adrienne Cannon; Staley Hitchcock; Fred Bauman; and especially to the patient and resourceful "archivist extraodinaire," Jeffrey Flannery, Library of Congress; Laura Kells, Library of Congress; Peter Drummey; Celeste Walker; William Fowler, Jr.; Nicholas Graham and Beth Krimmel, Massachusetts Historical Society; my old friend Elizabeth Safley, Harry S Truman Library; Brian Sullivan, Harvard University Archives; Michael Plunkett, University of Virginia Special Collections;

312

John Gable, Theodore Roosevelt Association; Nora Guthrie, Felicia Katz, and Jorge Arevalo, Woody Guthrie Archives; Bob Clark and Mark Renovich, Franklin D. Roosevelt Library; JoEllen Dickie, Newberry Library; Wallace Dailey, Houghton Library, Harvard University; Laura Kissell and Dr. Raimund Goerler, Richard Byrd Archives, Ohio State University; Anne Marie Menta, Beineke Library, Yale University; Edward Skipworth and Erika Gorder, Rutgers University; Jaqueline McKiernan, Harriet Beecher Stowe Center; Lynn A. Smith, Herbert Hoover Presidential Library; John Hooper, National John Steinbeck Center; Jean Becker, Office of George Bush; Marc Rothenberg, Joseph Henry Papers Project; Linda Seelke, Lyndon Baines Johnson Library; and Dr. Charles Beveridge, Frederick Law Olmsted Papers Project.

A number of people to whom I am grateful provided letters or helped to track down correspondence: Louisa Thomas, Jack Bales, David Rae Morris, Roger Lawson, Emily Morison Beck, Ann Marshall, John Powell, Anne Adams Helms, Joan Howard Maurer, Gloria Owens Hemphill, Kate Healy, Ian Schoenherr, and Wylie O'Hara Doughty.

My thanks also go to Barbara Shuster, for her translation of the Einstein letters; my sister, Melissa McCullough McDonald, for her meticulous proofreading of typescripts against original letters; Linda Konkel for typescripts; and Bentley Davis for her enormous help with requests for letters, tracking permissions, typing, and errands of all kinds. For suggestions, encouragement, advice, and help in a variety of capacities, I am grateful to Bob Wilson; Geoffrey McCullough; Melissa McDonald; Alice Hammerstein Mathias; Tim Newman; Phil Zeidman; Caitlin McDonald; Jim and Marty Carter; Margot Goodwin; David McCullough, Jr.; William McCullough; Shannon Gregory; Ed Adler; Susan Simpson Gallagher; David Alden; Jane Acton; Michael Beschloss; Martina Gonsalves; Melissa Marchetti; Kendra Harpster; Laura MacCarty; Molly Will; and Susan Peck.

My agent, Luke Janklow, and his father, Morton Janklow, with their immediate enthusiasm for the idea gave me confidence to get right to work. Luke's quick mind, sensitivity to tone and content, and terrific humor put me at ease throughout the project, knowing I have been in nothing but the best of hands. Bill Thomas of Doubleday and Katie Hall have provided me with terrific suggestions and valuable improvements to the manuscript.

I thank my husband, Tim, for his endless enthusiasm and help with everything, from making it possible for me to work on the book in the evenings and on Saturdays, to his experienced understanding and encouragement of creativity. My children, Ingram, Nathaniel, and Luke (who only made his presence known as the work neared its end), kept me hopping and by their energetic presence constantly reminded me of why this book was a worthwhile undertaking. Perhaps most importantly for the work, they made it possible for me to understand the letters from the perspective of a parent.

To my own parents, Rosalee and David McCullough, all of the gratitude in the world is not enough. Their encouragement, good sense, advice, judgment, and experience have guided me in everything. In working on this book I came to appreciate and respect, more fully than ever, all they know, all they have done, and all they do.

Photo Credits

Chapter 1: Continuity

William Henry Seward to William Henry Seward, Jr.: Rare Book and Special Collections, Rush Rhees Library, University of Rochester, Rochester, NY

Chapter 2: The Developing Mind

Alexander Graham Bell and family: Library of Congress, Washington, D.C.

Lincoln Steffens and son Pete, ca. 1931. Photograph by Edward Weston. © 1981, Center for Creative Photography, Arizona Board of Regents. Tucson, AZ

Chapter 3: Love

Alfred Thayer Mahan to Helen Evans Mahan: Naval War College, Newport, RI

Chapter 4: Good Work

Eugene O'Neill and Eugene O'Neill, Jr.: Charles E. Shain Library, Special Collections, Connecticut College, New London, CT

Laura Ingalls Wilder: Herbert Hoover Presidential Library, West Branch, IA

John D. Rockefeller and John D. Rockefeller, Jr.: Photograph by George Bain, Library of Congress, Washington, D.C.

Chapter 5: Struggle

Woody Guthrie and family: Woody Guthrie Foundation and Archives, New York, NY

General John J. Pershing and Warren: Library of Congress, Washington, D.C.

John Steinbeck, John Steinbeck IV, and President Lyndon B. Johnson: Lyndon B. Johnson Presidential Library, Austin, TX

Chapter 6: Strength of Character

Yolanda DuBois: W. E. B. DuBois Library, University of Massachusetts, Amherst, MA

Theodore Roosevelt: Library of Congress, Washington, D.C.

John O'Hara and Wylie O'Hara: Collection of Wylie O'Hara Doughty

Chapter 7: The Pleasures of Life

William James and daughter Margaret: Houghton Library, Harvard University, Cambridge, MA

Mark Twain and family: Mark Twain House, Hartford, CT

Chapter 8: Brace-Up

F. Scott Fitzgerald and daughter Scottie: Courtesy Matthew J. Bruccoli

Jack London and daughter Joan: JLP 458, Album 20, #08445, Jack London Collection, Huntington Library, San Marino, CA. Published with permission

Thomas Edison and Thomas Edison, Jr.: Library of Congress, Washington, D.C.

Chapter 9: A Place in Time

Harry S. Truman to Margaret Truman: Harry S. Truman Presidential Library, Independence, MO

Chapter 10: Loss

Rosetta Douglass: Frederick Douglass National Historic Site, Washington, D.C.

Woodrow Wilson and family: Library of Congress, Washington, D.C.

Chapter 11: Aging

Frederick Law Olmsted: Frederick Law Olmsted National Historic Site, Brookline, MA

Frederick Law Olmsted to John Olmsted: Manuscript Division, Library of Congress, Washington, D.C.

Chapter 12: Rules to Live By

Anne Bradstreet to Simon Bradstreet: *Works of Anne Bradstreet,* John Howard Ellis, ed. Peter Smith Publisher, Gloucester, MA, 1962